KV-371-959

Controlling Women

The Normal and the Deviant

Edited by
Bridget Hutter and Gillian Williams

HATFIELD POLYTECHNIC

CI	O2	STC
HAT	BL	BIE
BNB	OIP	VIP

CONTROL
070990469 X

CLASS
305.42   Con

ACC.
10-045937-9

CROOM HELM LONDON
In association with the
OXFORD UNIVERSITY WOMEN'S STUDIES COMMITTEE

© 1981 Bridget Hutter and Gillian Williams
Croom Helm Ltd, 2-10 St John's Road, London SW11

British Library Cataloguing in Publication Data

Controlling women. — (The Oxford women's
    series)
    1. Women — Great Britain — Social conditions
    2. Social control
    I. Hutter, Bridget II. Williams, Gillian
    III. Series
    305.4'2   HQ1597

ISBN 0-7099-0469-X
ISBN 0-7099-1218-8 Pbk

Printed and bound in Great Britain by
Biddles Ltd, Guildford and King's Lynn

10 0145937 9

C

CONTROLLING WOMEN

.D

iED

2 3 NOV 1988
BOOK RETURNED

THE OXFORD WOMEN'S SERIES

This volume, the fourth in the series, derives from a programme of seminars convened under the auspices of the Oxford University Women's Studies Committee, in Hilary Term 1980.

Other volumes

DEFINING FEMALES: The Nature of Women in Society
Edited by Shirley Ardener

FIT WORK FOR WOMEN
Edited by Sandra Burman

WOMEN WRITING AND WRITING ABOUT WOMEN
Edited by Mary Jacobus

CONTENTS

Preface

PREFACE

This book is the result of a programme of seminars organised by Oxford University Women's Studies Committee in Hilary Term 1980. It is one in a series of books stemming from the work of the Committee, which is described in greater detail in the first volume of this series (*Defining Females: The Nature of Women in Society*, edited by Shirley Ardener). The programme was made possible through a generous grant from the Ford Foundation. We are most grateful to them and to the Warden and staff of Queen Elizabeth House for providing the venue for the seminars. We would also like to thank members of the Women's Studies Committee and those who attended and contributed to discussion at the seminars. The contributors to this volume have waived part of their royalties from this book in favour of the continuing work of the Committee and we would like to thank them for their time and support. A considerable number of people have helped, not only with preparing this book but also in developing the ideas and interests of the editors. We would particularly like to thank Carol Smart for her support and for the work which she has done in this field.

Bridget Hutter
Gillian Williams

1 CONTROLLING WOMEN: THE NORMAL AND THE DEVIANT

Bridget Hutter and Gillian Williams

Women are controlled, and free themselves from control, in many ways. We are concerned with the nature of social control over adult women in contemporary British society. As Smart and Smart (1978, p. 2) succinctly point out, 'The social control of women assumes many forms, it may be internal or external, implicit or explicit, private or public, ideological or repressive.' It may also not even be perceived or experienced as control. The studies we include in this book examine some of the forms which this control may take and their effects upon women at various stages in the life cycle. They are concerned with the way that an image of the 'normal woman' is built into the formation and implementation of social policy and also into day-to-day relations between individuals. This image does not necessarily accord with actual behaviour. It does not merely delineate what is usual or con-ventionally appropriate female behaviour but also defines what is morally expected.

Examination of the explicit controls exercised over women who are seen as deviant because they act in ways beyond the bounds of 'normal society' helps us to clarify this concept of 'normal behaviour'. Further-more, it allows us to see more clearly the extent and nature of the covert controls employed to persuade all women to fit their behaviour into this 'normal' pattern. We suggest that such controls are divisive. They emphasise the differences between groups of women and prevent old and young, 'normal' and 'deviant' women from seeing what they have in common.

As daughters, wives, mothers, workers and friends, we, as other women, have experienced various forms of control. We are only beginning to realise the extent to which we have taken for granted this picture of what is normal, to grasp the all-pervasiveness of the controls and the extent to which the various forms of control are related. We considered originally a study of groups of 'deviant' women but rapidly extended this to groups defined as 'non-deviant'. In focussing on the controls exercised over both groups it became clear that the controls embodied a notion of normality that specifically referred to women rather than to people in general. They sought to contain their behaviour not only in one capacity, for example, as childbearer or purveyor of sexual services, but in many other aspects of their lives. It usually has to be claimed that men are less than adult, psychopaths, have inadequate personalities, are foreigners or, in the case of racist ideologies, are less than fully human, before justifying such extended control. With women it is sufficient justification that they are women.

Fay Fransella and Kay Frost (1977, p. 24) suggest:

> As a society, we construct the social world according to our interests and beliefs; and as individuals we construct our beliefs to make sense of our own particular experiences of the world. So shared beliefs and experiences support each other — at least for a good deal of the time. Sex-role norms do not exist only in people's heads. They influence people's behaviour. We are constantly giving each other evidence to support our beliefs.

Some of these beliefs may be embodied in explicit external 'rules', imposed from outside, but many are internalised to a point where they cease to be felt as assumptions or beliefs but are more like 'facts of life', which do not change and are not questioned. People 'ascribe to themselves the qualities of the group to which they belong; they want to do what is expected of them and they value the socially recognised goals'. (Fransella and Frost, 1977, p. 14). Men and women do this not because they are 'conformist', but because, in a particular social framework, it makes sense to do so. It is not easy to flout explicit norms of behaviour but it is very much harder to question norms which are not articulated at all.

Over the last two centuries, feminist writers have tended to focus on legal and other overt controls which acted as barriers to women's participation in public and political life. Mary Wollstonecroft (1792) addressed herself to 'The Effect of an Early Association of Ideas on the Character', but it is only more recently in this century that we have again returned to focus on the social mechanisms and personal responses involved in the learning of gender identity.[1] There is evidence to show that, even at three weeks old, babies of different sexes are literally handled differently (Murphy, 1962; Hartley, 1966; Moss, 1970 and Oakley, 1972, p. 174). In western society, by the time a child reaches the age of four s/he already has firm ideas of gender identity (Oakley, 1972, pp. 177–8). Furthermore, parents such as ourselves may have little or no awareness of what they are doing and may even wish, and believe, that we are merely responding to the child as an individual (Sears *et al.*, 1957; Oakley, 1972, pp. 177, 206). Merely to legislate for the removal of overt controls is insufficient to dissolve these more subtle, invisible restraints on the behaviour of women and men.

The pervasiveness of controls over women suggest that, as a group, their attempts to free themselves from their unequal position in society offer a particularly strong threat to existing social arrangements. There has been strong reaction to demands for the liberalisation of abortion legislation, extension of the franchise to all women and an end to overt discrimination against women in employment. An even stronger threat is posed in the demand for women's right to control their own bodies, with abortion on demand as of right, rather than depending on a doctor's judgement and permission. Women may now have the right to be seen as householders and guardians of their children but there is still strong resistance to the abolition of the 'cohabitation' rule which places women recipients of welfare benefits in a disadvantaged position, when compared to the male claimant's right to control over his own sexuality and privacy (Coote and Gill, 1977, pp. 170—6). In general conversation, the subject of women's rights at best produces embarrassed shuffling and a change of subject, at worst, near apoplexy. It would seem to bring into the public sphere matters which are firmly intended to remain in the private world of the individual. A close analogy is that of the rights of homosexuals. While private acts between consenting adults are no longer punishable by the criminal law, this still allows for continued, legally validated discrimination in the civil sphere, for example in guardianship and custody of children and in employment. Any move to place homosexuals in an equal position with heterosexuals produces the same sort of reactions as women's claims to rights for themselves.

Smart and Smart (1978, p. 2) state that 'there remains the problem of showing the existence of specific *covert* forms of oppression and control, and of revealing that their location lies in the public sphere rather than the individual psychologies or personal lives of oppressed women'. They might also refer to blacks, prisoners, the unemployed and to other groups whose unequal position is accounted for by reference to their failure as individuals. If we can expose the degree of control actually exercised over the most apparently private areas of women's lives, we shall develop a language and method of understanding and attacking such controls over the lives of others.

Deviance among Women

As we stated earlier, our original conception was of a series of studies looking solely at women and crime, concentrating upon the ways in which society seeks to govern the position and behaviour of women by formal methods of control such as the law and legal institutions. Gillian Williams' experiences as a social worker and probation officer, both in the community and in prison, had already caused her to doubt positivist accounts of the individual pathologies of such women. For a number of reasons, which we discuss below, we found the most attractive approach would be what Stanley Cohen (1971, p. 14) terms a 'sceptical approach' to deviant behaviour, which we will outline below. This would allow differentiation between sex and gender and would challenge taken-for-granted assumptions about women, and deviants in particular. It was the adoption of this approach which made us realise that we could not look at women whose behaviour bears the label 'deviant' without also looking at those whose behaviour is considered 'normal'.

The focus on methods of social control which the 'sceptical' approach demands led us to discover shared experiences between groups of 'normal' and 'deviant' women and ourselves. Similarly the narrow equivalence of crime and deviance proved inadequate, as members of the so called 'deviant' group could not be distanced from other women. The common thread running through both the age cycle and the differing lifestyles of the women studied was that of women seen as a 'problem' whose behaviour required control and containment within the predominantly male ideologies of British society. Consequently, it was the similarities between women, and not their differences, that arose as the most important factor in our understanding of the ways in which women's lives are controlled and the categories of 'normal' and 'deviant' are applied.

We also began to realise that one weakness of the 'sceptical' approach is its concentration on behaviour at the margins of society, a concentration which can disguise the powerful effect of controls in everyday life (Cohen and Taylor, 1976). The image of the 'normal' woman employed, time and time again, is of a person with something of a childish incapacity to govern herself and in some need of protection — a kind of original sin stemming from Eve's inability to control her desire to seek new knowledge.

The definitions we continue to employ may rather loosely be typified as follows. Deviance refers to behaviour that does not accord with those expectations and norms for individual behaviour which are generally shared and recognised within a particular social system. It involves the breach of social rules which are commonly thought of as necessary to cohesion and order within a social group. Criminality may be considered as a particular form of deviance; it represents the violation of society's laws, that is, an institutionalised body of rules which is officially recognised as legitimate and binding upon society's members. The problem of defining what is deviant, in accordance with the wide definition of this term, is inextricably related to the difficulty of establishing what is normal. Just as cross-cultural studies reveal that there is no consistent definition of gender characteristics (Mead, 1935; Oakley, 1972; Rosaldo and Lamphere, 1974), so do studies of the law reveal that neither has one specific rule ever been present in all societies (Turk, 1967, p. 11). Perceptions and definitions of the 'normal' and the 'deviant' vary from one social situation to another, as do definitions of male and female. Two simple examples would be the racial laws of South Africa and Nazi Germany and the various definitions of suicide as criminal in one society and legal in another.

One of the attractions of the deviancy approach for the study of the control of women stems from its recognition that the social significance of, and societal reactions towards, certain types of behaviour are not enduring across time and space. The deviancy perspective, or the 'sceptical approach' to deviance, represents a break with traditional criminological theories. It raises questions as to the whole concept of deviant behaviour and its control, rather than investigating the physical and psychological characteristics of criminals and their histories and social origins in such a way as to imply that those in the deviant and criminal categories are somehow quite different from the rest of society. Writers such as Cohen argue that the definition of certain acts as 'deviant' should itself be seen as a problem for study and propose that societal reaction to certain types of behaviour is no less important, if not more important, than the act itself in deciding the 'deviant' character of the act (Becker, 1963).

The situation of female deviancy as a topic of sociological research is accurately described by Frances Heidensohn (1968, p. 160) as 'an obscure and largely ignored area of human behaviour.' Criminological and sociological research has paid most attention to the male offender, and reasons for female crime and deviancy have tended to be overlooked (Smart, 1976) or merely 'fitted' into explanations of male criminality (Cohen, 1955). This neglect of the study of female criminality and deviance mirrors a general sociological and academic disregard of women as important or even fit topics of research (Oakley, 1974, chap. 1; Stacey, 1980). It may also reflect the comparatively low proportion of women who are convicted of criminal offences.[2] Several writers have pointed out that the reason for the small proportion of women involved in crime may simply be that much illegal behaviour of women is masked or invisible. It may be invisible in the sense that it occurs in a private rather than public space and thus remains undetected. Alternatively, it may be rendered invisible by the law and by other procedures for regulating women and their behaviour. Part of women's invisibility in the deviance literature stems from the common assumptions about normal women which prevent a series of questions from being posed and explored. If a woman does not behave 'normally' then questions are asked about her hormones (Lombroso and Ferrero, 1895; Thomas, 1907; Pollak, 1950) or her 'poor relations' with her father (Greenwald, 1958), not whether there is something wrong with the identikit picture of the normal woman.

The narrow equivalence of deviance and crime may also render female deviance invisible. It is not sufficient merely to comment that female deviance is in some sense 'privatised' because of the roles women are normally expected to perform, or to claim that specifically female misdemeanours have been considered insufficiently serious to warrant penal measures (Mannheim, 1965). We have to examine the forms that even apparently trivial 'abnormal' behaviour takes and the meaning that women may give to it. For example, a prostitute working for higher wages than she might otherwise be able to obtain may see herself as fulfilling the role of a good, providing mother. One married woman's paid employment on the factory assembly line may be seen by her as an escape and rejection of an imposed role of housewife; to another it may represent a disgrace occasioned by her husband's lack of ability to provide for his family or the state's lack of provision for mothers at home.

Some areas of overt control are extremely difficult to study. The Official Secrets Act applies not only to prisons but also to special hospitals such as Broadmoor. Consequently there is a seemingly immutable barrier to the study of the nature of control exercised in these institutions and the non-official meanings which the controllers give to their own actions. While mainstream criminology has been concerned with the pathology of criminals, little, until recently, has been available on the pathology of the penal institutions and agencies of control. As a result we know even less about the treatment of female criminals within the penal system and the effects of the taken-for-granted assumptions about female criminality which inform the Home Office policy makers.

Until recently those adopting the deviancy approach have been implicitly preoccupied with male deviancy. No account has been taken of gender differentiation in, for example, studies of the police and their enforcement of the law, the processing of 'criminals' by the courts and the effects of the 'criminal' or 'deviant' status upon women. The deviancy approach has tended to lead study away from the criminal and his behaviour to an examination of those who define misbehaviour and the various ways in which they enforce the law and process deviants. This perspective highlights the problems of enforcing and implementing the law and concentrates on examining the 'law in action' rather than the intention, structure and content of the law as stated in books.[3]

In Chapters 2 and 3, Carol Smart and Eileen McLeod examine the structure and formation of the 1950s legislation governing sexual behaviour and its implications and effects upon women/prostitutes. As McLeod shows, the provisions of this legislation have a profound influence both upon police surveillance of prostitutes' lives and upon their treatment in court.

The 'sceptical approach to deviance' regards deviance as a process which originates in the definition of deviant behaviour and the commital of a deviant act. In the case of criminal acts, application of the criminal label is dependent upon a number of factors. The 'crime' must, initially, be reported but, from thereon the reactions of the law enforcers in the interpretation and application of the law is regarded as decisive. For example, the police decision either to arrest a suspect or to release him/her with just a warning may be influenced by such factors as the ambiguity of behaviour or legal statutes, the record of the suspect or the dramaturgical skills of the suspect (Box, 1971). An important element in the process is 'stereotyping' by the law enforcers, which involves them in assigning a set of behavioural and possibly physical characteristics to particular types of offenders. The logical implication of this is that those members of the population who outwardly conform to the stereotype may be reacted to as if they have committed, or are liable to commit, an offence.

Stereotypes of Normal and Deviant Women

It is to this element of stereotyping that we now turn. We are interested specifically in the stereotypes which derive from gender divisions in British society and in the power of the stereotypical image to define normal female behaviour and, in turn, deviant female behaviour. Women's deviant behaviour may well be considered insufficiently serious to warrant penal measures, but it is sufficient to warrant other controls. We will therefore consider the relations between the stereotypical image of the normal woman and both criminal and deviant women.

Stereotypes are a complex set of shared images and conceptions which denote the general characteristics and appropriate behaviour of a given group in society, in this case women. The norms for appropriate male and female behaviour are learnt and may be internalised very early in life. Primary socialisation within the family and secondary socialisation within the education system and via the media teach children what women are like and what men are like and how they should behave towards each other and with members of the same sex. The complexity of this process is indicated by Shirley Ardener (1978, p. 89) when she writes: 'perceptions of the *nature* of women affect the shape of the *categories* assigned to them, which in turn reflect back upon and reinforce or remould perceptions of the *nature* of women in a continuing process'. As Ardener indicates, stereotypes are not static. In Chapter 2, Smart examines the changing image of women's sexuality in the 1950s, a period which may be contrasted with the Victorian era, as the sexual potential of the married woman was realised and she ceased to be viewed as someone devoid of sexuality.

A number of common images and assumptions about female behaviour are presented in the stereotypes. A prevalent image, which is incorporated not only into medical ideologies but also into legislation and the re-socialisation of female patients and criminals in Broadmoor (as Rowett and Vaughan show in Chapter 6), is that women's work and skills lie within the home. Smart examines the inclusion of this assumption in the 1950s legislation governing sexual behaviour. This period witnessed changes in the structure of the family and the position of women. The dominant ideology was that of the monogamous family and the sexual fidelity of women. The growth of the social-work profession and health visitors posited the central importance of the child. In turn, the legislation operated to reproduce the social order and the criminal law functioned to rein-force the ideology that a woman's place is in the home. This ideology was further legitimated, claims Smart, in social-security, health, tax and pension provisions, all of which assume the dependent status of women. While the minority of women in Britain may be financially independent, the majority are, of course, dependent because of their position in the home. Recent changes in the payment of child allowances have, implicitly if not explicitly, recognised the problems which may accompany the distribution of income within the family.

The major justification for keeping women in the home is in their position as mothers. However, as Chris Phillipson points out in Chapter 9, the caring role of women is maintained across the life span. Women in their middle age may face a double burden in their role as paid workers and in their responsibilities for the care of male partners and ageing parents. While paid employment may represent an intensification in the activities of middle-aged women, it at least provides a measure of economic independence and an escape from the limited opportunities within the home, family and community. However, the ethos that a woman's primary role is in the home is highlighted at times of contraction in the job market. We now hear calls for women to operate in a voluntary capacity as a source of physical and social support for the elderly (Uhlenburg, 1979, p. 240). Furthermore, present cuts in public expenditure also pose a threat to community care for the physically and mentally handicapped, a threat which, if it is realised, will force women rather than men back into the home to care for physically and mentally handicapped relatives.

In Chapter 4, Oakley notes the assumption of the medical profession that women will have children and will be mothers. This assumption is of course not confined to the medical profession. It is generally supposed that women will breed and that they will want to breed. Even in this age of relatively efficient and readily available contraception, women are not easily permitted the choice of whether or not to have children; the choice is rather restricted to when they will have them. Sally Vincent remarks in the *Observer* (28 September 1980): 'To ask the question "Why have babies?" is to pronounce a particularly seditious rhetoric. You must be at some kind of diabolical loggerheads with women's central role in the scheme of things.' She continues to remark that other women play a significant role in pressurising women to conform and have children:

> There is, as any childless woman will affirm, a gulf between
> women who are mothers and women who are not mothers that is
> more unbridgeable and fraught with peril than any that lies

between women and men. The chasms are similar only in that they are largely created by inarticulateness. We are accustomed to explain ourselves in terms of 'Did want' and 'Didn't want' and leaving it at that. The childless, however, are more likely to be pressed for further explanation for their non-conformity.

One can only speculate as to the reasons why women manufacture this division between the childless and mothers. Perhaps this may be partly accounted for in terms of the desire of some women to re-affirm and legitimate their position as mothers; the denial of the choice they may, or may not, have had to have children thus maintains the inevitability of the role of women as mothers in the home.

The question of whether or not to have children leads one to another 'uncomfortable' question: can we assume that the so-called 'maternal instinct' is natural? Oakley's findings, for instance, certainly do not support the notion that women have a natural instinct to mother. However, the assumption is so common that suggestions to the contrary elicit very hostile responses. One only has to witness the uproar caused by Elisabeth Badinter's (1980) claims that the maternal instinct is a myth created to subjugate women.

The image of women as mothers not only serves to reinforce the ideology that women's place is in the home but also controls other aspects of women's lives. For example, Otto suggests, in Chapter 7, that the possible root of the 'deviancy' label as applied to alcoholic women is that alcohol creates threatening behaviour amongst a group normally expected to be wives and mothers. She comments that 'no-one likes to believe that the hand that rocks the cradle might be a shaky one'.

The strength of the image of women as mothers in the home is perhaps indicated by Rowett and Vaughan in Chapter 6. They examine a group of women, many of whom have contradicted the female stereotype and been convicted of violent behaviour, the victims often being their children. Nevertheless, Broadmoor attempts to re-socialise these women into a stereotypically female role. The work areas to which female patients are assigned tend to be typically domestic. Furthermore, the rehabilitation programme for women in Broadmoor includes such topics as 'Home Management', 'Conception', 'Birth' and 'Contraception'.

In Chapter 9, Phillipson examines the way in which the typification that a woman's place is in the home may lead to problems for older women. He comments that widowhood may 'trigger off a downward spiral of withdrawal and social isolation' partly resulting from this typification. Widows may face the last twenty years of their lives living alone, while the only acceptable state prior to this has been marriage and living with children and a partner. The traditional role of women may lead to a relative inability to handle public affairs and the potential threat of removal to an institution conflicts with their domestic identity.

The 'normal woman' is constantly portrayed as a person with something of a childish incapacity to govern herself and in some need of protection. This child/woman must not be allowed to control her own child-bearing capacities. In Chapter 8, Madeleine Simms shows the widespread use of abortion before the 1967 Act. The Act is portrayed as being used by the unscrupulous to 'impose' abortion on the gullible, easily swayed woman. A liberal extension of the Act would still leave the ultimate power in the hands of the medical profession, in order to protect women from themselves and from exercising the responsibility for their own decisions that abortion on demand would entail. There are similar controls over a woman's right to choose where she has her baby. As Oakley shows in her study of the literature on pregnancy and child-birth, a woman's capacity for choice is seen as modified by her 'nature' and, again, renders her a fit subject for the care, protection and control of medical experts. This irresponsible image of the 'normal woman' extends to her performance of the mother role, again justifying the need for experts to protect mother and child.

Aside from protection from their own childish nature, pregnant women are seen to need protection from the nature of other women. Oakley suggests that what the medical experts term 'old wives' tales' might alternatively be termed the 'subversive power of sisterhood'. Both Simms (Chapter 8) and Oakley (Chapter 4) show that, in child-birth, motherhood and abortion, women actively seek the support and knowledge of other women, that this is no new phenomenon and that this has a subversive power that obstructs the medical experts in their 'self-assigned task of controlling reproduction and parenthood'.

Ironically, this childish image does not disappear with age. Helen Evers, in her study of geriatric patients (Chapter 5), found that female patients are depersonalised and treated as 'childish' and 'non-adult'. She illustrates three broad categories of female patients in long-stay geriatric wards, and compares the stereotypical images of these female patients to their male counterparts in order to reveal the importance of the gender order in the patient careers created by nursing staff. 'Grans', for example, were attributed child-like qualities and treated like children, whereas their male equivalent, 'Pop', tended to elicit more legitimate adult status. The same held for 'Nellies' and 'Awkward Alice', both of whom were treated as essentially 'non-adult' when compared to their male counterparts. Evers suggests that the ascription of a non-adult status to women and their depersonalisation may well be a direct result of the ethos that a woman's place is in the home. Thus women have no public identity, whereas men retain their occupational status. Geriatric patients, indeed patients in general, are a group who are very much under the control of the experts. Evers points out that patients surrendered their autonomy to the experts with varying degrees of submissiveness and challenge. Nevertheless, all patients were subject to the controls of a ward routine which even prevented them from making a cup of tea for themselves.

Old age is an element which is not seen as a characteristic of the 'normal woman', despite the fact that women live longer than men and thus constitute the majority of the elderly population. Phillipson notes in Chapter 9 that the age dimension tends to be invisible in both academic and feminist literature, especially in Great Britain. Phillipson and Evers both observe that the elderly tend to be desexed and regarded as a separate group, this process being especially severe for women as their sexual value decreases and they cease to be regarded as viable human beings. The rehabilitation programme offered to women in Broadmoor assumes an audience of child-bearing age. However, in reality, the women leaving Broadmoor tend to be moved to another institution and it is likely that they will be well into their middle age, if not older, by the time they are released.

Deviant women are stereotypically portrayed as 'sick' and not 'sinful', a characteristic which is consistent with the image of the 'normal woman', who is childish, irresponsible and in need of protection. The legislation against soliciting, for example, is based on the assumption that the women involved suffer from personality defects rather than that their activity is the result of difficult economic and social circumstances. In Chapter 2, Carol Smart describes the promiscuous girl or woman, who is not sinful but sick, as being the 'new psycho-social problem of the post-war era'. Similarly, prostitute's customers are commonly thought to be in some way perverted, whereas prostitutes describe them as being 'Mr Average'. However, the law only operates to control half of the actors in the situation and the prostitutes' clients tend not to be subject to the implementation of the law.

Female alcoholics are also considered to be either sad or mad rather than bad, and are often diagnosed as depressed or neurotic. In Chapter 7, Otto compares the female homeless alcoholic to her male counterpart and concludes that, where the male homeless alcoholic is assigned an individual political role, this individual responsibility for action is not attributed to women. The 'sick-rather-than-sinful' image also extends itself to women who have committed murder. The popular image of the 'sick' female convicted of homicide may be compared to the 'wicked' man who is guilty of the same offence. This is perhaps symbolised in Broadmoor where the nursing staff responsible for female patients wear a typical nurse's uniform which may be identified in any hospital. By comparison, the nursing staff responsible for male patients in Broadmoor wear a typical prison officer's uniform. Typically 'feminine' interests are also regarded as methods of 'recovery' and re-socialisation. Oakley notes that 'female' diversions are seen as a 'cure' to postnatal depression. Thus the Health Visitors Association recommend that depressed mothers go out with their husbands, go to a mother's club or find playmates for their children, as methods of recovering from the trials of motherhood. One wonders how successful these methods of 'recovery' can be for women who are depressed partly because they are in the most stereotypical of all female roles, namely mothers in the home. 'Pride in one's "feminine" appearance and ability to fulfil a stereotype' are cited as significant factors in the 'recovery' of mentally ill and psychopathic female patients in Broadmoor.

Underlying the stereotypical assumptions detailed above is a double standard of behaviour, which designates certain forms of behaviour as appropriate for men and inappropriate for women and vice versa. This is most clear in cultural attitudes towards sexuality, where the ideal is one of celibacy before marriage for women, whereas men may be encouraged to gain premarital sexual experience. Smart relates the legislation controlling prostitution to two main factors: efforts to restabilise the family; and a new sexual morality which is especially salient to women. She notes that monogamy has traditionally meant a restriction of female rather than male extra-marital sexual behaviour, and claims that the legal, as opposed to the moral, concern over the sexuality of young women has resulted in particularly strict supervision of women's sexual behaviour. The double standard also exists with regard to habitual drinking, which is considered normal behaviour for men and deviant amongst women. Otto explains how this double standard is maintained by means of stereotypes which portray men as aggressive when drunk and women as promiscuous. She comments that

female alcoholics tend to be portrayed as devoid of gender and personality characteristics. This mirrors the double standard adopted by
nurses towards male and female geriatric patients, where male patients
were regarded as persons with biographies and the female patients were
considered as less than adult, non-persons.

Male and female patients in Broadmoor are also treated according
to a double standard of behaviour. This double standard appears to be
significant in the admission route to Broadmoor. In the period 1972—4,
seven per cent of male admissions, as compared with 36 per cent of
female admissions, to Broadmoor were civil admissions. The majority
of female admissions were thus from other hospitals, whereas the
majority of male admissions were from the courts (Dell and Parker,
1979). As Rowett and Vaughan point out in Chapter 6, these figures
reflect a double standard which considers it necessary to treat self-
destructive women in the same conditions as outwardly aggressive
men.[4] Women patients in Broadmoor receive better preparation for
discharge than men but, ironically, the majority of them are transferred
to another psychiatric hospital, while a substantial number of men are
discharged directly back into the community (Dell, 1980).

The complex set of shared images and conceptions which are stereotypically attributed to women are mediated and maintained in a variety
of ways. Notions of appropriate female behaviour influence, for example,
governmental committees and penal-reform groups. These groups help
to define appropriate problems for control and specify groups which
may be subjected to these control measures. In turn, these groups
and committees inform the legislators and quasi-legal institutions which
may mediate the assumptions about appropriate female behaviour in
the form of external rules and controls (see Chapter 2). The media play
an important role in portraying, for example, the female alcoholic in a
negative light, either as a slut or as pathetic. Textbooks and manuals
provide a significant method of communicating appropriate behaviour
to pregnant women and, thereafter, they indicate appropriate methods
of child rearing. On a more informal level, women's interactions with
the medical profession are an important means of conveying to
pregnant and nursing mothers what types of behaviour are acceptable.
Indeed, interactions with the medical profession not only convey
notions of appropriate female behaviour to pregnant women; these
notions are also conveyed to the majority of women visiting GPs and
may also have a significant influence upon diagnoses of illness and
the treatment that women receive (Barrett and Roberts, 1978).

The imposition of moral assumptions and expectations, and their translation into 'natural' laws, is a forceful way of maintaining the female image. Thus the 'maternal instinct' is natural and it is 'natural' for women to assume a caring role. Conversely, it is 'unnatural' for a woman not to want children and it 'goes against her nature' to seek an abortion. 'Good' mothers listen to the experts and breast-feed their babies, whereas 'bad' mothers are 'selfish' in their quest for a career. Caring for elderly relatives and ageing partners is a middle-aged woman's *duty*. Deviant behaviour is often regarded as 'unnatural', and 'unnatural' behaviour is usually considered immoral and a freak of nature. The strength and power of the images and assumptions presented by stereotypes is reflected in the relative inability of men and women to negotiate their acceptance or rejection of certain labels and typifications. This is the case whether or not the stereotype is grounded in proven fact. Thus, Otto explains that the image of women as promiscuous when drunk persists despite the fact that there is no empirical evidence to support this notion. As Oakley illustrates in Chapter 4, the rise of the so-called 'experts' has played an important role in placing women in a powerless position in such negotiations. 'Inexperienced' women find themselves in an unequal relationship with professional 'experts', since their own sources of knowledge are denied or destroyed.

Women are particularly subject to the discretionary decision-making procedures of a number of quasi-legal agencies such as the DHSS, social services and probation. We cited earlier the case of the non-cohabitation rule which effectively denies women their own sexuality and their ability to negotiate social-security benefits. This discretionary element is also to be found and justified in the treatment approach for criminals and patients. Thus the inmates of Broadmoor, in effect, face indeterminate sentences and are powerless to find out the standards they need to reach in order to negotiate their own release (see Chapter 6). Evers remarks in Chapter 5 that female geriatric patients are unable to negotiate the 'labels' assigned to them by nursing staff. Thus, even when 'Awkward Alice' decides to 'behave' and conform to ward routines and nurses' directions, she is suspected of being 'up to something'.

Stereotypes are not necessarily consistent with actual behaviour, and women in any one society may even be presented with contra-dictory images which are considered to represent typical characteristics and behaviour. Otto remarks upon the contradictory pressures which exist to encourage women to drink, and yet punish excess drinking among women. Thus, one is presented with the glamorous drinking lady of the advertisements and the pathetic or sluttish woman who is drunk.

McLeod challenges the assumptions upon which the legislation controlling prostitution is based, by comparing the popular image of the prostitute with reality. Rather than a woman beset with personality defects, she finds mothers working to keep their children, with a business-like attitude to work. McLeod also remarks upon the counter-productive effects of the sanctions used against prostitutes: imprisonment and fines generate financial need amongst these women, and hence the necessity to find more work to compensate for the loss of earnings. Ann Oakley notes a number of contradictions in the stereotype of mothers who 'ought to be happy but are instead constantly beset with anxiety and depression'. Although the medical profession recognises the problem of post-natal depression, it explains it 'scientifically' in terms of hormones rather than acknowledging the social and economic conditions which might contribute to depression. Sally Macintyre observes the 'co-existence of two versions of reality', which posit that, whereas pregnancy and child bearing are normal and desirable for married women, pregnancy and child bearing for single women are abnormal and undesirable. As Macintyre (1976, p. 159) says, 'There is an underlying contradiction between the view of all women as essentially similar and endowed with strong maternal instincts, and the view that differentiates between women by marital status'.

Stigmatising Women

These stereotypes of normal and abnormal femininity are composed of a number of qualities attributed to particular women. Several of these attributes lead a woman to be seen as less than a whole human being and to her disqualification from full social acceptance. Erving Goffman (1963) deems such an attribute a *stigma*. When a woman has been labelled, successfully, in this way, it has consequences not only for how others identify and respond to her — her personal and social identity — but also for her sense of her own identity, her 'ego' or felt identity.

It has been suggested that women generally have lower self-images than men (Bardwick, 1971), but more recent studies do not necessarily support this view (Kaplan, 1973; Maccoby and Jacklin, 1974). However, there is some evidence that the basis of self-evaluation varies between the sexes (Carlson, 1970, 1971). Carlson found that men described themselves using adjectives of a personal, individualistic type, such as independent, confident, imaginative or fair-minded. Women responded in adjectives of a social and interpersonal nature, such as cooperative, friendly, tactful, sympathetic or dependable. We would therefore expect that, when women are labelled, successfully, as members of an 'abnormal' group, their sense of self-worth would be particularly affected by the response of others to them as an individual, and their ability to interact with others.

The stigmatising label may be assigned in a number of ways. It may be firmly attached, in legal form, as when a court declares a woman to be a 'common prostitute', or it may be the result of a long series of interactions with family members, doctors and other professionals before a woman is labelled 'alcoholic' or 'junkie'. For a woman who becomes pregnant, housewife, mother or old it takes time before she realises the force of the stigmatising attributes now applied to her. Goffman (1963, p. 45) says that:

> Persons who have a particular stigma tend to have similar learning experiences concerning their plight and similar changes in conception of self — a similar 'moral career' that is both cause and effect of commitment to a similar sequence of personal adjustments.

In the initial stages of such a *moral career* the stigmatised woman has to learn to incorporate the standpoint of the 'normal' person, together with a sense of what it would be like to possess a particular stigma. She also has to learn that she possesses such a stigma and, this time, the detailed personal consequence of possessing it. It is the timing and interplay of these two phases which forms the basis for the development of her moral career, and Goffman isolates various possible patterns.

The moral career of the alcoholic woman represents one discernible pattern. Long before she is clearly defined as an alcoholic, she will have learned what it is to be a 'normal' woman, wife and mother and will be aware of 'normal' views of the female alcoholic, the 'lush' portrayed in the media. Once she acquires the identity of 'alcoholic', she applies to herself the qualities of low esteem and failure as a woman which she has previously learned to associate with such women. This general feeling of failure is compounded by the views of her social and personal identity held by professionals who aim to help her. At first, these views will actually prevent professionals from considering the drink problems that may underlie her other problems (Sheehan and Watson, 1980), but they may form barriers to successful treatment. For example, in group therapy, not only therapists but also male patients may hold similar images of this double stigma of failed woman and alcoholic, which may prevent her from sharing with them or learning from the experience of other alcoholics (Page, 1980, pp. 165—8).

The prostitute will, similarly, have learned the 'normal' attributes of women and the public view of the 'whore', and then has to learn how others respond to her as a prostitute. Not only will a number of negative qualities be assigned to her, but these will affect her life in various ways. Her ability to function as a mother will be questioned (whether or not she is in prison), and her relationship with her husband or lover may lead to him being accused of 'living off immoral earnings'. She has to learn to cope with her new social and personal identity in the eyes of shopkeepers and neighbours. Her status and rights as a private citizen will be affected out of her working time. As a known prostitute, to wait for a friend in the street makes her liable to be arrested for 'loitering'. When she appears in court, unlike other defendants, her criminal record is known to the court before the current charge is proved, as the court will be told, at the beginning of the hearing, that she is a 'common prostitute'. The acquisition of the label 'prostitute' leads to her being subjected to a greater degree of control over all aspects of her life.

On release from Broadmoor, women patients share the employment and accommodation problems of all ex-inmates of prisons and mental hospitals. This double stigma of madness and criminality affects them within the institution, where the stigma of 'criminally insane' leads to a regime of tight control over all inmates dictated by the security risk occasioned by a few. Within such a regime, it is hard for the individual to ascertain and achieve the degree of 'normality' which would justify to staff recommendations for her discharge from Broadmoor. Even when this is achieved, her career is further affected by the reluctance of outside hospitals to judge her on any basis except those attributes which led to her incarceration. Suzanne Dell (1980), in a study of discharges from all special hospitals, illustrates this point very clearly. She shows that, when normal NHS mental hospitals are formally requested to receive a Broadmoor patient, they are very likely to refuse. The patient is judged purely on the basis of her identity on admission to the special hospital. If an informal approach is made, and a consultant from the outside hospital visits the special hospital, the patient has the opportunity to present herself in her new identity as 'improved patient', and she (or he) is much more likely to be accepted by the other hospital.

This sense of 'spoiled identity', with all its consequences for the individual, applies to areas where, at first sight, women may be seen as 'normal women' acting 'normally'. Oakley shows in Chapter 4 that many of the attributes of the stereotype of 'normal femininity' are sharpened and intensified in pregnancy. The 'unreliable-machine' model of the pregnant woman 'upset' by her hormones is used to justify her need for protection, and to account for her 'irrational' and 'childish' qualities. Elsewhere, Oakley (1974) has examined the work and attitudes of housewives. She examined, in detail, the different strategies of adaptation to their work and identity as house-wives, and showed that they shared the perception that the work is accorded low status and the housewife herself credited with various qualities summed up in the one derogatory phrase 'only a housewife'.

The women described so far might be considered as exercising some degree of choice as to whether to behave in ways which lead to them being placed in particular categories. To grow old is not a matter of choice but, as Phillipson and Evers show, growing old involves a woman in a moral career where she not only has to learn to manage her 'spoiled identity', but also, eventually, has difficulties in maintaining any strong sense of felt or personal identity. 'Normal' woman is pre-menopausal woman. The image is inextricably tied up with her sexual value, her ability to care for others, the performance of her domestic labour and her relationship to men, particularly her husband. The older, and ageing, woman is placed in a category where such attributes of 'normal femininity' are seen to have diminished or to have disappeared completely. Her declining sexual value, the death of her male partner, the devaluation of her caring skills and the threat of their eventual loss through hospitalisation place her firmly out of the range of normality. Loneliness, depression and a sense of alienation all contribute to a low sense of her own worth. As Phillipson says, there is a double standard of ageing for men and women, although, eventually, both will be consigned, in western society, to a category of 'old people', stigmatised as less than whole functioning members of the community. The woman's lack of money, impaired pension rights, sense of isolation and lack of friends from paid employment outside the home further prevent her from employing the means of maintaining her identity as a valued and valuable member of society.

Towards the end of *Stigma*, Goffman (1963, pp. 163—4) reminds us that:

> stigma involves not so much a set of concrete individuals who can be separated into two piles, the stigmatized and the normal, as a pervasive two-way social process in which every individual participates in both roles, at least in some connexions, and in some phases of his life . . . he who is stigmatized in one regard nicely exhibits all the normal prejudices held toward those who are stigmatized in another regard.

Women Controlling Women

Evers' geriatric nurses are socialised into female-dominated caring work, involving tasks which are accorded relatively low status in the field of medical care. They are subject to pressures towards ward efficiency which require them to control the behaviour of their patients. Their position in the hospital hierarchy leaves them, both individually and as a group, vulnerable and powerless to resist such pressures. To perform their controlling tasks, the nurses must maintain a sense of social distance from their patient, seeing her as 'other' than themselves. The behaviour of the articulate patient, who does not easily renounce her wish for personal autonomy, doubly threatens them. She challenges both their competence in the 'normal' woman's work of caring for others and their image of their future selves. As the picture of 'normal femininity' has no dimension of age, the nurses must treat their patient as a less than whole person firmly fitted into a separate stereotype of femininity which contrasts with their own identity as competent normal women.

As an officer of the court, parole officer and social worker with responsibility for prisoners and ex-prisoners, the probation officer is asked not only to befriend offenders but to exercise control over their behaviour.[5] The first probation officers were men and, although women were originally introduced to supervise women offenders, the departmental committee of 1909 suggested that male officers were 'often as successful if not more than' female officers in such supervision (Parsloe, 1972, p. 269). Despite this, the control of female offenders by female officers was embodied in legislation which specifically excluded women and girls from the supervision of male probation officers between 1934 and 1967. In 1969, Phyllida Parsloe began an investigation of the case loads of probation officers, followed up by discussions with them designed to explore their attitudes towards what she termed 'cross-sex supervision' of clients. On the whole, officers controlled clients of their own sex. The slightly greater tendency for women to supervise male clients was accounted for by the inclusion of young boys in their case loads. In discussion with officers, their fears as to the dangers inherent in cross-sex supervision of clients focused largely on women controlled by male officers. The authority role to be exercised by the female officer fitted closely with the stereotype of the normal 'good' mother, a worker who would not present a sexual threat to male clients. Male officers, however, were thought to be more vulnerable to sexual blackmail by their 'abnormal' female clients, and were particularly concerned about being sexually attracted by them. Some fears were expressed about the 'indignity' suffered by a male client controlled by women officers, but this was balanced by the view that the women would help him to work out particular forms of authority problems 'originally created between him and his mother'. This caring disciplinary role of the 'normal' mother was further brought out in discussion of women's control of female clients. It was felt that normal women officers could actually be firmer in such control and were less likely to be a 'soft touch' than male officers.

Five years later, a smaller study of three probation areas indicated few changes in the composition of case loads, with women and juveniles still more likely to be under the supervision of female officers (Brunner *et al.*, 1974). In Parsloe's sample, the allocation of cases was often justified in terms of staff shortages or distribution of staff, but two Principal Probation Officers specifically claimed that cases were allocated according to the needs of individual clients.

In this later study, the overwhelming claim was that officer and client were (and should be) matched entirely upon the basis of their individual capabilities and 'casework needs', rather than assumed gender characteristics. These claims are not borne out by the actual distribution of cases. A more likely explanation is that the allocation of cases reflects clear stereotypes of qualities attributed to the two groups of women, resulting in the selection of women officers to control women clients. These attributes and stereotypes, in turn, present problems for women chosen to exercise authority over other women, especially in the case of the Woman Prison Officer.

Thomas (1972, p. xiii) suggests that 'because writers have often found the prisoner more interesting, very little has been written about

the uniformed prison officer'. Even he excludes examination of the
work of women officers, and their role in the Prison Officers'
Association, on the grounds that female institutions have been, and are,
different. We have very little evidence, in Britain, as to how they see
their job. A male prison officer, commenting on his job to Tony Parker
(1973, p. 60), said:

> I think the prisoners despise us because we represent the public, and
> I think the public despises us because we are doing what they
> want us to do in their hearts but they pretend they don't. It's like
> they look down on lavatory attendants or dustmen: they couldn't
> do without them but they won't soil their hands doing the job.

The derogatory popular image of the male 'screw' takes on an
additional flavour, often comic, when applied to the uniformed female
officer. While the female prisoner may wear her own clothes, the
female prison officer wears a uniform which does not even have the
cachet of the Nightingale cap which adorns the head of the nursing
heroine of romantic fiction. As with men, present overcrowding and
understaffing of prisons mean that the women officers have to work
extra time, over rest days and even holiday periods. The small number
of women's prisons may often result in long journeys for officers
escorting prisoners to distant courts or prisons. The rigid hierarchy
and discipline of the prison regime has its impact on basic uniformed
staff just as it has on the prisoners themselves. As another officer
told Parker (p. 59):

> I work all my life within these walls and when I go home it's to a
> house just outside where I see the same walls, but from the other
> side, that's all. I often find myself thinking 'Well at least every
> prisoner knows the date when he won't have to look at them any
> more, which is more than I do'.

The official view of women's prisons is that they should provide
regimes more liberal and therapeutic than those in men's prisons. This
image suggests that women prison officers are chosen, as with women
probation officers, to act both as imitable models of 'normal
femininity' and with a firm but caring maternal discipline. The
regimes emphasise the need for prisoners to acquire the skills and
personality traits which mirror the stereotypes of the 'normal' female
(Giallombardo, 1966; Smart, 1976b; Fitzgerald and Sim, 1979). Not

only does imprisonment separate women prisoners from children and families, but the nature of the work of the officer similarly affects the time and energy she has to maintain such 'normal' female relationships. Fitzgerald and Sim (1979, pp. 81—5) suggest that female prisoners are subject to a greater degree of control than their male counterparts. They also point out that a consistently higher proportion of disciplinary charges are brought against women. Whether this merely reflects greater problems for women in submitting to prison rules or greater enforcement of prison regulations, it implies a considerable degree of rule enforcement in the work of the woman officer. Like geriatric nurses, the officer's 'caring women's work' is coupled with controlling the behaviour of others. Much of the work undertaken by prisoners is the domestic labour necessary to the maintenance of an establishment such as Holloway. Again, as with the nurses, the officer's competence to direct and teach such tasks may be challenged and criticised by prisoners, who may well have skills that officers lack. It further establishes the need to maintain a sense of social distance between officer and prisoner.

In her study of employers and servants in the Eastern Cape of South Africa, Jacklyn Cock (1980) explores the conditions necessary to the control of one group of women by another. She examines the intimate relationship of white 'madam' and black 'maid', showing that the patterns of control are maintained not only because of the underlying racist ideology of the society, but also because of other mechanisms which allow the similarities between the two groups of women to be obscured or ignored. She uses Lewis Coser's (1974) concept of the 'greedy institution' which makes total claims upon its members. It seeks their exclusive and individual loyalty, time and energy, by minimising and excluding competing claims from outside and is 'omnivorous'. Unlike hospitals, prisons and asylums, the 'total institutions' of Erving Goffman (1961), they do not rely on physical barriers. Although 'greedy institutions' such as domestic service, various utopian sects or modern American marriage may utilise the device of physical isolation (for example, rules for residential maids), they tend to rely on symbolic boundaries to separate insider and outsider.

Most of the white women in Cock's sample were well-entrenched in such marriages. Altogether, 60 per cent of them said that financial decisions were made by their husbands, and 35 per cent did not even know what their husbands earned.[6] This dependency on their husbands is also reflected in the fact that, despite the average 73 hours per week worked by their maids, 84 per cent of the white women were not in waged employment. As Cock remarks (p. 161):

> both domestic servants and their employers are caught in a dependent's situation . . . The paid domestic worker is dependent on her employer, but does not accept the legitimacy of her own subordination in the social order, she is not a deferential worker. The unpaid domestic worker, on the other hand, is dependent on her husband, but usually accepts the legitimacy of her own subordination and is a deferential wife.

The black maid is a *trapped worker*. She has double responsibilities in the reproduction and maintenance of labour power, not only in her own family but also in those of the dominant (white) class. The convergence of three systems of exploitation — sex, race and class — leads to her entrapment in a work situation bearing all the marks of a 'greedy institution'.

Gender and racial barriers affect her access to education or means of finding alternative employment. The imposition by the state of controls over the residence and mobility of black workers,[7] in turn, limits the time that she can spend with her husband. Once employed as a domestic worker, her very presence in that 'white' area is a right only accorded to her while she remains employed. Many women are there illegally, and are thus even more at the mercy of their employers. Her inability to challenge rates of pay, hours and conditions of work generally, coupled with the absence of day-care facilities for her children, lead to her inevitable exploitation by other women. Many of the maids were well aware of their vulnerability to exploitation on the grounds of class, and their primary commitment to their white employing families was made reluctantly. The 'madams', however, themselves subject to exploitation and discrimination, largely ignored the structural restraints on their own power, such as rigid abortion laws, limits on the legal rights of married women and institutionalised lower wage rates for women in general. There is no provision for maternity leave in South Africa; indeed, a female public servant such as a teacher automatically loses her job on getting married.

Maids and madams offered totally different pictures of each other, their interactions and the actual work. As Cock (1980, p. 261) points out, both racial and sexual stereotypes of women share a set of beliefs as to the 'inferiority of the group in question, its incapacity to perform certain roles' and to exercise authority. White women, however, are

believed capable of exercising certain authority, but only that concerned with the running of the home or the control over children or
women or men of an 'inferior' race. Most white women accepted the
prevailing definitions of 'normal' woman and her place within the
home.

This picture of 'normal femininity' is also linked to the class
position of a particular group of women. For the white female members
of a dominant class, the restrictive attributes of the lady are only made
possible by a process of exploitation of other women termed, by
Olive Schreiner, 'female parasitism'. Her description of these women
(Schreiner, 1911, p. 81) still applies to the white women in Cock's
study. These women who, 'clad in fine raiment, the work of others'
fingers, waited on by the labour of others, fed on luxurious viands, the
result of others' toil,' seek 'by dissipation and amusements to fill up
the inordinate blank left by the lack of productive activity.'

If white women were not only to recognise the nature of their
exploitation of black women, but also to destroy the social distance
between them by noting the similarities in the restraints upon their
power, they could not perform their present controlling roles.
Perhaps, however, if you see yourself as relatively, and appropriately,
powerless, it may still be possible, and even more comfortable, to
exercise power over another, stigmatised, individual if that individual
does not challenge your definition of your own realm of competence.

Breaking the Boundaries

We have asserted that these stereotypes of 'normal' and 'deviant'
women are interrelated and that they involve justification both for the
forms and extent of control over women's behaviour. This system of
classification is itself a form of moral regulation: it allows women to be
deviant, but only in particular ways. As one contributor to *Justice of
the Peace* (Samuels, 1974) remarked: 'But do not imagine that men are
sinners and women saints . . . female deviancy takes other forms' than
crime: 'nagging, quarrelling, lying, deceit and sexual irregularity.' It
also allows for rebellion to be incorporated as part of the 'typical'
response of such women. Thus the 'awkward' female geriatric patient
is seen as a 'typical' old woman, to be controlled in the interests of
order amongst other patients. Post-natal depression is not seen to be
related to birth technology but as 'typical' of women's emotionality,
and justifies control by experts. The housewife who reacts against her

role is a 'typical' nagging, hysterical woman, just as the battered woman, standing up for herself, 'deserves what she gets'.

This system of moral regulation allocates certain categories of 'normal' female deviance. When women start appearing in classifications which fall outside this system,[8] or reject the categories themselves,[9] this may be seen as a serious threat to fundamental aspects of the social order. If women seek only formal legal equality, this threat may be lessened and women may be made to remain, both symbolically and actually, within 'their place', retaining a primary commitment and loyalty to 'womanly tasks'. We would suggest that the attempts of various women's groups, in the 1970s, to redefine the classifications themselves has produced increasingly strong societal reactions, apparently out of all proportion to the threat to the social order presented by any one of their aims. These reactions come close to meeting the criteria of Cohen's conception of a *moral panic* (Cohen, 1972, p. 28). Why should there be such a reaction at this time?

Stuart Hall *et al.* (1978) have posed similar questions as to the 'moral panic' over 'mugging' in the early 1970s, and the ways in which it was used to legitimate a more coercive state role. In a detailed and sensitive study, they show that not only was there no new crime wave but there was actually a dramatic slowing down in the increase of violent crime. The incidence of crime could not be linked to a 'softer' sentencing policy on the part of the courts as, immediately prior to this period, the courts had tended towards harsher sentencing and the imposition of longer sentences. Hall *et al.* show how the typification of this 'new' crime of 'mugging' was linked publicly with various social themes: the breakdown of public morality, the collapse of law and order, and the 'evils produced by the permissive society'. All this occurred during a period of political, economic and racial conflict engendering social anxieties in members of all classes. This moral panic was orchestrated by public moralists in the media, and in the courts, to fit with these anxieties. The call for punitive action and a traditionalist, disciplining approach to crime, therefore, made a much more successful appeal across class lines than did that of a liberal, reformist approach.

We would suggest that in Britain and the USA we are witnessing a similar 'moral panic' over the apparently 'new' phenomenon of women seeking to free themselves from 'traditional' classifications. In this anti-feminist backlash, the liberation of women is linked with a cluster of social themes: the 'permissive society', breakdown in law and order and 'public morality'. Abortion, pornography, sexual promiscuity, drugs and public acceptance of homosexuality are linked together. The 'blackboard jungle' of the comprehensive school, rising crime and general 'lack of discipline' are variously blamed on women's 'failure' to continue in their 'voluntary' caring roles and to promote a 'traditional' morality within the home. In all this, women are seen as contributing to a general lessening and removal of 'civilised standards'.

In the USA the various factions of such public moralists have played a significant part in the election of President Reagan. A coalition called 'Moral Majority' was formed from various groups concerned with issues such as opposition to the Equal Rights Amendment, abortion and homosexuality. Not only was this group able to command considerable financial resources, but women played a large part in the organisation and leadership of the campaign, which achieved its dual objectives of electing Reagan and ousting a specified group of senators known for their liberal stance on various social issues. We also have to understand, given the success of the appeal across class lines, why the majority of *all* women who voted, voted for Reagan.

Associated themes, in Britain, have been taken up by such bodies as the Festival of Light, LIFE and SPUC, not only in their opposition to abortion laws but also in their general opposition to the 'permissive society'. The present Thatcher administration, despite a rhetoric of freedom, has been returned on policies calling for increased use of authority against 'childish' strikers, 'welfare scroungers' and law breakers in general. Many of their proposals are concerned, specifically, with returning women to their 'rightful place'.[10] Women are asked to leave jobs for 'men who need them', maternity-leave provision is being attacked, calls are made for women to undertake the 'voluntary' care of groups such as the elderly or handicapped and nursery-school places are being cut.

All these events take place at a time of social and economic upheaval. Soaring unemployment figures, inadequate housing provision, the loss of whole fields of employment in areas such as the textile industry and the threat to jobs offered by new technology all contribute to the fears of many men and women of all classes, who find the security of their personal worlds threatened. The world is 'falling apart' for many people, and women may only too easily be seen as potential scapegoats.

To reject these imposed classifications of women and to see common interests between the groups of women involves taking on new, and often frightening, responsibilities. We have to come to appreciate and to understand these fears, together with the others to which the anti-feminists appeal, before we can combat the effects of this growing 'moral panic', which could lead to the imposition of new controls over the behaviour of women.

Women do not 'naturally' or 'inevitably' fall within the classifications of normality and abnormality outlined in this chapter. As Gayle Rubin says (1975, p. 158), in a rephrasing of Marx's words,

What is a domesticated woman? A female of the species. The one explanation is as good as the other. A woman is a woman. She only becomes a domestic, a chattel, a playboy bunny, a prostitute or a human dictaphone in certain relations. Torn from these relations she is no more the help-mate of man than gold itself is money.

Classifications of British women have changed over the centuries but here, as in other countries, some women have always, in many ways, sought to free themselves from control and regulation (Rowbotham, 1972). Oakley (1972, p. 10) quotes this declaration of hope from a pamphlet issued in 1620, *Haec Vir* or 'the womanish-man':

We are as freeborn as Men, have as free elections and as free spirit, we are compounded of like parts and may with liberty make benefit of our creations.

Notes

Many people have helped us in writing this chapter. We are particularly grateful to Clive Briault, Kay Frost, the late Ellen Williams and Gavin Williams.

1. See, for example, Oakley (1972) and Maccoby and Jacklin (1974). For a discussion of women's perceptions of differences between the sexes, see Fransella and Frost (1977).
2. In 1978, 358,026 males and 66,036 females were found guilty of indictable offences in England and Wales (Home Office, 1979).
3. Note that both the American 'realist' school of jurisprudential writers and advocates of the 'sceptical' approach to deviance have been criticised for this emphasis on the 'law in action' (McBarnet, 1976).
4. Dr Ian Stewart, Consultant Psychiatrist at Rampton, recently commented (*The Sunday Times*, 16 November 1980):

There is delay in taking women into custody, for understandable reasons, but it means that their condition is chronic on admission. The length of stay of female patients is, on average, three years longer than that of males.

Hormonal factors help to perpetuate disturbed behaviour and so does the stress of mothers being separated from children. There is thus a far greater frequency of impulsive violent behaviour to those around them and to them-selves. It is little wonder that the female population was consuming at least double the quantity of drugs per head compared with the male wing.

5. For a discussion of the issues affecting women social workers and women clients, see Wilson (1977, 1980) and Jones (1980).
6. For a discussion of income distribution within British marriages see Pahl (1980).
7. See Wilson (1972). For a detailed account of the effects on the life of one black woman, see Joubert (1978).
8. For example, violent crime. See Smart (1976), especially pp. xiv—xv. The *Daily Express* (28 October 1977) carried a report headed *Deadly as the Male: Women Muggers who Terrified a Judge*, in which Judge Gwyn Morris is quoted as saying that this case 'highlighted the emergence of the female mugger in a sophisticated form'.
9. For example, Evers (Chapter 5) suggests that 'Changes in the relative status of female nurses and patients would, in turn, create new tensions and conflicts in the wider organisation of the health services.'
10. See Rowbotham (1972, pp. 160—2) for a discussion of similar reactions in Stalinist Russia. For a more recent account of responses in Eastern Europe, see Scott (1976), especially Chapter 7, pp. 138—63.

Bibliography

Ardener, S. (ed.) *Defining Females: The Nature of Women in Society* (Croom Helm, London, 1978)

Badinter, E. *L'Amour en Plus: L'Histoire de l'Amour Maternelle* (Flammoir, Paris, 1980)

Bardwick, J. *Psychology of Women* (Harper and Row, New York, 1971)

Barrett, M. and Roberts, H. 'Doctors and Their Patients: The Social Control of Women in General Practice', in Smart and Smart (1978)

Becker, H.S. *Outsiders* (Collier-Macmillan, New York, 1963)

Box, S. *Deviance, Reality and Society* (Holt, Rinehart and Winston, London, 1971)

Brunner, A., Macleod, L. and Williams, G.A.F. 'Cross Sex Supervision in the Probation and Aftercare Service Reviewed', *Probation Staff Magazine*, Cleveland County (May, 1974)

Camberwell Council on Alcoholism *Women and Alcohol* (Tavistock, London, 1980)

Carlson, R. 'On the Structure of Self-esteem: Comments on Ziller's Formulation'. *Journal of Consulting and Clinical Psychology*, vol. 34 (1970), pp. 264—8

——— 'Sex Differences in Ego Functioning: Exploratory Studies of Agency and Communion'. *Journal of Consulting and Clinical Psychology*, vol. 37 (1971), pp. 267—77

Cock, J. *Maids and Madams: A Study in the Politics of Exploitation* (Raven Press, Johannesburg, 1980)

Cohen, A. *Delinquent Boys* (The Free Press, Glencoe, 1955)

Cohen, S. (ed.) *Images of Deviance* (Penguin, Harmondsworth, 1971)

——— *Folk Devils and Moral Panics: The Creation of Mods and Rockers* (Macgibbon and Kee, London, 1972)

Cohen, S. and Taylor, L. *Escape Attempts: The Theory and Practice of Resistance* to Everyday Life (Allen Lane, London, 1976)

Coote, A. and Gill, G. Women's Rights: A Practical Guide, 2nd edn. (Penguin, Harmondsworth, 1977)

Coser, L. Greedy Institutions (The Free Press, Glencoe, 1974)

Dell, S. 'Transfer of Special Hospital Patients to the NHS', British Journal of Psychiatry, vol. 136 (1980), pp. 222–34

Dell, S. and Parker, E. 'Special Hospitals Case Register Triennial Statistics 1972–4', in Special Hospitals Case Register: The First Five Years, Special Hospitals Research Report no. 15 (1979)

Fitzgerald, M. and Sim, J. British Prisons (Basil Blackwell, Oxford, 1979)

Fransella, F. and Frost, K. On Being a Woman: A Review of Research on How Women See Themselves (Tavistock, London, 1977)

Giallombardo, R. Society of Women: A Study of a Women's Prison (John Wiley, New York, 1966)

Goffman, E. Asylums (Doubleday, New York, 1961)

—— Stigma: Notes on the Management of Spoiled Identity (Prentice Hall, Englewood Cliffs, 1963; Penguin, Harmondsworth, 1968)

Greenwald, H. The Call Girl (Ballantine, New York, 1958)

Hall, S. et al. Policing the Crisis: Mugging, the State and Law and Order (Macmillan, London and Basingstoke, 1978)

Hartley, R.E. 'A Developmental View of Female Sex-Role Identification' in B.J. Biddle and E.J. Thomas (eds.), Role Theory (John Wiley, New York, 1966)

Heidensohn, F. 'The Deviance of Women: A Critique and an Enquiry'. British Journal of Sociology, vol. 19 (1968), pp. 160–75

Home Office Criminal Statistics, England and Wales 1978 (HMSO, London, 1979)

Jones, C. 'Women in Social Control: The Case of Social Work' (seminar paper, Oxford Women's Studies, 1980)

Joubert, E. Die Swerfjare Van Poppie Nongena (Kaapstad, Tafelberg, 1978); translated as The Long Journey of Poppie Nongena (1980)

Kaplan, H. 'Self-derogation and Social Position: Interaction Effects of Sex, Race, Education and Age', Social Psychology, vol. 8 (1973), pp. 92–9

Lombroso, C. and Ferrero, W. The Female Offender (Fisher Unwin, London, 1895)

McBarnet, D.J. 'Pre-trial Procedures and Construction of Conviction', in P. Carlen (ed.), The Sociology of Law, Sociological Review Monograph 23 (University of Keele, 1976)

Maccoby, E.E. and Jacklin, C.N. The Psychology of Sex Differences, volume I: Text; volume II: Annotated Bibliography (Stanford University Press, Stanford, California, 1974)

Macintyre, S. 'Who Wants Babies? The Social Construction of "Instincts" ', in D. Barker and S. Allen (eds.), Sexual Divisions and Society: Process and Change (Tavistock, London, 1976)

Mannheim, H. Comparative Criminology (Routledge and Kegan Paul, London, 1965), vol. 2

Mead, M. Sex and Temperament in Three Primitive Societies (William Morrow, 1935)

Moss, H.A. 'Sex, Age and State as Determinants of Mother-Infant Interaction', in K. Danziger (ed.), Readings in Child Socialisation (Pergamon, Oxford, 1970)

Murphy, L.B. The Widening World of Childhood (Basic, New York, 1962)

Oakley, A. Sex, Gender and Society (Temple Smith, London, 1972)

—— The Sociology of Housework (Martin Robertson, London, 1974)

Page, A. 'Counselling', in Camberwell Council on Alcoholism (1980), pp. 159–75

Pahl, J. 'Patterns of Money Management within Marriage', *Journal of Social Policy*, vol. 9, no. 3 (1980), pp. 313–15

Parker, T. (ed.) *The Man Inside: An Anthology of Writing and Conversational Comment by Men in Prison* (Michael Joseph, London, 1973)

Parsloe, P. 'Cross-sex Supervision in the Probation and After-care Service', *British Journal of Criminology*, vol. 12, no. 3 (July 1972), pp. 269–79

Pollak, O. *The Criminality of Women* (University of Pennsylvania Press, Pennsylvania, 1950)

Reiter, R. (ed.) *Towards an Anthropology of Women* (Monthly Review Press, New York, 1975)

Rosaldo, M.Z. and Lamphere, L. (eds.) *Women, Culture and Society* (Stanford University Press, Stanford, California, 1974)

Rowbotham, S. *Women, Resistance and Revolution* (Allen Lane, Harmondsworth, 1972; Penguin, 1974)

Rubin, G. 'The Traffic in Women: Notes on the Political Economy of Sex', in Reiter (1975)

Samuels, J. *Justice of the Peace* (12 October 1974), p. 563

Schreiner, O. *Women and Labour* (Fisher Unwin, London, 1911); new edition, with preface by J. Graves (Virago, London, 1978)

Scott, H. *Women and Socialism: Experiences from Eastern Europe* (Allison and Busby, London, 1976)

Sears, R.R., Maccoby, E. and Levin, H. *Patterns of Child Rearing* (Row Peterson, Evanston, Illinois, 1957)

Sheehan, M. and Watson, J. 'Response and Recognition', in Camberwell Council on Alcoholism (1980)

Smart, C. *Women, Crime and Criminology: A Feminist Critique* (Routledge and Kegan Paul, London, 1976a)

Smart, C. and Smart, B. (eds.) *Women, Sexuality and Social Control* (Routledge and Kegan Paul, London, 1976b)

Stacey, M. 'The Division of Labour Revisited or Overcoming the Two Adams' (paper given at the British Sociological Association Annual Conference, 1980; to be published by Allen and Unwin)

Thomas, J.E. *The English Prison Officer since 1850: A Study in Conflict* (Routledge and Kegan Paul, London, 1972)

Thomas, W.I. *Sex and Society* (Little Brown, Boston, 1907)

Turk, A.T. *Criminality and the Legal Order* (Rand McNally, Chicago, 1967)

Uhlenberg, P. 'Older Women: The Growing Challenge to Design Constructive Roles', *The Gerontologist*, vol. 19, no. 3 (1979), pp. 236–9

Vincent, S. 'No Immortal Longings?', *Observer* (28 September, 1980)

Wilson, E. *Women and the Welfare State* (Tavistock, London, 1977)

—— 'Feminism and Social Work' in M. Brake and R. Bailey (eds.), *Radical Social Work and Practice* (Edward Arnold, London, 1980)

Wilson, F. *Migrant Labour*. Report to the South African Council of Churches (The South African Council of Churches and Spro-Cas, Johannesburg, 1972)

Wollstonecroft, M. *A Vindication of the Rights of Women* (Joseph Johnson, London, 1792); new edition, M. Krannick (ed.) (Penguin, Harmondsworth, 1975)

2 LAW AND THE CONTROL OF WOMEN'S SEXUALITY: THE CASE OF THE 1950s

Carol Smart

The nature of law and its relation to a given social formation is currently an issue of debate and enquiry, particularly within marxist schools of thought (Hall *et al.*, 1978; Hirst, 1979; Picciotto, 1979). However, such debates have consistently given priority to issues of social class and related economic and political forms of domination. They have not conceded the equal significance of sexual oppression to their general thesis. Thus, although there is a growing amount of feminist literature highlighting the way in which the law discriminates against, or disadvantages, women (for example, Land, 1976; Sachs and Wilson, 1978; O'Donovan, 1979), there is as yet little work available on the nature of law in relation to structures of patriarchy (see Harrison and Mort, 1980). This is no easy task; the difficulties of theorising the nature of the law in relation to a given formation are themselves considerable, but in addition feminists have not yet established a fully adequate conceptualisation of patriarchy nor its relationship to a given mode of production (cf. Beechey, 1979). Any attempt therefore to explore the relationship between patriarchal structures, law and the capitalist state must still be tentative.

The concept of patriarchy necessarily focuses analysis in the first instance on the family and the economic, sexual and reproductive relations between the sexes in a household unit. A major site of women's oppression has been identified as centring on male domination over female sexuality and women's reproductive capacity (Rowbotham, 1973; McDonough and Harrison, 1978), as well as the organisation of unpaid domestic labour (Delphy, 1977; Bland *et al.*, 1978; McIntosh, 1979). It is essential to comprehend these relations prior to theorising women's position in the waged-labour market precisely because women are never independent of the domestic sphere, or as McDonough and Harrison term it, the relations of reproduction. In other words, as waged workers women are still wives and mothers, and even as single women they are potential wives and mothers. Women, as Mitchell (1975) has argued, are still primarily defined in terms of the kinship structure and not as individual workers who can 'freely' sell their labour power. Women do not negotiate in the labour market on the same terms as men and to understand this difference their position within the kinship or family structure must be addressed first. As McDonough and Harrison (1978, p. 31) maintain,

> A wife's relation to capital is always a mediated one because of her primary responsibility to service the family: her relation to production is always mediated through her relations to her husband, precisely through the relation of human reproduction.

This necessarily problematises orthodox materialist conceptions of women's class position, because it is not only the domestic labourer whose class position is allocated via her husband rather than by her relation to the means of production, but also the female wage-labourer who cannot operate 'freely' on the labour market. The under-valuation of female labour (waged and domestic), which is justified in terms of women's wages being 'pin money' or the female labour force being unreliable or of housework not being *real* work, is precisely a consequence of patriarchal relations within the family. This economic weakness, or the essentially proletarian class position of most women regardless of their standard of living, is usually only revealed when a particular household unit breaks down. Much of the time it is hidden by the structure of the domestic economy, particularly the institution of housekeeping, which can masquerade as a wage, or simply by the privacy of domestic life, which obscures the extensiveness and specificity of the poverty suffered by women (Delphy and Leonard, 1980).

Patriarchal relations are therefore not confined to the domestic sphere, even though the relations of reproduction are necessarily given analytical priority in theorising women's oppression in the *present*. Patriarchy is as much a feature of the political economy as of the domestic economy or women's consciousness. Rowbotham is mistaken when she argues that an analysis of patriarchal relations produces two separate systems of oppression, one patriarchal and the other capitalistic. She maintains (Rowbotham, 1979, p. 970) that, with such an analysis,

> We have patriarchy oppressing women and capitalism oppressing male workers. We have biological reproduction on the one hand and work on the other. We have the ideology of 'patriarchy' opposed to the mode of production which is seen as a purely economic matter.

Such an outcome is not inevitable; giving analytic primacy to one aspect of the social formation does not imply the existence of opposed concrete structures in the 'real' world. Moreover the aim of such an analysis is to link biological reproduction to waged labour, to examine the extent to which a capitalist economy is dependent upon a sexually differentiated labour force and to consider how patriarchal relations may mediate the influences and development of capitalism (and vice versa).

It is with aspects of the latter issue that this chapter is primarily concerned. In as much as legislation provides the capitalist state with one of the predominant means of reinforcing and reproducing the social order, including gender differentiation, it is necessary, as part of an overall project attempting to understand the oppression of women, to examine the role of the law as it is produced under a capitalist economic order and, further, to examine how the law modifies, reinforces or undermines patriarchal relations initially in the realms of reproduction and sexuality but also in the realms of domestic and waged labour. However in analysing the nature of law in relation to patriarchy it is instructive to examine the problems of marxist theories of law, so as to avoid replicating the same inadequacies. It might, for example, be tempting to depict the law simply as an instrument of patriarchal oppression, asserting that it overtly and covertly serves the interest of the dominant male group or, more abstractly, the interests of patriarchy.[1] Such a position would tend to be supported by the existence of tax laws which treat a wife's earnings as her husband's; social security laws which ban a woman from living with a man whilst drawing benefit or which bar women from claiming certain benefits because they are not defined as 'breadwinners'; or divorce laws which define a woman's share of matrimonial property as only one-third of the total. But like capitalism, patriarchy has its contradictions, and there is not necessarily an homogeneous set of 'interests' for the law to serve.

It is worth considering, for example, that during the twentieth century the law has reversed its position on the question of custody of children on divorce or separation so that mothers now are far more likely to win the custody of children than fathers. This may be little more than a legal recognition of the social organisation of childcare, but it removes from most men the power they once had over their wives via their children. Moreover many of the law reforms that most concern women have been won only by women's struggle,[2] and so to imply that the law is only a reflection of the interests of patriarchy (whether overt or covert) is to deny the significance and the consequences of that struggle. Moreover much of the legislation that has been enacted over the last century in the area of family law has had an appreciable effect on the economic status of women, particularly on wives faced with divorce. Although the law cannot provide for a real equality of economic power within the family, the gradual erosion of disabilities placed on married women with regard to property rights and the growing recognition of the economic contribution of domestic labour have at least *reduced* the married woman's powerlessness. Feminist analyses of law should therefore be cautious of resorting to the simplistic metaphor of conspiracy, which has been shown to be manifestly inadequate elsewhere.

Similarly it is possible to appreciate, from an examination of other analyses, the problem of the concept of legal equality. As a political strategy, the Women's Movement is struggling for full formal legal equality with men, but in terms of a feminist analysis of law it must be recognised that real legal equality is illusionary within the prevailing social formation. The concept of legal equality is part of a powerful liberal ideology which has appeal because it apparently offers an impartial system of justice and regulation. But treating as equal, persons who are manifestly socially and economically unequal can actually operate to further discriminatory practices whilst perpetuating an ideology of total fairness and impartiality (Gregory, 1979[3]).

It is perhaps also important not to over-emphasise the significance of the law in the control of women and other minorities. As Hall *et al.* (1978) have argued, it is not only the content of the law that changes but also the position of the law. In other words, through law reform the content of legislation may become less obviously discriminatory but, equally significant, the centrality of the law may alter such that other agencies, often quasi-legal, may take over and develop certain controlling functions. Control is therefore mediated through numerous agencies which may ultimately have the backing of law but which, in appearance, are far removed from legal institutions. An example of this process is the cohabitation rule, which has removed the surveillance of women's non-marital sexual behaviour away from the operations of the courts (where a separated husband could once apply to have a maintenance order stopped if his wife simply committed adultery) to the operations of the Department of Health and Social Security with its special investigators. Moreover the DHSS can prosecute the woman for social-security fraud in addition to ending her benefits; its punitive sanctions are thus much more extensive. The law is therefore no longer a discrete, easily definable institution. It has expanded its scope immensely since World War II, not necessarily because of changing legislation but because of the development of new technologies and new professions (especially social work) which facilitate the surveillance of people's lives and intrusions into their privacy. This surveillance and intrusion does not have an overt legal appearance, however, and so the law itself remains in the background, relying on alternative agencies to operate control. It is, in turn, precisely the operations of these alternative agencies that allows the law itself to become more permissive and 'egalitarian'. A progressive body of legislation is therefore mirrored by extra-legal forms of control elsewhere.[4]

So far the law has been depicted as a purely coercive agency or force (Foucault, 1979) but it is possible to argue, as do Hall *et al.* (1978), that the legal system is also part of the 'production of consent' and that it has a positive and educative function which orchestrates 'public opinion'. The law therefore does not simply reflect 'public opinion' (itself a controversial concept), it is part of the production of consensus around such issues as the importance of law and order, the sanctity of private property and the sacred nature of the family. Again, the law may no longer be a primary agency in this respect; for example, the media, the structure of language and the education system may now be held to be of greater salience. Yet the law, through its refusal to recognise such phenomena as rape in marriage, by its treatment of wives' earnings as husbands' property, by its reluctance in practice to recognise domestic violence and by its criminalisation of women prostitutes, sustains, perpetuates and justifies a consensual view on sex roles and the relative rights and duties of men and women. The law can therefore be theorised as a mode of reproduction of the existing patriarchal order, minimising social change but avoiding the problems of overt conflict.

Finally any feminist analysis of law should not fail to make a distinction between the law as it appears in its legislative form and the law as it is routinely practised. The disparity between the spirit of the Equal Pay Act and the Sex Discrimination Act 1975 and their enforcement is a prime example of this. Apparently progressive legislation can be rendered virtually useless if the courts and other agencies fail to operate it as legislators intended, whilst the fact that the legislation exists at all sustains a liberal and egalitarian front to actual legal practices. This is not, however, to negate the struggle for legal reform, but rather to emphasise that the law itself is *not* a unified structure, and that the operations of the law can vary according to its different levels of jurisdiction,[5] or can be dependent upon the activities of the

Although divorce and illegitimacy rates rose during and immediately after the war, never returning to the pre-war level, the 1950s had a stable divorce rate, with an illegitimacy rate in England and Wales that fell consistently in the first half of the decade, rising again during the second half but not escalating until the 1960s (Gill, 1977). In spite of this, the 1950s was a decade that was apparently fearful of an imminent collapse of the family. The war had obviously had a destructive effect on many families and the government (which was Conservative from 1951 to 1964) placed considerable emphasis on re-stabilising the family. This policy took several overt and covert forms. Most significant, perhaps, was the refusal to reform the law on divorce during the 1950s in spite of much public and Parliamentary pressure. The Royal Commission on Marriage and Divorce (1956) could not ultimately contemplate a relaxation in the law for fear that the divorce 'contagion' would spread. Indeed the commissioners stated that they would recommend the total abolition of divorce if they felt it would end the high degree of family instability that they perceived to be a feature of post-war Britain.

Also of great significance during this decade was the development of the social-work profession and the increase in health visitors. These professionals were, in many ways, the 'carriers' of new bourgeois ideas on the nature of family life, the role of women and the centrality of child care. The period after the war marked the beginnings of a new emphasis on childhood. The work of Melanie Klein and other neo-Freudians stressed the vital importance of the mother/child dyad for normal development, while the work of Bowlby (1951) gave such theories credit through empirical research. One of the primary functions of the family became the socialisation of 'normal' children, and social workers and health visitors were pushing forward the frontiers of this, now widely accepted, ideology. The lack of waged work for many women was therefore complemented by scientifically sustained versions of the traditional belief that a woman's place is in the home. In turn this could be used to redefine women's unemployment, or inability to engage in wage labour, as a non-problem for the state. This is one instance in which the lack of demand for women in the labour market operated to reinforce patriarchal control within the family by re-emphasising the extent to which women's participation in that market is dependent upon the demands of the family structure. The state during the 1950s was therefore 'mobilised' to support the family and patriarchal relations, and this was gradually linked with a growing belief that stability in the family had benefits elsewhere, particularly in avoiding delinquency and other social problems.

Alongside this policy of restabilisation there developed what has been termed an eroticisation of the family (Shorter, 1977). Whilst the Victorian era might be typically viewed as a period when most sexual enjoyment (for men at least) occurred outside the family (and very little apparently occurred for women at all), the 1950s marked a distinct change in this tendency. The work of Chesser (1957) and the whole thrust of marriage guidance moved towards an appreciation of sex as a mode of sustaining and stabilising the family. Sex became, not so much an act of intrinsic enjoyment, but a method of maintaining sexual monogamy, which was increasingly defined as the cornerstone of family stability. Interestingly, this monogamy had consequences for men as well as women, as it was predominantly the 'discovery' of the married woman's sexual potential that was to be geared towards satisfying the needs of her husband in order to prevent his infidelities. The 1950s witnessed the beginning of the weakening of the link between sex and reproduction, particularly with the growing dissemination of knowledge about contraception. However, sex in turn became tied to sustaining the monogamous nuclear family. A wife was allowed, even encouraged, to be sexual but her sexuality had to be functional in terms of family stability and was consequently still constrained within very narrow limits.

Moreover, it appears that sex itself was being romanticised. Shorter (1977) in his history of the modern family argues that there is a close connection between sexual and sentimental patterns in the nineteenth and twentieth centuries which implies a growing association between love and sex. Sex increasingly required the justification of romantic love; it was not simply a duty or a necessary bodily function, but became a way of expressing love. It is precisely this link between sex and love, combined with the eroticisation of the family (particularly the wife and mother) and the instrumental nature of sexual pleasure, that provides a platform for beginning to understand why prostitution was so condemned in the 1950s and how its condemnation was specific to the decade and not simply a reaffirmation of traditional Christian values. The prostitute became a new folk devil *in spite* of an apparent liberation of female sexuality in discourses on sex.

However, in spite of these apparent changes in the 1950s, it seems that for a great many women sex was still a duty, the clitoris was unheard of, and orgasm rare. It is of course impossible to know this without reservation, but such studies as occurred during this period of Britain (for example, Slater and Woodside, 1951; Gorer, 1971) at least reveal that, in speaking about sex, women and men (particularly in the working classes) adhered to the ideology of superior male sexuality, double standards of morality and of the essentially spiritual nature of sex for women. How the subjects' sexual practices may have varied from their statements on sexual practices is unknown, but regardless of any degree of variation it is significant in itself that in speaking about sex the subjects conformed to fairly traditional discourses on sexual behaviour. This would tend to reflect the power of ideologies concerning 'normal' sexual behaviour which were not transformed at that time by the 'new sexuality' of the post-war sexologists and psychologists.

The Moral Panic over Prostitution

The emphasis on the value of family life in the 1950s cannot itself explain why attitudes towards prostitution hardened so much at that time. Throughout the first half of the twentieth century there had been attempts to increase police powers over prostitutes and to clear the streets of their presence (Storch, 1977). These attempts had been strongly resisted by civil libertarians, who feared that a general increase in police powers would be extended to cover all citizens and would reduce 'personal freedom' in a blanket fashion. In fact there had been several lobbies and a departmental report on prostitution (Macmillan, 1928) which argued that police powers should be reduced and that the category of 'common prostitute' should be removed from the wording of the legislation on street offences. In other words, not only was there a fear that the police would try to establish greater controls over the general population but, prior to the 1950s, there was also a desire to give prostitutes the same protection from police harassment as other citizens. Such progressive aims had disappeared by the end of the war, however, mainly because the police had gained a greater legitimacy and also because the state offered strong reassurances to concerned lobbies that only a specific, socially undeserving and undesirable, sector of the community would be affected by new legislation giving the police greater powers.

Even so, changes in legislation would probably not have occurred if there had not been such a successfully orchestrated moral panic over prostitution in the 1950s. The first wave of the panic occurred prior to the establishment of the Wolfenden Committee (1953—4), whilst the second occurred around the time of the publication of the Report of the Committee on Homosexual Offences as Prostitution (Wolfenden, 1957), prior to the enactment of new legislation. The first wave focused on two issues, one being the number of tourists in London due to the

Coronation and the shameful reputation that the capital was acquiring as the vice centre of the western world. This was not welcomed at a time when a new, young Queen had just acceded to the throne, and it was also felt that undesirable, mafia-type figures would be attracted to Britain. But perhaps more important still was the second issue, that of immigration (Gosling and Warner, 1960). In the 1950s the 'problem of prostitution' became linked with the 'problem of immigration'. In post-war London many of the pimps were Maltese, Italian and West Indian, and this combination of black or foreign men, said to be 'living off the bodies of white women', was utilised to enrage public opinion. Magistrates and judges spoke of a desire to bring back whipping, and MPs raised questions of deportation for black and foreign pimps. Unease about the visibility of prostitution, particularly in residential areas like Stepney and Paddington, was sufficient, when coupled with a racialist ideology, to allow the press to orchestrate the ensuing panic.

There is, in fact, some doubt as to whether prostitution was actually increasing during the 1950s, even though police statistics were used to imply this. There are reasons to suspect that, in reality, the police increased their arrest rates, thereby creating an apparent crime wave, in order to further the pressure on the government for new legislation. But whether or not there was an increase, a new theme developed during this period, namely that the visibility of prostitution was harmful to family life and particularly to the psychological development of the young. The prostitute was engendered therefore with the ability to 'deprave and corrupt' by her mere presence. Unlike the prostitute of the nineteenth century, her twentieth-century counterpart was not as socially distant from the respectable woman and the monogamous family. Streetwalkers were undoubtedly predominantly working class but, in post-war Britain, class distinctions, although they had by no means disappeared, were very different from those of the previous century. The prostitute could no longer be held as a class apart from respectable women; the separate spheres were merging, and in this way the prostitute became more of a threat to respectable family lifestyles. Her proximity, both socially and spatially, presented a challenge to all the values embodied in ideologies of family life and motherhood so prevalent in the 1950s.

The Wolfenden Report, which was in part an outcome of the first wave of panic, requires close analysis (see Bland *et al.*, 1978). The major concern of the report was homosexuality, with prostitution appearing as something of an after-thought, an additional problem for the committee to resolve as a consequence of the pressure exerted over the

Government. The committee therefore spent disproportionate amounts of its resources and time on the two issues. In its recommendations on legislation pertaining to prostitution, the report was surprisingly illiberal and far more oppressive than the Macmillan Report on Street Offences had been almost 30 years previously. Yet Wolfenden is popularly taken as an enlightened document with a liberal philosophy underlying it. This is essentially because the significance of the report has been read in terms of its proposals on homosexuality, which have been thought of as progressive in spite of its pro-heterosexual ideology and its perpetuation of legal discrimination, whilst the section on prostitution has largely been ignored or glossed over.

The guiding principle of Wolfenden was the distinction between law and morality, and the individual's right to make his/her own moral choices without legal interference as long as harm is not inflicted on another. Privacy became the key note to this principle. What this concept of privacy entailed for certain classes of prostitutes who needed to be publicly visible to meet their clients was, however, little more than a justification for an extension of policy control over them. Thus, whilst Wolfenden was recommending that the control of homosexuality should be partially removed from legal agencies to medical, psychiatric or other professional bodies, he surrendered the street prostitute even further into the control of the criminal law.

Having justified the extension of police powers over street-walkers by reference to a pragmatic and liberal concept of freedom of moral choice in the confines of privacy, Wolfenden could not foresee that even that privacy would be violated in practice as soon as the legislation was implemented. Within a year of the 1959 Street Offences Act becoming law, the courts extended police jurisdiction over prostitutes into their own homes. A woman who solicited from her doorway or window was deemed to be, for the purposes of the Act, *soliciting in the street*.[7] Publishers of contact magazines were prosecuted for 'corrupting public morals'[8] and the managers of saunas, etc. could be prosecuted for procuring prostitutes.[9] In the sphere of prostitution, the fragile concept of privacy was very rapidly destroyed, and even the most discreet forms of prostitution, which Wolfenden had not been concerned to eradicate, came under the new law.

The 1959 Street Offences Act [10]

Hall *et al.* (1978) have defined the moral panic as a principal form of ideological consciousness through which the so-called silent majority comes to support increasingly coercive forms of control by the state.

In the case of legislation on soliciting, it would seem that the moral panics of the 1950s achieved precisely this end. The 1959 Act, which was based almost entirely on Wolfenden's recommendations, was warmly received even though it was in fact a reactionary reformulation of the nineteenth-century Vagrancy Acts, with additional powers for fining and imprisoning given to the courts. Prostitutes in legal practice had never been constituted as persons with the same rights as other citizens. The term 'common prostitute', dating from common law, defined them as non-persons in a legal sense, while the nineteenth-century Vagrancy Acts cast them as 'idle and disorderly' persons or 'incorrigible rogues'. As such, they were always placed outside 'respectable' society. The 1959 Act merely translated this exteriority or exclusion into a more contemporary setting, changing the terminology of vagrancy legislation but retaining the concept of the 'common prostitute'. In so doing it perpetuated a legal practice, which in turn perpetuated a social acceptance, of constituting prostitutes as a pariah group with no access to the civil rights taken for granted by most of the community. The retention of the term 'common prostitute' meant in effect that a woman's previous record was read out in court before she had been tried, whilst at the same time the Act made it possible for her to be convicted on police evidence alone. Although Wolfenden had been concerned about eradicating the 'nuisance' of prostitution that the moral entrepreneurs had been so anxious about, the legislation he ultimately recommended made no reference to this by requiring proof of annoyance to the public by a prostitute. The law could therefore be used against the most inconspicuous and inoffensive streetwalker miles away from the respectable families she was supposedly corrupting.

The debates on the Street Offences Bill in both Houses of Parliament reveal that most MPs were fully aware of the repressive nature of this legislation. Women in the Commons, led by Eirene White, were particularly vociferous in their condemnation of the legislation. However the Conservative Government, which refused to act on legislation on homosexuality so close to a General Election, did not have the same reservations about legislation on soliciting. In fact the highly visible effect of clearing the streets of 'undesirables' and increasing the penalties for soliciting and living off immoral earnings was congruent with the popular ideology of law and order espoused by the Conservatives and general public even in 1959. It should be remembered that the latter half of the 1950s saw the impact of youth countercultures for the first time. The permissive age was dawning and the reaction then, as now, was to attempt to reassert authority and to implement more punitive controls. The legislation was, therefore, popular rather than controversial, a benefit to the election campaign rather than a disadvantage.

The production of new legislation on prostitution in the 1950s therefore needs to be understood in terms of, firstly, the efforts to re-stabilise the family and, secondly, a new sexual morality which was particularly salient to women. This morality was no longer of the repressive Victorian variety but rather in the mould of the 'sexual mother figure', where sexuality was not excluded, but used instrumentally to increase pair-bonding and provide stability for developing children. The prostitute was as much an anathema to this morality as she had been to nineteenth-century morals. In addition, the catalyst for creating the legislation in the 1950s was the moral panic based on the power of prostitution to corrupt the vulnerable nuclear family, coupled with racialist sentiments about undesirable immigrants exploiting simple-minded, depraved white women. Ironically the outcome of the legislation was to force prostitutes further into the control of the very pimps and exploitative criminal organisations there had been so much panic over. It became extremely difficult for prostitutes to work independently, precisely because they could no longer legitimately make direct contact with their clients. If they did attempt to solicit on their own behalf, they became subject to increased control from the police. Ultimately, virtually police-designated 'red-light' districts became established, within which prostitution was contained and controlled directly by agents of the state, namely the police.

Legislation on Sexual Offences – the Victorian Heritage

The only other major piece of legislation governing sexual behaviour in the criminal sphere during the 1950s was the Sexual Offences Act of 1956. This was an act to consolidate a wide variety of existing legislation on sexual offences.[11] Prior to this Act, criminal activities such as running a brothel, rape or incest were all dealt with under separate legislation, some of it dating back to the 1885 Criminal Law (Amendment) Act and the 1898 Vagrancy Act. Consolidation acts allow Parliament to up-date and rationalise statutes without going through the usual procedures of debates in both Houses, as long as no change is actually made to the law. It is interesting that the law on sexual offences should be consolidated at this time, as by 1956 the Wolfenden Committee had been sitting for a year and was already considering some of the legislation embodied in the consolidated Act.

Clearly there was a particular concern about sexual offences in the 1950s and it was felt that a rationalisation of existing laws could not await the deliberations of Wolfenden.

Although it is clear that the Wolfenden Report and the subsequent Street Offences Act overshadowed the 1956 Sexual Offences Act because they produced controversy and change, while the 1956 Act produced 'sameness' and continuity, the 1956 Act is nonetheless of considerable significance. This is precisely because it did *not* effectively change legislation that had been on the statute books for over 50 years and which, in some instances, stemmed from common law.[12] The Conservative Government in the 1950s apparently felt that, in the prevailing moral climate, it would be insensitive to raise the issues of incest, rape or sexual assault with a view to reform of the law, even though so much of the existing legislation had been formulated under very different social and economic conditions. Ultimately, therefore, the 1950s represent a 'holding operation' on legislation regarding most sexual offences, with the criminal law maintaining its jurisdiction over much sexual behaviour. It was therefore, and still is, an offence for a man to bugger a woman, even though she consents (it is no longer criminal for a man to do it to a man as long as there is consent and both are over 21), and the law then, as now, provided a maximum penalty of two years imprisonment for an indecent assault on a woman but a maximum of ten years for a similar assault on a man.

Whilst the Government in the 1950s failed to address itself to the antiquated and often inadequate laws on sexual behaviour (such as legislation on rape) that stemmed from a Victorian morality, it was also rejecting reforms in non-criminal areas. At this time the Government successfully avoided any change to the laws on divorce and separation and on the provision of maintenance to wives. Adultery by women was still punished by a denial of, or reduction in, maintenance and could result in the loss of children. Neither would the Government consider changing the laws on illegitimacy, for fear that a removal of the stigma of bastardy would weaken the bonds of marriage. When all of these features are taken together, it becomes clearer that the law in the 1950s did operate to reproduce the social order and, in particular, established patriarchal relations of sexual exchange and familial structure.

The Origins of the 1956 Act

The central figure of the 1956 Act is the female subject; she is essentially the source of almost all the sections in the statute. The male subject, where he appears, is consistently depicted as the aggressor, with the woman or child as his victim.[13] Most of the 1956 Act is therefore oriented towards the protection of women and girls from sexual exploitation by men. For example section 17(1) reads

> It is a felony for a person to take away or detain a woman against her will with the intention that she shall marry or have unlawful sexual intercourse with that or any other person, if she is so taken away or detained either by force or for the sake of her property or expectations of property.

Whilst this legislation appears to be little more than a legal representation of actual sexual politics (as women are most usually the sexual victims of men and *do* need protection), a deeper reading of the Act reveals that beneath the appearance the legislation is in fact a mode of reproducing the oppressive order from which it purports to protect women. We need to ask how it is that 'woman' is always constituted as the victim and to point to the consequences of this consistent categorisation. To do this we must briefly analyse the historical processes that produced the legislation.

The origins of the 1956 Act reside in the nineteenth century, a period which marked a distinct era in sexual mores which were the culmination of processes occurring over two centuries. Sexuality was increasingly perceived as an area in need of control or policing (Foucault, 1979), a dangerous area that could do harm to the individual and corrupt others. The 1885 Criminal Law (Amendment) Act, which provides the basis for the 1956 Act, is essentially about corruption. Within it, sexuality was construed as a contagious evil which could contaminate. Those who were then defined as the most vulnerable to this contamination were women and children. The 1885 Act was, moreover, the embodiment of the ideals of the bourgeois Victorian family, which held that children were innocent and asexual (Aries, 1979), that sex was for procreation only and that it should only occur within wedlock, and finally that it was particularly important that women and girls should remain pure and virginal.

This is not to argue that the law was a simple imposition of bourgeois morality on the Victorian working classes. In fact it was the bourgeois male who would appear to have much to lose by this type of legislation, as it was he who benefitted most from the procuration of prostitutes and the organisation of brothels. There was indeed a considerable resistance on the part of Victorian middle-class men to the implementation of such legislation. However, in effect the enactment of the 1885 Act had little impact on the trading of commercialised sex at the end of the nineteenth century (Henriques, 1968) and working-class women and girls still provided fodder for the so-called white slave trade. Ultimately, the Act did little more than *confirm* women's special status with regard to sexuality and to property. It was this special status that was carried over from 1885 to 1956. Hence in the 1956 Act there are sections concerned with intercourse with girls under 16 years although not with boys, intercourse with women who are mental defectives but not men, the abduction of women and girls but not males, and on procuring and causing the prostitution of women but not men.

A major consequence of these two Acts has been the growing *legal*, as opposed to moral, concern over the sexuality of young women. The statutory definition of women as persons in need of special protection has engendered a particularly stringent surveillance over female sexual behaviour rather than male. The legal legitimation of this basically moral view has been mirrored and reflected in the twentieth century by medical and psychoanalytic discourses. The work of Karen Horney (1967) and other neo-Freudians and also the later work of Chesser (1978) provided psychoanalytic and psychological justifications for why 'normal' women should be monogamous and sexually reserved, although not frigid. Increasingly, the promiscuous girl or woman became, not sinful, but 'sick', a new psycho-social problem for the post-war era. The 1950s therefore witnessed the demise of the masturbating schoolboy so prevalent in the works of Aries and Foucault, and the rise of the precocious schoolgirl, soon to become the unmarried teenage mother and supposed cause of a whole new generation of social problems.

The law has played a significant role in this process in that, by the 1950s, this new social and moral problem was already defined as a legal matter. Masturbation may have been sinful and even sick, but it has never been illegal or unlawful. But if a girl has sex under the age of 16 or a woman sells her sexuality for economic gain, she does encounter the controlling agencies of the law. The law entitles state agencies to intervene, not only to punish but also to control physically by curtailing the woman's or girl's liberty (e.g., care orders, Borstal or prison). Persistent promiscuity or public prostitution, even though the female subject is defined as the victim, invariably leads to some form of restriction or incarceration for young women. The paternalism of the 1956 Act has therefore provided a justification for, and a means of, extending and increasing the state's surveillance over female sexuality (Casburn, 1979; Bowker, 1979).[14]

Conclusion

This chapter reflects the beginnings of an attempt to understand the recent historical development of specific legislative measures which have been identified as particularly salient to an analysis of contemporary patriarchal structures. This entails considerable emphasis on the structure of the family in post-war Britain, which, in turn, must be situated in the wider political and economic context. During the 1950s the state intervened directly in family life, particularly through the vehicle of welfare legislation, but also significantly through family law and legislation on sexual behaviour. Such legislation was overtly oriented towards maintaining family stability, reproducing, in some instances, patriarchal relations within the family, and containing and controlling social change that was seen as harmful to the family. The family did not, however, simply have ideological significance; the organisation of the domestic economy and the division of labour between the sexes at home and at work was (and is) a part of the material structure of the capitalist economy. This is not necessarily to endorse a functionalist position which implies that the structure of the family is dependent upon, and reflects, the needs of the economy. Rather, it is to assert that they are part of the same process and that we need to make a closer examination of precisely how it is that the social, economic and political order is so fundamentally reliant upon a power inequality between the sexes. Intrinsic to such an analysis is both an examination of the way in which the state operates to reproduce that power inequality and an enquiry into the role of the law in that reproduction. As Harrison and Mort (1980, p. 81) explain,

> The state can be seen to draw on, transform and modify particular sets of patriarchal relations, through legislation governing the transmission of property, marriage and sexuality, but it cannot be seen to *create* those relations.

This chapter has attempted to reveal the significance of legislation governing sexual behaviour (which is defined as criminal) to the reproduction of patriarchal relations. However, such an analysis must necessarily be partial until there is a further examination of the actual practices of the law. Feminists have long been aware that legislation at the Parliamentary level does not necessarily produce expected results in court or elsewhere. The practice of law can therefore be more subtle and obscure than an initial reading of statutory legislation would imply. The differentiation of law by the courts and the changing structural position of law itself can further complicate analysis, to the point where general theoretical propositions on the relationship between the capitalist state, patriarchy and the law need to be abandoned in favour of more specific, concrete studies that can accommodate essential detail and complexities. This chapter is part of such a project.

Notes

1.   This position would have its parallels in marxist theories which either view the law as operating in the interests of individual owners of capital or, more sophisticatedly, in the interests of capital. Such positions ignore that there may be contradictions in the interests of individual capitalists or even in the overall interests of capital. Moreover they ignore the existence of class struggle, which has modified and influenced the passing of legislation.

2.   Examples of women's resistance to repressive legislation would be Josephine Butler's struggle over the Contagious Diseases Acts in the nineteenth century and the National Abortion Campaign's struggle against regressive reforms to the abortion law in the twentieth century.

3.   Jeanne Gregory gives one reason for the failure of the Equal Pay Act as its reliance on a juridical notion of formal equality. Where so many women have to work part-time or where their work is categorised differentially to men's work, they cannot fulfil the basic criteria of the Act of 'broadly similar work' and therefore do not qualify for formal equality. Hence women's wages remain at two-thirds of men's average earnings.

4.   A most notable example of this was the government's exclusion of itself from its own sex-discrimination legislation. Thereby it left the operations of welfare and tax agencies unaffected by the law.

5.   That different levels of jurisdiction may be in conflict is reflected in the use of the one-third rule in matrimonial issues. Whilst Sir Jocelyn Simon, President of the Family Division of the High Court, has made it clear that the one-third rule is now a discredited concept, the majority of registrars still use it as a rule of thumb in deciding financial matters on divorce or separation (Barrington Baker *et al.*, 1977).

6.   The implementation of the legislation on domestic violence, particularly 'wife battering', is extremely dependent upon how the police choose to operate it and whether the courts are willing to use their powers.

7.   Smith *v* Hughes [1960] 1 A11 E R 859.

8.   Shaw *v* DPP [1961] 2 A11 E R 446, [1962] A C 220.

9.   R *v* Webb [1964] 1 QB 357.

10. The 1959 Street Offences Act provides that:

S1 (1) It shall be an offence for a common prostitute to loiter or solicit in a street or public place for the purpose of prostitution.
   (3) A constable may arrest without warrant anyone he finds in a street or

public place and suspects, with reasonable cause to be committing an offence under this section.

Only a 'common prostitute' can be guilty of this offence and a woman is deemed such if she has been cautioned for soliciting on two previous occasions. Once she is known as a 'common prostitute' it requires only police evidence to convict her of soliciting. A man cannot become known as a 'common prostitute'.

11. The 1956 Sexual Offences Act covered such offences as rape, indecent assault, incest, buggery, indecency between men, soliciting by men (this was only used against homosexuals), abduction, procuring and brothel keeping.

12. Much of the content of the 1956 Act is still in force at the turn of the 1980s. As a consequence we are governed by laws, many of which were formulated 100 years ago. The major exception to this is legislation on homosexuality.

13. The exceptions to this are sections 13 and 32. Section 13 provides that it is an offence for a man to commit an act of gross indecency with another man or to procure such an act. This section has been repealed by the 1967 Sexual Offences Act. Section 32 provides that it is an offence for a man to solicit or importune in a public place for immoral purposes. However in practice this section relates only to men soliciting other men and not women, and so it is essentially concerned with homosexual males.

14. There are parallels here with the surveillance of homosexual male sexuality in the 1950s and 1960s prior to the 1967 Sexual Offences Act, which decriminalised a number of homosexual acts.

Bibliography

Aries, P. *Centuries of Childhood* (Penguin, Harmondsworth, 1979)

Barrington Baker, J. *et al. The Matrimonial Jurisdiction of Registrars* (SSRC, London, 1977)

Beechey, V. 'On Patriarchy', *Feminist Review*, no. 3 (1979), pp. 66–82

Beveridge, W. *Social Insurance and Allied Services*, Cmnd 6404 (HMSO, London, 1942)

Bland, L. *et al.* 'Women, Ideologies and Theories of Reproduction', Paper presented to BSA Annual Conference on 'Culture' (April 1978)

Bowker, Lee H. *Women, Crime and the Criminal Justice System* (Lexington Books, Lexington, 1979)

Bowlby, J. *Maternal Care and Mental Health* (WHO, Geneva, 1951)

Brownmiller, S. *Against Our Will* (Secker and Warburg, London, 1975)

Burman, S. (ed.) *Fit Work for Women* (Croom Helm, London, 1979)

Casburn, M. *Girls Will Be Girls* (Women's Research and Resources Centre, London, 1979)

Chesser, E. *Love and Marriage* (Pan, London, 1957)

—— *Love without Fear* (Arrow, London, 1978)

Delphy, C. *The Main Enemy* (Women's Research and Resources Centre, London, 1977)

Delphy, C. and Leonard, D. 'The Family as an Economic System', Paper presented at the Conference on Institutionalization of Sex Differences (University of Kent, 13 April 1980)

Foucault, M. *The History of Sexuality* (Allen Lane, London, 1979), vol. 1

Gill, D. *Illegitimacy, Sexuality and the Status of Women* (Blackwell, Oxford, 1977)

Gorer, G. *Sex and Marriage in England Today* (Nelson, London, 1971)

Gosling, J. and Warner, D. *The Shame of a City* (WH Allen, London, 1960)

Gregory, J. 'Sex Discrimination, Work and the Law', in B. Fine *et al.* (eds.), *Capitalism and the Rule of Law* (Hutchinson, London, 1979)

Hall, S. *et al. Policing the Crisis* (Macmillan, London, 1978)

Harrison, R. and Mort, F. 'Patriarchal Aspects of Nineteenth-century State Formation: Property Relations, Marriage and Divorce, and Sexuality', in P. Corrigan (ed.), *Capitalism, State Formation and Marxist Theory* (Quartet, London, 1980)

Henriques, F. *Prostitution and Society. A Survey* (McGibbon and Kee, London, 1968)

Hirst, P. *On Law and Ideology* (Macmillan, London, 1979)

Horney, K. *Feminine Psychology* (Routledge and Kegan Paul, London, 1967)

Jaget, C. (ed.) *Prostitutes, Our Life* (Falling Wall Press, Bristol, 1980)

Land, H. 'Women: Supporters or Supported' in D. Leonard Barker and S. Allen (eds.), *Sexual Divisions in Society: Process and Change* (Tavistock, London, 1976)

McDonough, R. and Harrison, R. 'Patriarchy and Relations of Production, in A. Kahn and A.-M. Wolpe (eds.), *Feminism and Materialism* (Routledge and Kegan Paul, London, 1978)

McIntosh, M. 'The Welfare State and the Needs of the Dependent Family' in Burman (1979)

Macmillan *Report of the Street Offences Committee* Cmnd 3231 (HMSO, London, 1928)

Mitchell, J. *Psychoanalysis and Feminism* (Penguin, Harmondsworth, 1975)

O'Donovan, K. 'The Male Appendage – Legal Definitions of Women' in Burman (1979)

Picciotto, S. 'The Theory of the State, Class Struggle and the Rule of Law', in B. Fine *et al.* (eds.), *Capitalism and the Rule of Law* (Hutchinson, London, 1979)

Rowbotham, S. *Woman's Consciousness, Man's World* (Penguin, Harmondsworth, 1973)

———— 'The Trouble with Patriarchy', *New Statesman* (21 December 1979)

Royal Commission on Marriage and Divorce *Report*, Cmnd 9678 (HMSO, London, 1956)

Sachs, A. and Wilson, J.H. *Sexism and the Law* (Martin Robertson, Oxford, 1978)

Shorter, E. *The Making of the Modern Family* (Fontana, London, 1977)

Slater, E. and Woodside, M. *Patterns of Marriage* (Cassell, London, 1951)

Storch, R.D. 'Police Control of Street Prostitution in Victorian London', in D.H. Bayley (ed.), *Police and Society* (Sage, London, 1977)

Wilson, E. *Women and the Welfare State* (Tavistock, London, 1977)

Wolfenden Report of the Committee on Homosexual Offences and Prostitution, Cmnd 247 (HMSO, London, 1957)

3 MAN-MADE LAWS FOR MEN? THE STREET PROSTITUTES' CAMPAIGN AGAINST CONTROL

Eileen McLeod

After a gap of a century, a campaign has again been formed to end discrimination against street prostitutes. In 1869 Josephine Butler began what was to prove a successful campaign against the Contagious Diseases Acts as the embodiment of the existing double standard in sexual morality. In the name of preventing the spread of venereal disease, these Acts had instituted the compulsory medical examination of prostitutes frequenting the barracks and streets of garrison towns and naval dockyards. They also provided for the detention of such prostitutes until presumed to be free from infection. Meanwhile, the troops themselves were not subject to any legislation in this respect (Sigsworth and Wyke, 1973). A less well known feature of the campaign was the participation of a substantial number of prostitutes. Aided by reformers, they refused to be examined or to go to hospital voluntarily and petitioned for their own release (Walkowitz and Walkowitz, 1974). The distinctive feature of the current campaign by PROS – Programme for Reform of the Law on Soliciting – is that, whilst not exclusively so, its active membership is largely composed of street prostitutes and it aims to represent their interests. This chapter will discuss the context in which PROS developed, the dimensions of the problems that street prostitutes face and the lessons that can be gained from the campaign itself. It is mainly based on the author's experience in the probation service and as a founder member of PROS and the following summary gives some idea of the tenor and extent of PROS' activities.

PROS' specific aims are:

(1) to remove prison sentences for the offences of loitering and soliciting for the purposes of prostitution;
(2) to abolish the term 'common prostitute' in legal proceedings;
(3) ultimately, to remove the offences of loitering and soliciting for the purposes of prostitution from the Statute book.

It is primarily concerned with the position of street prostitutes, since 'high-class prostitutes' operating in hotels and through escort or contact

THE LIBRARY
THE HATFIELD POLY
P.O. BOX 110
HATFIELD, HERTS.
TEL HATFIELD 68100   TELEX 262418

agencies are rarely subject to legal penalities. In general, PROS wants to ensure that the street prostitute's voice is heard and that she participates in any discussion about the issue of prostitution. It therefore has educative and consciousness-raising objectives.

PROS was founded in November 1976 by two prostitutes, two social workers and a solicitor. Its registered members now number several hundred and it has organising groups in Birmingham, Manchester, Bristol, Sheffield and London. The campaign strategies have concentrated on developing a national network, forming alliances with sympathetic groups, extensive use of the media to stimulate public debate and parliamentary lobbying.

The Development of PROS

Redefining the Problem

In the early 1970s a particular assumption was in evidence throughout the penal system. This was that the problem regarding street prostitutes was not that they were simply involved in soliciting and loitering, but that they were psychopathologically drawn to prostitution. The 1959 Street Offences Act remained unaltered[1] and embodied the conclusions of the Wolfenden Committee (1957, p. 79), which had been reached against a background of full employment and the fashionable belief that poverty was finally being conquered: 'Whatever may have been the case in the past, in these days, in this country, at any rate, economic factors cannot account for it', that is, the prevalence of prostitution, 'to any large or decisive extent', and

> Prostitution is a way of life consciously chosen because it suits a woman's personality in particular circumstances . . . the great majority of those women who are prostitutes are those whose psychological make-up is such that they choose this life because they find it a style of living which is to them easier, freer and more profitable.

Accordingly, one reason why the Act incorporated provisions for two cautions before a woman was brought to court was in the hope that she would be referred to the probation service and reformed before becoming too entrenched in prostitution. Imprisonment was also included not simply as the ultimate sanction, but because the threat of it might make offenders more willing to accept an attempt at rehabilitation through probation (Home Office, 1974).

When reviewing the workings of the Street Offences Act, the Home Office Working Party (1974, paras 234–5) counselled against the removal of the term 'common prostitute' in legal proceedings on the following grounds:

> There seems little doubt that the motivation of a prostitute goes much deeper than a simple reaction to the phrasing of the criminal law. We were impressed by a suggestion made to us that the way of life of a prostitute is so remarkably a rejection of the normal ways of society as to bear comparison with that of the drug addict.

Well-established penal-reform groups such as the Howard League were already arguing against the continuing use of imprisonment under the Street Offences Act. However, they did so in terms which also perpetuated the image of a street prostitute as a pathetic woman whose defective personality formation could only be worsened by the operation of the current law. *Their* argument (Howard League, 1974, p. 5) regarding the use of the term common prostitute was as follows: 'So many of these girls and women are inadequate and depressive, with very low self-esteem and lack of a sense of identity, that they will take on the label "common prostitute" feeling that is what they will become.'

The hall-mark of the probation services' work with prostitutes was the attempt to steer women away from soliciting through counselling about emotional and material problems (McLeod, 1979). This implicitly reinforced the idea that an individual propensity to solicit was the problem to be tackled rather than more general issues. One of the most widely read works on the subject of prostitution among probation officers at the time was the pamphlet by Glover (1969), *The Psychopathology of Prostitution*, produced by the Institute for the Study and Treatment of Delinquency. This propounded the idea that young women's entry into prostitution and continuation in it should be seen as directly related to various personality defects (Glover, 1969, p. 15): 'the fact that the prostitute barters her body for filthy lucre is psychologically speaking – neither so surprising nor so unnatural as it seems. It is . . . one more proof that prostitution is a primitive and regressive manifestation.'

As she made contact with a large number of street prostitutes, the author was in the process of developing a feminist perspective. This meant that she was on her guard against tolerating adverse social conditions among women, nor was she in favour of seeing them as necessarily rooted in individual shortcomings. Most of the women she met who were established in prostitution also struck her as being highly independent, shrewd and competent. Their involvement in prostitution seemed a reasonable choice in the face of difficult economic and social circumstances (McLeod, 1979). The majority were young, unskilled single parents[2] with sole responsibility for their children, no cohabitee or husband in long-term employment and few resources to fall back on in their family of origin. In such a situation the alternatives to the material rewards of prostitution were low earnings in conventional shop and factory work, with difficult working conditions to combine with childcare, or living at subsistence levels on social security. The author therefore rejected the psychopathological perspective on prostitution as incorrect. She came to see that, more importantly, once acting as a street prostitute a woman was subject to a law which left the service she provided intact, whilst seriously undermining her civil liberties in terms of her rights under the law.

Prostitution is legal in Britain. However, certain activities connected with it are not. The law relating to street prostitution sounds straightforward enough. A woman soliciting or loitering receives two cautions. On the third occasion she is charged and brought to court. Once in court, the fact that she is known as a common prostitute is read out as she is charged. The maximum penalty for a first conviction is £50, for a second conviction £200, for a third conviction £200 and/or three months imprisonment. In operation, however, the law is sexist and unjust. Once a woman is known as a 'common prostitute', all the police have to do in practice to bring a charge of loitering is to prove that she has been seen standing or walking in an area known for prostitution. As many prostitutes live in or near such areas they are in danger of being apprehended as soon as they leave their homes.[3] In the case of other offences, a past criminal record is not revealed until the current charge is proved; however, the fact that a woman is known as a 'common prostitute' is referred to in court before the current charge is found, and may prejudice her chances of a fair hearing. There are two equally active parties to the act of soliciting: the prostitute and the customer. However, only the prostitute is subject to legal process. Charges rest on police evidence alone; therefore it is not necessary for anyone to have been annoyed by the activities of a particular prostitute and to make a complaint for a charge to be brought. So a situation exists whereby the female of the two parties, in the preliminaries to an act which is legal, can face imprisonment without anyone having been affronted by her activity.

Besides such injustice, it seemed to the author that imprisonment[4] was a particularly harsh and ineffective measure in the case of street prostitutes. When it occurred, it meant separation of many mothers and young children. On release from prison, difficulties in retaining accommodation, meeting outstanding bills or, on occasion, keeping belongings were often acute and led back to soliciting to obtain the necessary capital.[5] As a lot of women continued in street prostitution to provide for their children's material well-being, they also regarded this as their highest priority, overriding the risks of imprisonment which they were well aware they ran.

The Dimensions of the Problems that Street Prostitutes Face

The problem of the law was PROS' initial working brief, and to a large extent remains its main concern. However, the problems that street prostitutes face have many facets, some of which are highly contentious. They require discussion before proceeding to a detailed examination of the campaign, so that the situation can be put into perspective.

'The Law'

From the outset, PROS' members have identified the problems that they face as street prostitutes as going beyond the letter of the law. In their experience, the machinery of police detection and prosecution incorporates a number of oppressive manoeuvres designed to maintain arrest rates. As other studies have brought out (Cain, 1971), such activities may reflect the pressures the police themselves are under to sustain levels of arrests. It is such common practice for police to set up arrests in connection with soliciting that this routine was selected by the police themselves to illustrate their procedure in a recent documentary on prostitution (Brasstacks, 1979). Susan describes what can be involved,[6] 'There are usually two in a car posing as clients. One asks you how much, you tell him, then the other one — who may have been hiding in the back — pops up and does you for soliciting' (McLeod, 1978). Examples of the repeated arrest of a particular prostitute without good foundation and of violence towards individuals are also known to the Birmingham group. By common agreement among street prostitutes, such events are not a simple case of good and bad policemen, but intrinsic to the nature of the job of being in a vice squad. Its brutalising nature was brought home to the author by a chance encounter with a member of one squad. Commenting on a recent spate of arrests of prostitutes he boasted, 'we rounded up forty in three days'.

All Part of the Game

Violence is a serious problem in prostitutes' work but its significance may be more correctly related to the position of women generally. Contrary to popular belief, the majority of established street prostitutes are not in the thrall of a ponce using violence to send them out on to the streets, although such ponces do exist.[7] Nevertheless, violence from customers is a constant threat. All the street prostitutes in the Birmingham area known to PROS have experienced at least one serious physical attack. This is usually accepted as an integral part of the job. However, recent work on marital violence (Dobash and Dobash, 1980) has demonstrated the extensive nature of male and female assumptions that women are the appropriate victims of male violence. Therefore the prostitutes' experience of violence and their attitude towards it may not be predominantly a feature of a criminal subculture with a deviant tolerance of brutality, as is the conventional view. It may have more to do with street prostitutes being women in an especially unprotected situation and reacting as such. The feminist 'Reclaim the Night' Campaign in Birmingham, organising to free women from the threat of violence on the streets, made this connection. As a result, they invited PROS to collaborate with them as representing a group of women who were particularly vulnerable to attack on the streets from men.

The stigma attaching to prostitutes and their customers would seem to cloak a more complex situation than the operation of a double standard in sexual relations (Smart, 1977). Admittedly, street prostitutes can have great difficulty in their private lives as a result of the stigma attaching to their job. Some find it very hard to tell their children what they do for fear of rejection. Others have found that they were perfectly acceptable to people outside prostitution until they learnt that they were prostitutes. The experience of two members of Birmingham PROS is typical: 'There was this little old lady — I used to deal at her shop. Me and her got on great and she thought I was golden, until someone told her what I did' (Carol); and, 'I've had a lot of trouble with my neighbours because of what I do. It's not so bad now (after living in the same house for ten years) but it can still be very, very difficult.' (Betty).

The popular view of prostitutes' customers, which explains the persistence of prostitution in the days of supposed sexual liberation, is that such men are bound to be sexual perverts or to have unusual difficulty in finding sexual partners. Prostitutes may cater for some men with unusual sexual tastes or for those for whom exceptional circumstances such as physical handicap or extreme isolation render sexual relations difficult. Nevertheless, several general features of prostitutes' custom undermine this argument. The consensus among prostitutes is that their customers are 'Mr Average': 'You get all ages and from all walks of life, from a bloke on the scaffolding to your posh executive in a company car' (Susan) (McLeod, 1978). Most customers are married, though their wives have no idea that they are going with a prostitute, whether street prostitute, call girl or working in a 'bent' sauna.

Another view, popular among feminists, is that prostitution caters for and reinforces the idea of male desires — particularly *macho* sexual desires — being given primacy (McIntosh, 1978). Discussion with numbers of prostitutes and some clients about what men want from prostitutes suggests — albeit tentatively — a rather different picture. Great variety characterises what men request. However, a common feature of clients' sexual activity with prostitutes is the opportunity it provides men to escape conventional heterosexual roles which place heavy emphasis on masculine prowess and domination. Thus, significant proportions of clients want to dress as women or children, be prostitutes' maids, be masturbated by prostitutes or masturbate themselves as the desirable form of sex or ask prostitutes to supply them with men. Not only do they keep visits secret from their wives but, significantly, the content of their activity with prostitutes tends to be kept secret from other men, suggesting that such an escape from conventional male sexual activity is under heavy taboo. A substantial number of men also discuss their emotional difficulties with prostitutes. 'They'll be going to the door then they'll say, I've been having such and such a problem' (Nancy).

If prostitutes spoke out more freely, their revelations about the extent to which modern marital relations are riddled with hypocrisy might be as striking in their way as the revelations of battered women about the integral part that violence plays in contemporary marriage. Beyond such revelations could lie further uncomfortable truths about the nature of men's emotional and sexual needs.

Your Own Boss

The main advantages to their work that street prostitutes put forward are relative to the generally poor employment opportunities open to women. The net amount that is earned may be less than is commonly supposed — about £10 a time, often for masturbation, the prices rising if women are working indoors or meeting unusual sexual demands. With expenses, evading the vice squad and trade ebbing and flowing — 'Summer holidays with the wife and kids is a slack time' (Sandra) — most street prostitutes probably clear about £100 per week. Nevertheless this is rather better than the rate they would get if dependent on social security or in unskilled jobs.[8] Working on the streets means that you can set your own pace and work hours that fit in with family commitments. While some prostitutes regard state-licensed brothels as a progressive development, most are against them because of the loss of control over their work that would be implied. Besides being dubious about the idea, on the grounds that many men might hesitate to be identified as resorting to brothels and because of the illogicality of VD checks on prostitutes alone, they spurn the notion of brothels because they could turn out to be a form of sex factory. This element of regimentation is one aspect of working in 'bent' saunas that comes in for a good deal of criticism as well. Most prostitutes I have spoken to on the subject say that, ideally, they would like to work on a cooperative basis with other prostitutes and would happily pay tax and insurance in return for freedom from legal harassment.

In one important respect, the street prostitute has limited room for manoeuvre relating to her work. With very few exceptions a swift advance to 'high-class call girl' work, say with Arab customers at the Hilton, is a romantic fantasy against the class-ridden reality of 'the trade'. At most, a woman may go on to work indoors. If she is on her own she then faces the danger of violence from customers arranged over the telephone or through contact magazines. Or she may progress to sauna work with no job security and unionisation a remote dream.

Selling Sex

Prostitutes are aware that their work can be seen as threatening other peoples' interests. One example of this is the effect on local residents and local property values of the circulating custom of the streets. The existence of activities associated with prostitutes and customers meeting up would seem to be a feature of urban blight rather than a factor determining it. Nevertheless, some residents feel genuine distress about the significance of what is going on for their neighbourhood's standing and their own feelings of social well-being (Means,

1979).[9] If there is a real nuisance it would seem to lie in the activities of 'kerb crawlers' rather than with prostitutes standing discreetly plying their trade, while keeping out of the vice squad's eye. Whether this is a sufficient problem to warrant special legal measures against kerb crawlers is a moot point.

Pride in offering a good service is often mentioned by prostitutes when discussing their work — 'You try to do your best for your customers' (Jean) — and reflects the ethos of the small independent tradesman. This endorses rather than counteracts the charge that prostitutes commercialise interactions that hopefully would spring from spontaneous emotional regard. But it may be less than fair to pillory prostitutes for commercialising sex when all around are examples of legitimate commercial exploitation. Furthermore, as Zaretsky (1976) points out, the idea of a relatively 'pure' zone of emotional expression in the family and marriage may exist as a palliative for enduring more exploitative relationships in the workplace.

Perhaps the most daunting charges that have been levelled against prostitutes come from within the Women's Movement. PROS has gained support from feminists who see street prostitutes as belonging to a particularly oppressed minority of women and also for the most part as belonging to the extensive ranks of single parents with concomitant social disadvantages. On the other hand, some members of the Women's Movement have seen the activities of prostitutes as antithetical to a feminist position, becaue they reinforce men's view of women as sex objects. They also argue that, instead of being concentrated on a narrow reformist platform, the energies going into PROS should be redirected. They should be used to bring about a situation where the need for prostitution is abolished because male/female relations will not be dominated by sexism and material inequality.

Taking these points together, I hope the foregoing discussion indicates that prostitutes occupy a more active and subtle role than merely being passive sex objects. Their activities indicate that two of the central institutions of our society, romance and marriage, do not necessarily cater for men's — or women's — sexual and emotional needs and may frustrate them. Prostitutes may meet some of these needs for men in return for some payment for their services — their time and their trouble. Their work is also suggestive of the material disadvantage that women still face. Prostitution may therefore be a sad reflection on our society. But should one be prepared to stand by while the prosecution of prostitutes continues, as a substitute for attacking society's shortcomings as such?

Getting Started

Moved by such a situation, realising that many street prostitutes were privately convinced of the injustice of their circumstances and that some were prepared to act, the author talked to individual women about their position, the law and the possibility of change. Amongst street prostitutes, her colleagues and some solicitors, she then canvassed the idea of a group to look at the situation of local prostitutes as representative of the situation more generally and at what could be done by them and probation officers to improve it. This group set up a 'drop-in centre' in a local red-light area in order to extend contact with prostitutes and initiated the following chain of events.

> For a few months the centre became a focal point in the area for considerable discussion and dialogue concerning the laws relating to prostitution and the situation of the prostitute in society generally.

> The probation service felt that it could only provide an 'advice/welfare' function, which was desperately needed at that time. However, there were prostitutes, lawyers and social workers (including the author who was by now teaching social work) who felt that this fell short of the expectations aroused by the discussion — particularly as many prostitutes felt that 'something should be done' about them being referred to as a 'common prostitute' in legal proceedings and their suffering prison sentences. PROS was formed from this base and with a mandate from street prostitutes.[10]

From the beginning, therefore, PROS did not follow a purely self-help model, that is, with the campaign being initiated and directed solely by people with immediate personal experience of the social injustice in question, as is the case with groups such as PROP (Preservation of the Rights of Prisoners). Instead the formation of PROS adhered more to the pattern of consciousness-raising between some women with immediate experience of a particular social problem and others keen to tackle that problem but with a more general interest in improving women's position (Hanmer, 1977; *Women*

Against Rape, 1978). In its campaign PROS incorporated the belief that social problems can be susceptible to change through specific campaigns (Mayo, 1977), and that concern for law reform should be an integral part of such a campaign (Wilson, 1980).

Lessons from the Campaign

Speaking Out

There is a circular problem in street prostitutes 'coming out' publicly. If they do so, their social position makes them very vulnerable. But unless campaigns such as PROS develop, then the general situation of street prostitutes is unlikely to be improved. In this respect the experience of PROS' members parallels that of members of other groups who have 'come out' (compare, for example, 'Action for Lesbian Parents', in Collins *et al.*, 1978).

Prostitutes joining PROS have faced a range of difficulties. There are the fears of repercussions from relatives, friends and neighbours if they publicly identify their work. Police harassment has occurred; in the case of one member who was interviewed in a television documentary, the social club she used was subsequently told it would lose its licence if it did not ban her. Further complications arise from the law relating to immoral earnings. A man cohabiting with a prostitute can be charged with living on immoral earnings and face a heavy prison sentence if he draws on the prostitute's con-tribution to their joint living expenses knowing that she is a prostitute. One of the Birmingham group's most talented original members withdrew from PROS after being beaten up by her cohabitee to warn her off taking part in any more public meetings, because of his fear of the consequences for himself. Without demoting the role of personal courage it is no accident that the street prostitutes who have stayed the course as prominent members have had unusually independent positions in respect of men and other social ties.

As the campaign has developed, such problems have been eased in various ways, even if the underlying difficulty has not been resolved. Acquiring a degree of formal organisation such as a name, a permanent address and a telephone number has helped to deflect outside attention away from individuals and onto the campaign as such. More powerful allies have offered protection. An official of the charitable trust that has recently funded PROS made it clear that he and his trustees would like to hear of any subsequent police victimis-ation. Developing its own media resources, as in the documentary film, *A Particular Kind of Job*, produced two years ago (PROS, 1978), has had a joint representative/protective function. The five prostitutes on film who discuss their work, their experience of violence and the campaign can represent prostitutes who as yet find it impossible to stand out. An important side-product of the development of the campaign as such has been the increase in self-respect it has brought to prostitutes who are members. Coupled with this, in many cases, has been a sharpened awareness of the extent to which their experience reflects problems affecting women generally. An extract from *PROS Bulletin* no. 3 illustrates this process at work:

> When talking on the radio to local people answering to the phone-in, I felt a hell of a lot better in myself. I didn't imagine people were so understanding and sympathetic towards us. One woman even said that if she had no other way to support her children then she would definitely take our way of life (Paula, Sheffield PROS).

PROS for Pros

Like NWAF (National Women's Aid Federation; Hanmer, 1977), PROS has found it difficult to guarantee that it is under the control of the women whose interests it is meant to serve. After years of collaborating together in the original Birmingham group, the author overheard one of the stalwart prostitute founder members refer to the social workers and solicitor as 'the meeting people'. PROS' first national event in 1979 was a forum for groups to meet, exchange views of their work and agree on some kind of policy for the coming six months. This was decided by a series of votes of all those present, nevertheless, the non-prostitute members at the meeting held the floor for a length of time quite disproportionate to their number.

The rule of sharing tasks as widely as possible has been adhered to. As a result, all members have had to take on work that is daunting to the most socially assured — such as speaking at public meetings, appearing on TV and in films and organising complicated events. Street prostitutes hold their own with anyone in the campaign in these respects and are now in a position to encourage others who have more recently joined PROS. As Kim put it, 'We've come a long way — we used to get in a right flap when the television was coming and think it was the end of the world'. The whole business of establishing and evolving a campaign platform is quite wearisome at times, involving detailed discussion between and within prostitutes' groups as policies come and go. The result is that the organisation has credibility with prostitutes encountered as potential supporters.

Street prostitutes are consolidating their position within the campaign. Those in the Bristol group who are responsible for producing *PROS Bulletin* no. 4 are adamant that it should be renamed *Streetbeat*, arguing: 'After all it's about us'.

In Sisterhood

The Women's Movement has underwritten PROS' existence. The fact that the campaign developed, in the first place, access to a wide variety of media (Collins *et al.*, 1978, p. 33; Omen, 1979; Green, 1977) and the support of sympathetic and talented activists[11] both stem from the Women's Movement as such. To take one example, a group of women caucussing within NAPO — the probation officers' union — in close collaboration with PROS were successful in getting decriminalisation of offences relating to prostitution established as official NAPO policy and securing the affiliation of NAPO to PROS. This has enhanced the campaign's public standing, besides providing support and cover for probation officers around the country who want to organise in connection with it.

Meanwhile, the relationship between PROS and other feminist groups needs to remain a dialectical one. Without the 'specialist' representations of PROS it might be very easy for feminists to 'overlook' the plight of street prostitutes for another hundred years (Toynbee, 1978). If the general perspective of the women's movement died away, the thrust within PROS beyond a legalistic solution to street prostitutes' problems and towards prostitutes determining their own living and working conditions in concert with other women might also fade.

The Media

It is very difficult to assess the value of participation in various sorts of media for such a campaign. A thousand talks to small, obscure groups do not necessarily influence public opinion that much, nor do they guarantee social change. There are also particular problems resulting from the stigma and hypocrisy surrounding street prostitutes. Early on in contact with the press, TV and radio, a definite pattern emerged. Sensational publicity could readily be obtained, as when one brief press contact with the Birmingham group's solicitor produced the headline: 'Vice Girls' Sexy Sticker Campaign'. Alternatively, while progressive research assistants would be keen for peak broadcasting time to come the way of PROS, their own middle management ensured that items were censored into off-peak hours or non-appearance. Campaign members are now more adroit in handling the media, and have learnt the lesson that the moment to assert maximum control is at the point of initial contact. Even with such strategies, however, editorial control remains theirs not ours.

Despite these drawbacks, involvement in the media of press and broadcasting seems essential to gaining substantial support, bringing matters to public notice and making it possible to start arguing that public opinion is on your side. Contributors to radio phone-in programmes on which PROS has featured have frequently commented that they did not realise before that prostitutes were still sent to prison. The national 'Reports-back' phone-in to local radio stations after the BBC 2 Brasstacks programme on prostitution (1979) in which PROS participated was overwhelmingly in favour of PROS' aims. This has provided most useful evidence of the extent to which public opinion is in favour of radical changes in the Street Offences Act.

There have also been distinct advantages in developing the campaign's own media — notably the film and bulletins. Besides reaching potential supporters and providing a forum for discussion on PROS' terms, the bulletins have also been encouraging to campaign members as achievements in their own right. The film has both extended the range of audiences PROS attracts and proved a useful tool in increasing the audiences it can reach; for instance, it has now been shown twice, informally, in a woman's prison. PROS groups vet requests for the film to be shown so as to decide whether a showing would further the campaign's interests. In addition, a showing can only occur with a PROS speaker, both to enhance the chances of developing informed discussion and to serve as further precaution against the film being used out of context.

In Parliament

Controversy about the extent to which reforms in the law are conducive to radical social change is alive in feminist social-work literature (Wilson, 1980). As yet, PROS has no specific law reforms to its credit from which to judge the issue in respect of prostitution. Nevertheless, the time is past when any MPs contacted by PROS with a view to introducing Bills declined to do so, for fear of jeopardising support from their constituents if they associated themselves publicly with prostitutes' interests. However, the campaign as such is still in the foothills of parliamentary lobbying, despite evidence to a number of select

committees, the pledged support of a number of MPs and the presentation of a Bill in the House of Lords incorporating PROS' aims
(*Hansard*, 1980). Selma James and Helen Buckingham of ECP[12] must
take credit for many of the initiatives behind Maureen Colquohoun's
Private Member's Bill in 1979, which also covered PROS' aims. The
Bill passed its first reading by a substantial majority, but got no
further as a result of a change in government, thereby illustrating,
perhaps, the juddering reality of this aspect of the work.

The Limits of Spare Time

PROS passed through a crisis prior to the appointment of a paid
national co-ordinator in March 1980. Ironically, through everyone's
efforts the campaign had developed to a point where it was in danger
of falling apart, unable, through lack of co-ordination and resources, to
carry out the tasks that the progress of the campaign had generated.
The specifics of the situation were succinctly described in the
application for funding the co-ordinator:

(1) To maintain the democratic basis and unity of PROS – it is
vital that a national structure is organised to co-ordinate the
work of the five PROS groups.

(2) To develop more local groups without any more fragmentation
so that each group positively effects the campaign.

(3) To develop more resources in order to continue to be self-
sufficient both at local and national level.

(4) The co-ordination of press and media coverage nationally is a
vital part of the campaign. At present with everyone working
in their spare time there is a danger that we 'miss the boat' on
important issues, i.e. the present Southampton situation. We
have also had to 'rush' our evidence to the Criminal Law
Revision Committee this year.

(5) The parliamentary campaign requires considerable national co-
ordination.

The plan is that, after a couple of years under the management of a
committee composed of street prostitutes, the present co-ordinator,
who was elected (unpaid) at the 1979 national event and is a founder
member and social worker, will hand over her job to a street prostitute,
who again will be paid. These developments do not guarantee future
success. However, the whole episode demonstrates a point that is not
well documented in the community-work literature – just how early

on in a campaign substantial material resources and sufficient human resources to maintain a sophisticated level of co-ordination are indispensable to any further progress.

Evaluation

At present, PROS has not achieved its declared aims, although it seems set fair. Nevertheless, the criteria for evaluating campaigns such as PROS are difficult to arrive at. The foregoing discussion has indicated how fragile the campaign still is in terms of its aims and membership. It could soon disappear: how could or should it be evaluated then? It might, alternatively, achieve some of its aims but in such a way that they backfired: for example, if decriminalisation were carried out along the lines PROS suggests, it might make it easier for middle men to move in and run the trade, thereby dictating street prostitutes' working conditions — unless they were well prepared against this eventuality. To this end, PROS is exploring the possibility of prostitutes organising their work in cooperatives, perhaps as part of a national PROS cooperative. From a marxist, feminist and moralistic standpoint it is still possible to conclude that prostitution is undesirable *per se*. However, PROS' existence means that it is no longer quite so easy to condemn prostitutes, as opposed to prostitution, and go unchallenged. Street prostitutes now have a public voice. By speaking out, prostitutes have emphasised the need for change in the most intimate and entrenched forms of social relations.

Notes

The contact address for PROS is: c/o Peace Centre, Moor Street, Birmingham 4.

1.   It still does, apart from increases in fines from £10 to £50 as a maximum for the first offence, £25 to £200 as a maximum for the second offence and £25 to £200 as a maximum for the third offence.

2.   For further corroboration of this point see *Hansard* (1980, cols 1508—9). Lord Avebury, in moving his Street Offences Amendment Bill, refers to figures provided by the inner-city probation office in Sheffield for the 17-month period from January 1979 to May 1980:

> Of 21 statutory clients referred to them by the court no fewer than 17 were single parents and this tallies with the estimate given to me by PROS that in their judgment as many as 75 per cent of prostitutes may be single parents.

3.   For the legal definition of loitering, under the 1959 Street Offences Act, see Chapter 2, note 10. Charges rest on police evidence, and so it is not necessary

for an individual to have been annoyed by a particular prostitute's activities and to make a complaint for a charge to be brought. In the Birmingham area alone, the author has direct personal knowledge herself of several instances of wrongful arrest occurring as cases of 'loitering'.

4. On average, approximately 3,000 street prostitutes pass through the courts each year on charges relating to the Street Offences Act and about 300 are imprisoned (Home Office, 1974).

5. No records are kept of the numbers of children received into care as a result of their mothers' receiving custodial sentences. But figures from the inner-city probation office in Sheffield for the period from January 1979 to May 1980 indicate the high incidence of this in respect of street prostitutes. Altogether, 17 women were imprisoned for soliciting, among whom six had children received into care. As prostitutes tend not to have close ties with their families of origin, this may make it especially difficult for them to obtain financial help from that source (Lord Avebury, *Hansard*, 1980, cols 1507–8).

6. The street prostitutes who are quoted are PROS members interviewed at various stages by the author. Some names have been changed.

7. Perhaps this notion is reinforced by assumptions regarding prostitutes' lack of initiative as part of the psychopathological view discussed earlier.

8. The rates earned by prostitutes stand in particularly sharp contrast to standard rates for outwork. Brown (1974) gives the hourly rates for fifty women interviewed who were doing jobs ranging from making plastic pants to mascara brushes. The rates run from up to 3p an hour to a maximum of 72p an hour.

9. Over the question of housing, Means (1979) counsels caution with regard to 'radical' social workers' unthinking espousal of deviant groups' part against 'unperceptive' local residents. Local residents may be only too aware of the extent to which they are in a state of competition for scarce resources and of the threat that the activities of deviant groups can pose to their chances.

10. This is an extract from an application for the post of national co-ordinator of PROS (1980).

11. Workers in the press, television, political parties, films and even medicine have offered specific assistance in this way.

12. ECP is the English Collective of Prostitutes – an organisation centring upon the efforts of Helen Buckingham, whose background is in the upmarket call-girl trade, and Selma James of Wages for Housework to gain publicity for decriminalisation. ECP is good at making an impact on the press. Its forerunner, PUSSI, was founded in 1975 in connection with the publication of *Prostitutes* by Jeremy Sandford (1975), and in 1976 was renamed PLAN (Prostitution Laws Are Nonsense).

Bibliography

Brasstacks *The Name of the Game* (BBC TV, 22 May 1979)

Brown, M. *Sweated Labour* (Low Pay Unit, London, 1974)

Cain, M. 'On the Beat: Interactions and Relations in Rural and Urban Police Forces', in S. Cohen (ed.), *Images of Deviance* (Penguin, Harmondsworth, 1971)

Collins, W., Friedman, E. and Pivot, A. *Women: The Directory of Social Change* (Wildwood House, London, 1978)

Dobash, R. and Dobash, R. *Violence against Wives: A Case Against the Patriarchy* (The Free Press, Glencoe, 1980)

Glover, E. *The Psychopathology of Prostitution* (Institute for the Study and Treatment of Delinquency, London, 1969)

Green, V. 'Prostitutes Organise', *Spare Rib*, no. 56 (March 1977)

Hanmer, J. (1977) 'Community Action, Women's Aid and the Women's Liberation Movement' in Mayo (1977).

Hansard (1980) vol. 409, cols. 1501–32 (Lords)

Home Office *Working Paper of the Working Party on Vagrancy and Street Offences* (HMSO, London, 1974)

Howard League *Comments on the Home Office Working Paper* (Howard League, London, 1974)

McIntosh, M. (1978) 'Who Needs Prostitutes? The Ideology of Male Sexual Need', in C. Smart and B. Smart (eds.), *Women, Sexuality and Social Control* (Routledge and Kegan Paul, London, 1978)

McLeod, E. 'Prostitutes Organise', *Spare Rib*, no. 69 (April 1978)

———— 'Working with Prostitutes: Probation Officers' Aims and Strategies', *British Journal of Social Work*, vol. 9, no. 14 (Winter 1979), pp. 453–69

Mayo, M. (ed.) *Women in the Community* (Routledge and Kegan Paul, London, 1977)

Means, R. 'Which Way for Radical Social Work?', *British Journal of Social Work*, vol. 9, no. 1 (Spring, 1979), pp. 15–28

Omen *Guardian* (9 October 1979)

PROS *A Particular Kind of Job* (film) (1978)

Sandford, J. *Prostitutes* (Secker and Warburg, London, 1975)

Sigsworth, E.M. and Wyke, T.J. 'A Study of Victorian Prostitution and Venereal Disease', in M. Vicinus (ed.), *Suffer and Be Still: Women in the Victorian Age* (Indiana University Press, Bloomington and London, 1973)

Smart, C. *Women, Crime and Criminology* (Routledge and Kegan Paul, London, 1977)

Toynbee, P. 'Guardian Women', *Guardian* (2 October 1978)

Walkowitz, J.R. and Walkowitz, D.J. ' "We Are Not Beasts of the Field", Prostitution and the Poor in Plymouth and Southampton under the Contagious Diseases Act' in M. Hartman and L.W. Banner (eds.), *Clio's Consciousness Raised* (Harper, Colophon, 1974)

Wilson, E. 'Feminism and Social Work', in M. Brake and B. Bailey (eds.), *Radical Social Work and Practice* (Edward Arnold, London, 1980)

Wolfenden *Report of the Committee on Homosexual Offences and Prostitution*, Cmnd 247 (HMSO, London, 1957)

Women Against Rape (Falling Wall Press, Bristol, 1978)

Zaretsky, E. *Capitalism, The Family and Personal Life* (Pluto, London, 1976)

4 NORMAL MOTHERHOOD: AN EXERCISE IN SELF-CONTROL?

Ann Oakley

In their functions as biological reproducers of children and social reproducers of the family, women are doubly important in the capitalist
world. One of the guiding illusions of this world is that the family is a
private place, a haven of protected, positive emotion safe from the
stresses of public labour, commercialism and power (Lasch, 1978).
Yet as Graham (1979), Land (1979) and others have shown, there is
nothing really private about the family, the state intrudes at every
point. Its policies both presume and dictate a division of labour by
gender and generation which is presented as 'natural', yet is actually
predicated on the culturally induced domesticity of women. In this
chapter I want to examine one particular manifestation of the social
importance of women in family life, and that is their role as 'normal'
mothers.

The questions I shall be asking are: In what sense is motherhood
normal? Who says what is normal about it — and why? I shall be looking at the frames of reference on motherhood employed by health-care
professionals on the one hand and mothers on the other, and asking
how far these frames of reference coincide. The data I shall draw on to
do this come from three sources: from interviews with women having
babies; from a series of observations I conducted in hospitals and GP
clinics of encounters between health care professionals and mothers;
and from an extensive, but by no means exhaustive, survey of the
advice literature currently available to mothers.[1] As Margaret Mead
and Martha Wolfenstein (1955, p. 145), noted some years ago, 'child-
training literature is as much expressive of the moral climate of the
time and place in which it is written as the state of scientific knowledge
about children'. I take this literature to be a reflection of the ortho-
doxy of both social and medical policies towards mothers, although
the messages are, of course, somewhat uneven both in their willingness
to stereotype and in their dogmatism.[2]

Medical Descriptions of Normal Motherhood

Five themes are particularly prominent in the advice literature as medical descriptions of normal motherood: normal mothers, or mothers to be, are people especially in need of medical care and protection; they are essentially childish, but at the same time fundamentally altruistic; they are married; and they ought to be happy but are instead constantly beset with anxiety and depression. I shall consider each of these descriptions in turn.

Doctor Knows Best

The first theme — that of medical care and control — is, of course, the primary reason why an advice literature exists. The Family Doctor publication *You and Your Baby* puts it nicely when it says (British Medical Association, 1977, p. 8)

> You decide when to see your doctor and let him confirm the fact of your pregnancy. From then onwards you are going to have to answer a lot of questions and be the subject of a lot of examinations. Never worry your head about any of these. They are necessary, they are in the interests of your baby and yourself and none of them will ever hurt you.

It appears that the only decision a pregnant woman has to make is to visit the doctor in the first place: after that the whole matter is taken out of her hands.

Dr Hugh Jolly (1975), considers that medical counselling is a normal prerequisite for motherhood because mothers themselves demand it. He says that mothers these days take it for granted that they will be able to rely on the advice of experts. The Health Visitors' Association booklet (1979, p. 6) adds

> Perhaps you have no relatives nearby to reassure you about your baby. It's natural to have queries . . . and nice to know there is a team of people to help you after, as well as before, your baby too . . . These services (the 'family doctor', the midwife, the health visitor, the infant welfare clinic) . . . for over 50 years have been helping children to grow up safe and healthy. Why not use them for your family too?

In other words, to be what child psychiatrist Donald Winnicott called 'an ordinary good mother' you need to listen to the experts.

The imputation of ignorance to mothers is common. 'Many women are very hazy indeed about the timing of the last monthly period', says one doctor (Pitt, 1978, p. 33), without citing any evidence that this is so. It could be argued that this version of womanhood is an essential formula, for if women knew everything they wouldn't need to consult doctors or read books. Although the historical development of antenatal literature, from the first decades of the nineteenth century onwards, reflects a felt need to communicate the 'right' way of doing things to mothers, it is interesting that certain ambiguities remain un- solved. Medical authorities were not, and indeed still are not, sure whether pregnancy is normal or abnormal; and whether motherhood as a whole is natural or medically problematic.[3]

The earliest antenatal guides did not take the line that medical care was necessary for pregnant women, but they did insist that medical advice on how to control habits of diet, exercise and elimination was essential, so that women's bodies could be brought into harmony with nature. Nature, not medicine, delivered women of their babies and enabled them to adjust to motherhood.

'A wife', said Dr Chavasse (1832, p. 3), 'may be likened to a fruit tree, a child to its fruit. We all know that it is impossible to have fine fruit from an unhealthy tree as to have a fine child from an unhealthy mother.' By the 1920s these guides to mother's health reflected a widening medical jurisdiction over pregnancy. The advice became not that of letting nature have the upper hand, but of allowing doctors to do so instead. Truby King's *Mothercraft*, a popular manual of the 1930s, introduces this theme (King, 1934, p. 8): 'As soon as possible after a woman knows she is pregnant she should visit a doctor for a complete examination. This should always take place before the third month.' In almost 1970s style, King went on to say 'Be very frank with your doctor and ask him freely about anything which is worrying you or which you do not quite understand.'

Women as Children

If pregnancy is a time for medical care, the underlying model of relationships between mothers and health-care professionals is one of inequality. First of all, it is not the mother who is the professional on the subject of motherhood. As the Family Doctor booklet says (British Medical Association, 1977, p. 21): 'Listen carefully to the advice your doctor or midwife gives you. As they are professionals at their jobs they know what they are talking about.' But, secondly, what is communicated in this advice literature is an image of women's essential *childishness*. They are portrayed as not properly grown-up people — as people beset with distracting whims and foolish fancies which make them *irresponsible* towards their children.

Take the Family Doctor booklet's remonstration (British Medical Association, 1977, p. 22):

> Do remember to take the tablets your doctor has given you. No matter how well you feel both you and your baby need them and they can't do either of you any good if you leave them sitting around on your dressing table.

There is an absolute moral certainty about the attributes of mothers in much of this literature, as indicated, for example, in such dictums as 'Every woman enjoys shopping for the pram' (British Medical Association, 1977, p. 42) and in the very common portrayal of women as bent on the particularly hazardous occupation of moving house in pregnancy. Most authors advise against this as a piece of idiocy guaranteed to jeopardise the baby's wellbeing. Note, however, that it is also widely recognised that scrubbing the floor and cleaning out the kitchen cupboards during the last weeks of pregnancy is a sign of women's genetic capacity for nest building; it seems that what biology legitimises and what it doesn't in the case of normal motherhood is also a matter for medical decision.

A further way in which normal mothers are childish is in their lack of forethought, their inability to engage in deferred gratification. Hugh Jolly (1975, p. 191) illustrates this tendency when he says, 'Don't start spooning food into your contented baby who is longing to sleep after a satisfying milk feed merely because your neighbour's baby started early.' The most patronising caricatures of this genre suggest that the sense of disorganisation about what to do when, and how, that possesses many normal mothers is actually abnormal and stems from the woman's own personal disorganisation. Brice Pitt (1978, p. 113) remarks in his chapter on 'Homecoming':

> If she has been in hospital for a week or more there is hardly a woman who is not dying to get home. Once back, though, and especially when her husband has returned to work and she is for the first time alone, she often finds herself in a state of anxiety. She wishes she could have the midwife back at her elbow to tell her what to do now, and reassure her that everything is alright.

How on earth is she to get everything done? There's the shopping and the baby to see to, the washing and the baby to change, the cleaning and the baby to feed, the dinner to cook, and, oh dear, why is he[4] breathing like that/crying so loudly/so quiet/so red in the face? . . . She is so afraid of doing the wrong thing, or that she'll forget or neglect to do what she should. And there simply aren't enough hours in the day. So when the husband comes home he may well find no dinner ready, the baby howling and his wife in tears. If he is mature and understanding . . . he will give her a kiss and a hug and tell her he loves her.

Note the reference to the husband's maturity. This passage indicates how a typification of mothers as generally unable to plan ahead and cope with the demands made upon them converts a common problem into a feminine disorder.

The association of feminine personality with childish characteristics is, of course, not confined to motherhood: it is an integral part, as Helen Hacker (1969), Jean Baker Miller (1976) and others have shown, of women's cultural treatment as a subordinate social group. However, motherhood does have a special status here, in that it is held by some to make women grow up and to bring about women's adulthood in a manner for which there is no parallel in the case of men. The theories of Helen Deutsch (1944), and other psychoanalytic thinkers (Chertok, 1969) who regard pregnancy as a period of maturation illustrate the underlying theme in all medical characterisations of normal motherhood, which is that motherhood is never normal because it is only normal to be a man. According to this standard, all women are defective, and it is just a matter of working out what particular deficiencies women, or subgroups of women, suffer from. A recent study asked doctors to list the various characteristics they saw as being typical of a 'normal healthy adult', 'a normal healthy male' and a 'normal healthy female', respectively. Most doctors saw normal healthy adults and normal healthy men as indistinguishable, but typical traits for normal healthy women were very different. They included being conceited about their appearance, being 'excitable in minor crises', being highly emotional, being submissive and unaggressive and being uninterested in science (Broverman *et al.*, 1970).

Altruism and the 'Maternal Instinct'

The attribution of childishness to women coexists uncomfortably with another message of the advice literature, which is that normal mothers are essentially altruistic, the servers of others' needs rather than their own. What this means is that mothers who consider their own needs are bad mothers. In their book *Breast Is Best*, Drs Penny and Andrew Stanway (1978, p. 138) discuss employment and breastfeeding in the following terms:

> Many mothers today say that living is so expensive that they simply can't afford to run a home on one income. That may seem to be the case but it's a thought that's worth challenging. Just think what you'd have to go without if you didn't work for nine months, for instance, and weigh up the advantages of being with your baby and feeding him the best way you possibly could. Very often going back to work is shrouded in economic excuses when really the mother wants to keep in the swim, maintain her career or even simply her own self-image. Mothers who take to mothering naturally don't want to leave their babies — they'll go throught all sorts of hardships to stay at home.

The moral of this is very obvious. It is only mothers who are 'unnatural' who go out to work. There is, of course, an unspoken equation between normal, natural and ideal in much of the advice literature. If what is held up to be ideal can also be said to obtain in nature and for most women (the statistical idea of normality), then it can more persuasively be argued that there is something wrong with those mothers who do not measure up to ideal standards of motherhood. And the ideal (despite the post-Bowlby enlightenment of child psychology in the 1970s) is, undoubtedly, that the interests of the child are served best by its mother's constant presence. 'From a mother's point of view it is highly convenient to have proxy mothers, who can release her for short periods to get her hair done, visit the dentist or have an evening out', observes the *Good Housekeeping Baby Book* (Vosper, 1974, p. 117), thereby making the point that the rest of the time mothers are supposed to be with their children.

Putting the baby first is perhaps the primary definition of normal motherhood in modern industrialised society. It owes much to the rise of a child psychology and the creation of a feminine psychology that takes self-immolation as a sign of proper womanhood. Normal mothers not only see the world in terms of their children's needs, but are highly sensitive to those needs and are able to gauge them by a process of intuition, so that they do not even have to be spelled out. Although the idea of a maternal instinct is not often directly stated in the advice literature, there are many appeals to 'maternal feelings', 'motherly behaviour', the natural feelings' a mother has for her child and so on. For example, 'It is absolutely natural for you to be very concerned about the health of the baby inside you. This is all part of normal maternal feelings' (Jolly, 1975, p. 26). Even Penelope Leach (1975, p. 170), a relatively emancipated adviser on motherhood, observes that 'many mothers have a permanent baby-shaped space at their left hip and shoulder; many instinctively pick up a baby if he cries'.[5] The natural-childbirth literature, I would add, is no more immune to such characterisations than the rest of the literature for mothers. Take this passage from Sheila Kitzinger (1962, p. 152), in which the author describes the end of the second stage of labour:

The woman feels as if her whole body is becoming a gateway into the world for her child. The head begins to ooze out . . . The gates swing back and open wide. This is the moment of triumph and exaltation. The baby is sliding down . . . even before the body is born the chest may flutter and then swell and the child may open wide its mouth and cry — a high-pitched wailing scream. He suddenly turns red, and the mother gasps with pleasure at this . . . She wants to take him into her arms immediately, to hold him tight and soothe him. The child's legs slither out and his screams get louder and louder, and all the muscles of his little body seem to be clenched in protest, in indignation at being born. His mother laughs; he looks so annoyed, so helpless, his rage is so futile, and she wants to protect him from himself and his own violent emotions. Whether boy or girl she realises that this child is exactly what she desired.

To be overcome by such spontaneous feelings of 'natural' maternal warmth and acceptance is not, as I shall show later, the destiny of most mothers at this particular moment in their motherhood careers. But it is, on the other hand, a very definite image of how mothers expect childbirth to be — and how they imagine that they themselves will feel and act.

Wives as Well

The fourth theme I have picked out from the advice literature is so obvious it perhaps hardly needs to be stated. Normal mothers are married. Certainly this representation is not articulated most of the time, but references to the husband's role in pregnancy, birth and parenthood make it clear that the scene is not complete without him. Under 'month 6' in the BMA's guide to pregnancy (1977, p. 61), it says, for instance, 'Because of the possibility of damage to your baby . . . it's safer to let your husband drive', which is fine, if you've got a husband (not to mention a car).

Jean Comaroff (1977) has pointed out that recognising the existence of husbands and fathers is the main strategy medical authorities have devised for acknowledging the social/emotional dimension of women's feelings about child bearing and motherhood. In fact, men have a dual and somewhat contradictory role in these manuals of advice. In the first place, normal motherhood requires wifehood, and the implication is that when men do not share their wives' pregnancies and labours the ideal has not been attained. As Dr Jolly (1975, p. 52) phrases it, 'Even after a long or difficult labour a mother usually has a special energy to respond at once to her baby. If the father is there too the moment is perfect'. But, on the other hand, the presence of men in mother's lives also creates problems. The most charitable view of this situation is taken by Betty Parsons in her *Expectant Fathers* (subtitled *A Practical Guide to Pregnancy for the Anxious Male*). She lists as one of the after-effects of childbirth the creation of a new family unit (Parsons, 1975, pp. 93–4):

> It is very important for a woman to remember that she is a wife as well as a mother. The husband-wife relationship is basic to family unity and something that must be nurtured. Because a baby has been born, it does not mean that romance is dead.

Hence, a babysitter must be arranged:

> For the mother it is a wonderful boost to her morale to be able to put on a pretty dress and get out to enjoy herself as a woman and a wife; and, for the father, it is pleasant to have his wife to himself for a little while.

The message comes over loud and clear that motherhood is an addition to, and not a simplification of, woman's responsibilities. There is no more direct demonstration of this than the manuals' construction of the duties of the new mother as including the desire for sexual intercourse as soon as possible after the birth.[6] Not wanting sex may indicate depression, say various of these specialists in normal motherhood. This is not surprising, since, as I said earlier, it is a prominent theme of the advice literature that normal mothers are more or less constantly anxious and depressed. This is the last theme I want to take up before moving on to consider how women themselves view normal motherhood.

Depression: The Normal Condition of Women

While the books don't say that normal mothers are depressed, they do say that depression both before and after childbirth is normal. What is normal in pregnancy, however, differs slightly from what is normal afterwards, and pregnant women are widely expected to be worried, anxious or moody. They are expected to worry about their physical and emotional symptoms, their babies' health, development and normality, the rest of the pregnancy, the birth, how they will cope as mothers. Indeed, dispelling worries of this kind is taken to be a main purpose of the advice literature, but there is also the acknowledgement — as in the quotation from *You and Your Baby* at the beginning of this chapter — that medical information, examinations and tests are themselves anxiety-provoking.

For Gordon Bourne (1975, p. 3), 'the idea that your child is growing inside you is sufficient to create a degree of emotional instability', a somewhat odd statement to make, perhaps, since it seems to suggest that the very image of a child in the uterus drives women mad. Reassuringly, Bourne goes on to observe that the rapid rise in hormone levels in early pregnancy is the cause of all this trouble. But the most normal sort of depression mothers get comes after birth. The Consumers' Association (1974, pp. 1—2) comforts mothers with the dictum that

> This emotional seesaw is normal after the birth of your child. It is also common for the mother to find herself deeply depressed in the first week after the baby is born, a depression associated with not wanting to do anything for the baby, not being interesting in visitors, the slightest careless statement producing floods of tears, and so on.

Advice from Professor McClure Brown (British Medical Association, 1977, p. 86) that the 'blues' about six days after birth are so common as to be unimportant is echoed by the Department of Health and Social Security (1977, p. 45). They say that mothers 'should be prepared for possibly feeling temporary depressed or "let down" for a few days after having a baby — this is normal.' Along with many others, Drs Jolly

(1975, p. 159) and Spock (1979, p. 28) advise that chemical changes are responsible.

When the advice manuals discuss postnatal depression, they are effectively recognising the frequency with which negative feelings about normal motherhood occur. Yet this is predominantly viewed as a problem of 'adjustment'. 'Getting back to normal', a ubiquitous phrase, includes getting and recovering from the postnatal blues, regaining one's waist, making up for lost sleep, learning to fit the housework into the baby's non-demanding spells, visiting the family-planning clinic to plan the next baby and generally settling down to a routine of family life. 'Physical and nervous weariness is mostly to blame', says the *Good Housekeeping Baby Book* authoritatively. 'The confinement may have been long and tiring, there is often an emotional "let-down" after all the excitement, and depression due to hormone changes' (Vosper, 1974, p. 78). Resting and acting *as though* you love your baby are recommended as ways in which a depressed woman 'will truly be able to fulfil her role as a mother'. 'Feeling blue?' asks the Health Visitors' Association pamphlet (1979, pp. 12–13):

> If so, talk things over to work out why. Could be you're run down and should see the doctor. Or that as much as you love your baby, you're missing adult company . . . so make the effort to see your friends. Go out with your husband whenever you can . . . Find out about local . . . mothers' clubs . . . Or put a notice on your front door: 'Baby wants playmates'!

In other words, snap out of it, not by *escaping* from motherhood but by choosing some paradigmatically feminine diversion. ('A movie', a visit to the 'beauty parlour' or a new dress are recommended by Dr Spock, 1979, p. 28).

The treatment of postnatal depression in the advice literature for mothers is essentially ambiguous. What the medical experts have to contend with is the contrast between the idealised paradigm of normal motherhood as a cherished happy state, on the one hand, and the very evident fact of some women's misery on the other. Hence the importance of hormones: although evidence as to any causal relationship between levels of the various hormones and depression in pregnancy or postpartum is almost totally lacking,[7] the hormonal interpretation is attractive because it suggests that normal mothers are basically suspended in their state of normality by nature; that is, most of the time they're happy because their hormones engender natural maternal feelings, but if they're not happy it's because their hormones have let them down. This 'unreliable machine' model is the dominant view of women in modern obstetrics.[8] Not only does it allow obstetricians a free rein in controlling reproduction, but it makes sure that mothers' attitudes and reactions are not seen as influenced by the social and economic conditions in which motherhood occurs.

The themes of the advice literature discussed so far could be summarised by saying that normal motherhood is an exercise in the denial of the self. Putting one's body, one's child and one's future as a mother into the hands of medical experts — the first theme — is acknowledging that one's own knowledge, feelings, theories and choices must be subject to the overriding authority of others. The expectation of altruism, that normal mothers always put the needs of the child first — the third theme — similarly denies the legitimacy of any needs the mother herself has. Relating to and servicing the baby's father in the name of the institution of marriage — the fourth theme — pretends that mothers' own social-emotional needs can be met exclusively by mothers' husbands.

The second and fifth themes — childishness and being depressed — are a little different from the other three in that they appear to accede the right of mothers to display emotions which express their own requirements. However, as we have seen, the childish behaviour attributed to pregnant women is a caricature of normative feminity, and the depression defined as a normal experience in pregnancy and afterwards is not held to be an expression of any fundamental, generalisable problem about the situation of mothers, but rather an index of women's biologically female status.

Mothers' Descriptions of Motherhood

In the second part of this chapter I want to draw on data from my own study of mothers in order to illustrate how some of the issues raised in the first part are perceived by mothers. I shall argue that it is precisely these features of medical definitions of normal motherhood which are regarded as problematic by mothers, and that the basic conflict of women in becoming and being mothers centres on the abnegation of self which is taken as such a central feature of normal motherhood by medical authorities.

Is Your Doctor Really Necessary?

Taking the theme of medical care and protection first: do women[9] feel they need it; do they believe that only doctors, midwives, health visitors, etc., are the experts on motherhood; and do they find medical care and advice reassuring in its effects?

Conflict over the extent to which childbearing is a pathology and over who are the experts — those who have the babies or those who deal in the medical management of pregnancy and birth — was endemic in the encounters between mothers and health-care professionals I observed in my own study and in the interviews with mothers. The same conflict was evident when it came to rearing children.

The most straightforward evidence for this comes from the interviews with mothers.[10] When first seen in early pregnancy and again a month or so before the birth, the women were asked whether they thought of pregnancy as an illness or a normal condition which required few, if any, changes in the mother's ordinary pattern of living. Only two women said they thought pregnancy was an illness — one had severe nausea and vomiting in pregnancy, for which she was hospitalised twice, and the other had a cardiac murmur and haemorrhaged on three separate occasions, for which she also was admitted to hospital. Another index of the non-medical importance of motherhood is provided by answers to a question asked in pregnancy and in the two postnatal interviews about who a woman would consult if she had a problem to do with her pregnancy or her baby. In the first pregnancy interview, 29 per cent of women said they would first consult their GP, 'clinic' (unspecified), doctor at the hospital or the health visitor if they had a problem with which they needed help. The other 71 per cent said they would first ask a member of the family, a friend or a neighbour who was herself medically qualified or who was a mother, or they would read a book. By the time of the first postnatal interview (five weeks after birth), the percentage saying they would consult a medical expert in the first instance about a problem had risen to 55 per cent. By five months after the birth it had declined to 40 per cent.[11]

The presumption that child bearing and child rearing are not necessarily legitimate terrains for the medical expert underlies the desire many women express to allow nature to take its course in determining when and how a baby is born. The following conversation took place between a doctor and a woman in the final stages of her first pregnancy:

Doctor   I've got to do an internal.
Patient   Okay.
(Doctor does so.)
Patient   It's a bit sore there.
Doctor   You're very near to starting off — the cervix is very ripe.
If I give it a little stretch that might start you off.
Patient   Oh don't, I wanted to make it St Valentine's Day.
Doctor   Your blood pressure is up a bit.
Patient   Yes, but I'd rather do it nature's way.
Doctor   If we brought you in today we'd start you off.
Patient   Having seen that programme on television (*Horizon*)
you'd have to give me tranquilizers.
Doctor   You shouldn't believe all that.
Patient   It's the idea of being wired up to all those machines.
Doctor (still poking around inside)   Alright?
Patient   Yes but I'd like you to stop.
Doctor   You may get a spot of blood after that, alright?

Wanting to do it 'nature's way' rather than 'wired up to machines' is
not a choice that is respected by the doctor, who proceeds with his
intention to provoke the woman's uterus into action by what is called
'sweeping the membranes' — a covert, and by no means wholly safe,
method of inducing labour.

A constant theme in the interviews was that women themselves
felt that they were knowledgeable about motherhood. They felt they
knew a certain amount about their own pregnant bodies, and hence
about their unborn children; once the child was born they said no
expert on motherhood could know their own child and what was
best for it as well as they did. One rather striking instance of the
maternal claim about knowledge in pregnancy is that, contrary to the
assertion cited earlier that most women don't know that most crucial
date, their last menstrual period, 91 per cent of these women did
know the exact date. The rest of the women knew the date within a
week. In addition, one in four of the women had information to offer
about the date of conception which would have been helpful
clinically, and certainly would have obviated the need in some cases
for an ultrasound examination to determine the stage of gestation.
Out of these 14 women, ten gave a date for conception which pre-
dicted the date of delivery within three days.

Whether or not a woman knows when her baby was conceived is
not, however, a routine question in antenatal clinics. On the other

hand, dating the pregnancy and calculating the expected date of delivery is a common preoccupation, and six per cent of the questions asked and five per cent of the statements made by mothers in the antenatal encounters with doctors I observed concerned dates, mothers usually trying to negotiate the 'correct' date of expected delivery with doctors who did not see this as a subject for negotiation — as a legitimate area of maternal expertise.

It could be pointed out that none of the women who knew the date of their child's conception insisted on making this private information available to the staff in charge of their care. In fact, although I have identified some ways in which normal mothers do not see a monopoly of expertise lying in medical hands, I would also say that some attitude of deference to the *probably* superior knowledge and skills of health-care professionals is common. About half of the women interviewed indicated that, on such subjects as whether an induction was necessary or whether certain immunisations in childhood were a good idea, they would generally accept the medical advice offered them. An intriguing feature of this deferential attitude to medical authority was that, in pregnancy at least, it was associated with a higher level of anxiety in mothers about pregnancy and birth than an attitude of querying medical opinion. 'Deferential' women were more likely to get an epidural in labour and to experience other kinds of birth technology. This, in turn, was associated with a higher rate of the kind of postnatal depression which mothers found particularly disabling. From the doctor's point of view, however, deference is a good thing: levels of declared satisfaction with birth management and with antenatal care were both higher among women who thought that doctors automatically know best.[12]

I want to note two other features of mothers' attitudes to medical care before moving on to the next theme. One concerns the image of the doctor-patient relationship in the antenatal and child-rearing advice literature. This, as even a casual reader will notice, is dotted with references to 'your own doctor', 'your own family doctor' and so forth. What normal mothers are supposed to believe in is the paradigm of a consistently available benevolent and wise counsellor/technician.

In fact, not only do mothers feel that many doctors are inadequate counsellors and deficient technicians, but they also have the greatest difficulty in forming any one-to-one relationship, given the common situation of a constantly changing and expanding team of care-givers. Of the mothers interviewed, 62 per cent were not examined at all by their GPs when they first attended as pregnant patients, and only 16 per cent received any advice — usually cursory — about the conduct of pregnancy in general. Though there were a few mothers whose attitude was that they couldn't be in and out of the GP's surgery fast enough, most complained that they expected the GP to do more in his advertised role as a family doctor than this. The women in my sample saw an average of nine different doctors in pregnancy in an average of thirteen antenatal visits.[13] Despite the fact that GPs might have been remiss in not doing all they were expected to, the 30 per cent of women who had shared antenatal care (between the GP's clinic and the hospital) would prefer this for their next pregnancy because it gave them an opportunity to develop a relationship with a far smaller number of care-providers — usually one doctor and a midwife.

Such a relationship makes it much easier to ask questions and get them answered honestly. This is another area of discrepancy between the perceptions of normal motherhood held by mothers and those who look after them. For example, many women want to know what is happening to them in pregnancy and what doctors and midwives are doing to them: of all the questions asked by mothers in the series of hospital encounters I observed, 20 per cent concerned the size or position of the baby, fetal heart sounds, maternal weight and blood pressure. A further 20 per cent were questions about the physiology of pregnancy or birth in general. Nearly a third of all the questions posed by mothers concerned technology — ultrasound, blood tests, induction and so forth. These questions are not simple requests for reassurance as the advice literature supposes; being told not to worry is worrying when what you want is your questions answered. However, in most cases answers were given that were intended to reassure and not to inform.

The same was true of another important category of questions. Of the questions asked in the clinics I observed, 12 per cent concerned pains, uncomfortable sensations or puzzling symptoms which, because they were of no clinical significance to the doctor or midwife, tended to be casually answered or dismissed. For example:

Doctor	Not much longer to go now.
Patient	Two weeks.
Doctor	Two weeks. How are you feeling?
Patient	Oh, terrible.
Doctor	Why do you feel terrible?
Patient	The pain's really bad in my back and down here.

Doctor   I shouldn't worry about that, you can take aspirin, you know.
Patient   I've been doing that, but it doesn't make any difference.
Doctor (palpating abdomen)   That's fine.

The contrast in medical and maternal perceptions of pregnancy is particularly clear in such examples. Normal pregnancy occasions physical experiences which mothers want to have explained — even if they are not on the list of symptoms doctors and midwives are looking for. The fact that medical experts are the socially approved people to ask does not mean that they know the answers, or are even prepared to count the questions legitimate.

These difficulties in the communication between mothers and health-care professionals point to the existence of different definitions of normal motherhood held by the two groups. They can be summed up by saying that, while mothers feel that doctors, midwives and health visitors all have some legitimate role in reproduction, this role is not as all-encompassing as some providers of health care, and certainly the purveyors of knowledge about normal motherhood in the advice literature, would like it to be. Lastly, a point I have not stressed but which a variety of other evidence also emphasises, medical care can itself generate the kind of anxiety and stress that is not conducive to mothers' happiness.[14]

Who's Being Childish Then?

It is implied in what I have already said that the second theme of the advice literature — women's inherent childishness — is also a motif of their actual communication with health-care providers. It is almost redundant to observe that most women find an attitude of patronising condescension — whether in the antenatal or in the baby clinic — unhelpful to them in the problems they as mothers have to face. I will briefly take up a few of the points I made in my earlier discussion of this theme, drawing on the accounts given by mothers interviewed in my study.

Firstly, the allegation that women are especially idiotic and child-like in choosing to move house in pregnancy ignores the material circumstances in which reproduction in our society happens. Pregnancy does not occur in a vacuum removed from the social and economic constraints of the 'real' world in which normal mothers live. Babies need homes and moving in pregnancy is the obvious way to secure this. Secondly, mothers' irresponsibility is seen to proceed from their

ungrown-up state in a way which denies the evidence about how
women actually feel towards their maternal, wifely and housekeeping
duties. One concrete example of this mystification is smoking, the
elimination of which in pregnancy is a major goal of current health-
education and preventive-medicine campaigns. The message of such
campaigns is that mothers who smoke in pregnancy are wilfully
irresponsible towards their unborn babies. My own observations of
conversations between health-care professionals and mothers on this
subject support what other research (Graham, 1976) has shown – that
mothers who continue to smoke do so for two main reasons: (a) they
take a different view of the evidence about the dangers of smoking
from doctors; and/or (b) they smoke in order to cope with the stress
that results from the fact that mother-to-be is only one of their many
roles. In the first case, women will cite friends and acquaintances
who have smoked regularly in pregnancy and nevertheless had large,
healthy babies – or they will cite their own experience of a previous
pregnancy. While this may be a mistaken view of the evidence according
to its orthodox medical interpretation, it certainly does not suggest
an attitude of not caring about one's baby. In the second case, we
come back to the shortcomings of the medical paradigm which views
mothers as full-time patients who have nothing else to do but follow
doctor's orders. In fact, of course, normal mothers have a great deal to
do: 70 or so hours of housework a week; looking after the other
children they have; keeping their marriages going and their husbands
happy; and/or working in the only one of these capacities that is
socially accredited work, that is, in paid employment. More than a
third of mothers of young children in Britain are now employed and,
contrary to the assertions of Drs Penny and Andrew Stanway (1978),
earning money is a necessity for most of them, however naturally or
unnaturally they take to motherhood.

Thirdly, moving on to the point made in Dr Jolly's remark about
not spooning solids into a contented baby just because your neighbour does, other mothers are, as I have hinted already, an important
reference group for normal mothers, whether health-care professionals
like it or not. Advances of the kind indicated by the move from breast
or bottle to jars and tins are an essential mechanism of self-reward for
normal mothers in what is otherwise often experienced as a static and,
despite the glowing images in the books, not altogether rewarding role.

Fourthly, and most crucially, I would argue that the gap between
expectations and reality which leads normal mothers to be characterised as incapable of forward planning is not a problem of their own

making. Women could be said to have the innocence of childhood in this respect, for the shock of discovering that normal motherhood is not as one had been led to think it would be is the greatest problem women have in becoming mothers today.[15]

Nature versus Nurture

Altruism and maternalism as attributes of normal mothers — the third theme of the advice literature — are experienced as deeply problematic by many; they certainly do not come naturally. Women speak of the belief that physiological reproduction automatically leads to (or proceeds from) a maternal instinct. For many, this is an aspect of the ideology of femininity they have not questioned before pregnancy and do not question until it seems to them they are deficient in it. For example, one woman, eight months pregnant, said:

> It's amazing how *boring* pregnancy is . . . I expected to feel much more *maternal*, feathering the nest, making things for the home — this sort of thing — but it's just not *me*. I expected — strangely — to undergo some change and have these maternal feelings. I haven't.

Three-fifths of the women believed in the maternal instinct before their babies were born: less than half did so afterwards. As many as 70 per cent were shocked to discover that they did not feel what Kitzinger says they should feel about their babies immediately after birth: indeed, it is clear that the rush of maternal love is an exception and not a general rule — though the question of how far this might be due to the whole environment of hospital birth and the family separation it entails cannot be answered until a proper comparative study is done.

But the disjunction between the expectation of maternalism and instant altruism and the shock of discovering that motherhood is not like that is judged poorly from such statistics. The sacrifice of one's own needs to the needs of the child is, I suggest, a chronic problem throughout all the ages and stages of normal motherhood, though differently experienced at different times, differently expressed and differently resolved by individual mothers. What I am saying can perhaps best be clarified by noting some of the ways in which the mothers in my study expressed this conflict between their identity as people and their identity as the mothers of other people with a prior claim in the business of need gratification. Four main areas of conflict were articulated. Firstly, women's *physical* needs were felt to compete with the demands of motherhood. In the early weeks this was expressed chiefly as maternal exhaustion and a need for sleep that babies didn't recognise. 'In the night, oh, you think it's never going to end. You think she's *never* going to go to sleep – she'll go on all night . . . I haven't taken to motherhood very well, I don't think.' Secondly, mothers' *emotional* needs were stated as conflicting with infants' demands:

> from a purely selfish point of view, your time is not your own. If I feel like it I can't just sit and read a book all day . . . I used to say to Keith, you wait till you have to get up in the night and do night feeds, but I never realised, it was very stupid of me, exactly what was involved.

Thirdly, even small babies have characters of their own and they convey to mothers a wilfulness that is not necessarily welcomed: 'he's going to be *strong-willed* . . . when he makes up his mind he wants to do something, he sort of keeps on'. Fourthly, children often challenged mothers' concepts of their own identity, causing at best a revision and at worst a sense of total demolition:

> I would like to go back to work . . . it has been so intense with her, because it has been every minute of the day thinking baby things, which I haven't particularly liked . . . I haven't had time for any other interests . . . It is really baby, baby, baby, 24 hours a day . . . I am not really living through this period of time, I am existing through it . . . It doesn't matter what you feel before you have a baby, you are just going to be shifted into the category of being a mother and being a housewife.

Although these dilemmas of normal mothers are abstracted from a study of women in the early stages of child rearing, I believe that other work on mothers' attitudes to employment, housework and motherhood project essentially the same problems. For example, Susannah Ginsberg (1976) has shown that most women are dissatisfied with full-time housewifery and motherhood and report an intense conflict between feeling that they ought to stay at home and knowing that they don't like it. In a Cambridgeshire study of fifteen-year-old girls, Shirley Prendergast and Alan Prout (1980) have discussed the way in which the contradiction between the normative and the actual sides of motherhood is embedded in how girls describe their own mothers and mothers in general: motherhood is both deeply fulfilling and intensely depressing. This leads to the suggestion that, when women have babies, they are actually experiencing a conflict they have known about for some time, and that the new personal immediacy of the discrepancy between idealised image and actual situation is one reason why mothers get depressed.

The Problem of Men

The fourth theme of the advice literature I discussed in the first part of this chapter was the location of normal motherhood squarely within the institution of marriage. The first thing to be said about this is, of course, that ten per cent of babies born today are born to unmarried mothers, and these women therefore cannot relate to the marital paradigm of the medical advisers on normal motherhood.[16] For those mothers who are married, the main difference between their perception of the situation and those conveyed in the advice literature is that husbands are a problem.

Why are they a problem? The first reason is that they represent *work*. One young mother complained:

> I find I'm not able to look after my husband as much as I wanted to. I feel that he feels neglected. But I just can't do anything. If at a quarter to eight he [the baby] wakes up, who do I feed — my husband or the baby?

The second reason why men are a problem is that marriage legitimates the sexual intercourse of its parents. Discrepancy between the views held by mothers and mothers' partners as to when intercourse ought to be stopped in pregnancy and resumed after birth occurred in 52 per cent of the couples in my study. From the point of view of mothers in the period after birth, it was not only the soreness of a cut and stitched perineum (98 per cent had episiotomies) that got (literally) in the way. A less tangible obstacle was mothers' feelings that their need for physical closeness was being met by the baby. Breast-feeding mothers, particularly, felt this; breastfeeding is a source of physical pleasure for women which is culturally underplayed and omitted from the advice literature, except in an ideological association with some concept of the natural maternal comfort that women's breasts and arms can give to babies.

The third reason why men are a problem is that the husband-wife relationship is ideally supposed to be a focus of equal emotional intensity for both participants in it. But who does a normal mother love most — her husband or her child? In my study, 73 per cent of mothers described a lessening of emotional closeness in the relationship with their husbands over the year or so from the first to the last interview. At the last interview the women were asked the incredibly unfair question, 'Out of being a mother, being a wife and being a housewife, which would you say is the most important to you?' For 48 per cent, the answer was their role as a mother; 27 per cent said they couldn't choose between their roles as wife and mother; and 25 per cent said that being a wife came first. The most conservative interpretation of these figures is that women are pulled in two opposing directions of commitment.

Getting (and Staying) Depressed

The manuals of advice do acknowledge some of the difficulties normal mothers have in reconciling their responsibilities to husbands and children and in devoting themselves wholeheartedly to children's needs. Indeed, the label 'postnatal depression', together with its ill-worked out package of contents, causes and treatments, can be seen as the major ideological strategy within the medical model for validating some degree of ambivalence and dissatisfaction in normal mothers. But the implication of medical descriptions of postnatal depression is that negative feelings are a temporary aberration, from which normal mothers quickly recover to settle down to a life of contented domesticity. Postnatal depression may be normal, but so is getting over it. What is not normal is continuing to feel depressed, worn down and/or under-utilised by the emotional and physical labours of motherhood.

I have discussed this fifth theme of the advice literature at length elsewhere (Oakley, 1980), but it is relevant to summarise the main points of my argument here. Firstly, and as the medical advisers on motherhood are aware, some form of depression or dissatisfaction after birth is common. In my study, four out of five mothers experienced a short-term 'blues' reaction; three-quarters experienced an anxiety state on first assuming responsibility for the baby; a third had depressed moods; and a quarter had a more serious symptomatic depression in the early months of motherhood. In addition, a third were not satisfied with the social role of mother, and two-thirds expressed negative feelings and ambivalence in their relationship with their babies. Briefly, my argument was that, if you listen to women themselves, you learn that postnatal depression is probably neither caused by hormones nor by improper feminity (the two favourite themes of medicine and psychiatry on normal motherhood). It is, instead, a complex reaction which has two main origins. Firstly, it is a response to the enormity of the change childbirth brings in our culture: medical patienthood, institutionalisation (in hospital), surgery, retirement from employment, occupational career change and so forth. Secondly, postnatal depression is a form of bereavement reaction in which a woman mourns her former identity. In both these senses, childbirth can, and should, be seen as a human life-event, that is, as a major change in *people's* lives rather than as an archetypally feminine experience.

The importance of these considerations is brought out by the fact that in my study a disabling postnatal depression was most likely to occur when the birth had been characterised by a high degree of technology, and when a woman was socially vulnerable in not having any form of employment, in living in poor housing, in lacking an intimate relationship with her baby's father and in knowing little about childcare before her own child was born.

Beyond the limits of this study, postnatal depression is, as I said earlier, not unconnected with other forms of depression from which women suffer — though the connection is not, so far as I know, made by those who study the epidemiology of either. It seems rather clear from evidence generated in a fairly wide range of studies that depression in women — particularly married women, particularly mothers and particularly mothers at home, throughout the whole period of child rearing and beyond — is the major legitimate strategy available to women for expressing the fact that the conditions of their lives are not congenial to them (see, for example, Porter, 1970; Gove and Tudor, 1973; Brown and Harris, 1978). In this sense, I would suggest that adjustment to motherhood in normal mothers is not normal — on the contrary, the pictures sketched in the advice literature of temporary problems in settling down represent the landscape on which the whole of normal motherhood is lived.

The conflict I have identified in this chapter between medical descriptions of normal motherhood and normal mothers' own accounts suggests that medicine has a particular interest in advertising a particular paradigm of women, their psychology and experiences. Such an observation is not original. It is, equally, not original to observe that the presence and effect of these typifications acts as a way of controlling women, of obstructing women's recognition that their lot is not an entirely happy one and could do with some radical change. The social-control function of the medical and allied professions *vis-à-vis* women is not a unique case of sexual chauvinism; other social institutions, from the law to the national-insurance and social-security systems, from the church to education, from the media to politics, also present an image of women which compresses the breadth and variety of their psychologies, lifestyles, satisfactions and dissatisfactions into the basic model of a childish, married, domesticated and neurotic dependent. However, I think there is one particular reason why medical experts on normal motherhood are motivated to present a distorting and limiting stereotype.

The Subversive Power of Sisterhood

This reason is the existence of a community of alternative purveyors of knowledge about normal motherhood, namely other women. Competition between medical experts and women as a group in this area does, I suggest, help to explain the historical development and importance today of advice literature on child bearing and child rearing. This literature has the important function of combating received wisdom among women about what normal motherhood is. In turn, women's collective definitions of normal motherhood mediate between the medical paradigm and the subjective realities of motherhood as experienced by individual women. The subversive power of these female definitions obstructs the medical experts in their self-assigned task of controlling reproduction and parenthood.

It is not a flight of imagination to say that those who write the advice manuals see themselves as waging war on the influence women have over each other. When Hugh Jolly observes that modern mothers take it for granted that they will have experts to rely on, what he means is that, if mothers are going to listen to experts, they must stop listening to their own mothers — or, for that matter, to any woman who offers an opinion on motherhood, from the neighbour who starts solids early to a sister who warns that childbirth might actually *hurt*. Jolly is not alone in recommending non-communication between women; indeed, this is a recurrent theme of the advice manuals. Bourne (1975, pp. 7–8) talks of 'the wicked tongue that tells nothing but stories of doom, disaster and death' to women approaching childbirth:

Why do women have to recount such stories to one another, especially when the majority of them are blatantly untrue? Even the most sensible of pregnant women seldom have the presence of mind to tell the purveyors of these wicked stories to be quiet[17] and however much a woman may laugh about the story it nearly always sows a tiny seed of doubt in her mind; doubt about herself, or her baby, or perhaps even the ambulance service, or the nurse or doctor or some other member of the staff of the hospital, or some aspect of the hospital itself. Probably more is done by wicked women with their malicious lying tongues to harm the confidence and happiness of pregnant women than by any other single factor.

Why do they do this? Perhaps it is some form of sadism or as a revenge payment for an unhappy experience of their own that they wish to magnify and share with someone who cannot answer back.

It probably is. After all, why should women not transmit their own experiences, whether happy or not, to other women? Indeed, might there not be something to be gained from women sharing experiences in this way — a sense of solidarity, the destruction of romantic myths of motherhood, at the very least a consumer's guide to which medical professionals and institutions offer the most satisfying form of care? Bourne (1975, pp. 6—7) rightly observes that if the medical experts are to counter the collective wisdom of women about motherhood, they must sabotage the power of what, significantly, are called 'old wives' tales':

> The problem of 'old wives' tales' is really one of confidence because the majority of old wives' tales are essentially destructive or demoralising . . . The majority of people today realise that these old wives' tales are a cartload of rubbish but even so they leave behind an unhappy legacy that is not difficult to understand . . . If you have heard some story or tale that has caused you any apprehension then mention it the next time you see your doctor or midwife.

Bourne's description of old wives' tales significantly highlights their role as destructive of a deferential confidence in the advisability, safety and appropriateness of medical care.[18] The fact that health-care professionals whose defined area of expertise is normal motherhood do, frequently, come up against the alternative know-ledge of women as a group has been demonstrated by some of the data I have presented in this chapter. For example, the proportion of women who consulted neighbours, friends, mothers, etc., in preference to medical professionals when they had a problem in pregnancy or with the baby points to the existence of women's collective knowledge about motherhood as a non-medical source of information and support. There were many other signs of the importance that women attached to asking other mothers for information, advice and help. Three-quarters of the women had practical help from their own mothers following childbirth. Other mothers were also important influences on decisions about feeding — breast versus bottle, what kind of milk, what to do about night needs, what kind of solid food to offer when. While other mothers fairly frequently offered advice about the processes of pregnancy or birth, there was no evidence that this, or any other advice, provoked anxiety in the mother at whom it was aimed. On the contrary, the anxiety felt in relation to medical encounters and medical sources of information was often allayed by the reassurances of other women.

Women's information and mutual-help networks are a finding of many post-war sociological studies of community in Britain and elsewhere (for example, Rees, 1950; Dennis *et al.*, 1956; Young and Willmott, 1957; Kerr, 1958). Some studies in the field of medical sociology have also highlighted the importance of mothers and other female relatives as sources of reproductive advice. For example, John McKinlay, in a study of working-class women in Aberdeen, deemed the women's mothers 'lay consultants' in the management of pregnancy. Those women who attended for antenatal care late or not at all, and followed the same pattern in their dealings with the child health services, were those who used the counsel of their own mothers instead. Interestingly, health visitors were the most tolerated of all health-care professionals by those who rejected medical care, on the grounds that they were either mothers themselves, or could be talked to like mothers. Interestingly too, the under-utilisers of professional health care regarded pregnancy as a normal life-event and shared a perception of pregnancy which excluded the possibility of any medical need (McKinlay, 1970).

To sum up, what I have suggested in this chapter is that there are considerable discrepancies between medical typifications of normal motherhood and normal motherhood as it is actually experienced. It seems probable that the non-medical knowledge which mothers have, and which they pass on across the generations has a fairly profound function in mediating this contradiction. Another way to put this is to say that if women aren't powerful in obvious ways — if, as maternity patients, they are frequently reduced to a state of inaction and dependence; if, as mothers, they are victims of the social and economic poverty of housewives and of a child psychology which reduces mothers to the status of servants of their children's needs — then, at least, women are powerful in other ways. For, in speaking of the realities of motherhood to each other, and in continuing to so speak, despite the ever-increasing volume of medical messages, they are actively countering the myth of their own infant and passively accepting natures.

Notes

1.   The survey is restricted to the British literature, with the exception of Spock (1979).
2.   The work of Leach (1975) is notable for its avoidance of generalisations about the personalities and attributes of normal mothers.
3.   Graham (1977) discusses the historical development of antenatal advice literature in terms of this ambiguity.
4.   Most babies in the advice literature are male. Some recent authors (for example, Leach, 1975) apologise for this. The revised version of Spock (1979, p. xvi) tries 'to get away from the implied assumption in previous editions that the child is always a boy and that the parent is usually a woman'.
5.   Leach (1975, p. 17) says that the impression of parenthood given in her own book, as in advice manuals generally, is 'an unrealistically dedicated one'. However, she makes no apology for this, contending that, 'In these days of good contraception and world overpopulation there is a moral obligation to rear as well as we can the children we choose to have.'
6.   The Health Visitors' Association pamphlet *New Baby* (1979, p. 49) says it is safe to make love two weeks after the birth. The general message of other authorities is that women certainly don't need to wait until after the magic date of the postnatal examination (at six weeks postpartum).
7.   For a discussion of research in this field see Oakley (1980, pp. 53–6).
8.   See Oakley (1979b, 1980, chap. 1).
9.   By 'women' or 'mothers', of course, I mean the people who were interviewed in this study, not women or mothers in general — although for reasons argued elsewhere (Oakley, 1979a, 1980) I believe the findings of this study to be of general relevance to the institution of motherhood today.
10.   There were 66 women in the study. Four interviews were done, either by myself or by a research assistant — two in pregnancy and two after the birth. All the women had their babies at the same large London maternity hospital in 1975–6. (See Oakley, 1979a, 1980.)
11.   It is worth pointing out that this sample (young urban women booked for hospital delivery) is one for which the proportion of 'medical consulters' would be expected to be fairly high.
12.   I am not suggesting here that medical expertise is redundant in the management of reproduction. There are clearly many mothers and babies whose lives have been saved by medical intervention. From an epidemiological point of view, however, the problem is to disentangle the benefits of modern obstetrics

for those child-bearing women and their babies who need them from its hazards to healthy women and babies who do not (Chard and Richards, 1977).

13. Through a lamentable process of selective perception on my part, and because the hospital notes afforded no way of calculating the number of midwives or pupil midwives the women saw, I do not know if there were as few familiar faces among the midwives as among the doctors.

14. That medical care may be experienced as stressful is the conclusion arrived at in many studies of patients' attitudes. Garcia (1980) provides a summary of surveys of how mothers feel about antenatal care. Graham and McKee's study in York (1979) is also very relevant. Newton *et al.* (1979) recently attempted to document the consequences of stress for the physical outcome of pregnancy. They found that the incidence of premature labour was raised in women who retrospectively described socially stressful pregnancies. Such a study does, of course, omit non-physical measures of pregnancy outcome such as how the mother feels about, and after, her experiences of pregnancy and birth.

15. The reasons why 'society' conspires to pull the wool over mothers' eyes are complex. For some suggestions, see Oakley (1980, pp. 284–91).

16. In my study, 13 per cent of the women were not married when first interviewed, although they were living with the baby's father. I apologise for using the term 'husband' to include these unions.

17. Note the usual characterisation of women as incapable of control.

18. See Chamberlain (in press) on the general social, medical and feminist significance of old wives' tales.

Bibliography

Bourne, G. *Pregnancy* (Pan, London, 1975)

British Medical Association, Family Doctor Publication, *You and Your Baby, Part 1, 'From Pregnancy to Birth'* (1977)

Broverman, I., Broverman, D., Clarkson, F., Rosencrantz, P. and Vogel, S. 'Sex Role Stereotype and Clinical Judgements of Mental Health', *Journal of Consulting and Clinical Psychology*, vol. 34 (1970), pp. 1–7

Brown, G.W. and Harris, T. *Social Origins of Depression* (Tavistock, London, 1978)

Chamberlain, M. *Old Wives' Tales* (Virago, London, in press)

Chard, T. and Richards, M. (eds.) *Benefits and Hazards of the New Obstetrics* (Heinemann, Spastics International Medical Publications, London, 1977)

Chavasse, P.H. *Advice to a Wife on the Management of Her Own Health* (Cassell, London, 1832)

Chertok, L. *Motherhood and Personality* (Tavistock, London, 1969)

Comaroff, J. 'Conflicting Paradigms of Pregnancy: Managing Ambiguity in Antenatal Encounters', in A. Davis and G. Horobin (eds.), *Medical Encounters* (Croom Helm, London, 1977)

Consumers' Association, *Pregnancy Month by Month* (1974)

Dennis, N., Henriques, F. and Slaughter, C. *Coal is Our Life* (Eyre and Spottiswoode, London, 1956)

Department of Health and Social Security *Reducing the Risk: Safer Pregnancy and Childbirth* (HMSO, London, 1977)

Deutsch, H. *The Psychology of Women: A Psychoanalytic Interpretation* (Heinemann, London, 1944)

Garcia, J. 'Mothers' Views of Antenatal Care'. Paper presented at Human

Relations in Obstetrics Seminar (University of Warwick, 21–3 March 1980)
Ginsberg, S. 'Women, Work and Conflict', in N. Fonda and P. Moss (eds.),
   Mothers in Employment (Brunel University Management Programme, 1976)
Gove, W.K. and Tudor, J.F. 'Adult Sex Roles and Mental Illness', *American
   Journal of Sociology*, vol. 78, no. 4 (January 1973), pp. 812–35
Graham, H. 'Smoking in Pregnancy: The Attitudes of Expectant Mothers',
   Social Science and Medicine, vol. 10 (1976), pp. 399–405
———— 'Images of Pregnancy in Antenatal Literature', in R. Dingwall, C. Heath,
   M. Reid and M. Stacey (eds.), *Health Care and Health Knowledge* (Croom
   Helm, London, 1977)
———— 'Prevention and Health. Every Mother's Business. A Comment on Child
   Health Policies in the 1970's', in C. Harris (ed.), *The Sociology of the Family:
   New Directions for Britain*, Sociological Review Monograph 28 (University of
   Keele, 1979)
Graham, H. and McKee, L. *The First Months of Motherhood* (Health Education
   Council, 1979)
Hacker, H. 'Women as a Minority Group', in B. Roszak and T. Roszak (eds.),
   *Masculine/Feminine: Readings in Sexual Mythology and the Liberation of
   Women* (Harper and Row, New York, 1969)
Health Visitors' Association, *First Three Years* (1979)
Jolly, H. *Book of Childcare* (Allen and Unwin, London, 1975)
Kerr, M. *The People of Ship Street* (Routledge and Kegan Paul, London, 1958)
King, T.M. *Mothercraft* (Simpkin, Marshall, London, 1934)
Kitzinger, S. *The Experience of Childbirth* (Gollancz, London, 1962)
Land, H. 'The Boundaries between the State and the Family', in C. Harris (ed.),
   The Sociology of the Family: New Directions for Britain, Sociological Review
   Monograph 28 (University of Keele, 1979)
Lasch, C. *Haven in a Heartless World* (Basic Books, New York, 1978)
Leach, P. *Babyhood* (Penguin, Harmondsworth, 1975)
McKinlay, J.B. 'Some Aspects of Lower Working Class Utilisation Behaviour'
   (Unpublished PhD thesis, University of Aberdeen, 1970)
Mead, M. and Wolfenstein, M. (eds.) *Childhood in Contemporary Cultures*
   (University of Chicago Press, Chicago, 1955)
Miller, J.B. *Toward a New Psychology of Women* (Beacon, Boston, 1976)
Newton, R.W., Webster, P.A.C., Binn, P.S., Maskrey, N. and Phillips, A.B.
   'Psychosocial Stress in Pregnancy and Its Relation to the Onset of Premature
   Labour', *British Medical Journal* (18 August 1979), II, pp. 411–13
Oakley, A. *Becoming A Mother* (Martin Robertson, Oxford, 1979a)
———— 'A Case of Maternity: Paradigms of Women as Maternity Cases', *Signs:
   Journal of Women in Culture and Society*, vol. 4, no. 4 (1979b), pp. 607–31
———— *Women Confined: Towards A Sociology of Childbirth* (Martin
   Robertson, Oxford, 1980)
Parsons, B. *Expectant Fathers* (Robert Yeatman, London, 1975)
Pitt, B. *Feelings about Childbirth* (Sheldon Press, London, 1978)
Porter, A.M.W. 'Depressive Illness in a General Practice. A Demographic Study
   and a Controlled Trial of Imipramine', *British Medical Journal* (28 March
   1970), I, pp. 773–8
Prendergast, S. and Prout, A. 'What Will I Do?: Teenage Girls and the
   Construction of Motherhood', *Sociological Review*, *28*, 3 (August 1980),
   pp. 517–35
Rees, A.D. *Life in a Welsh Countryside* (University of Wales Press, Cardiff, 1950)
Spock, B. *Baby and Child Care*, revised edn (Star, London, 1979)
Stanway, P. and Stanway, A. *Breast is Best* (Pan, London, 1978)
Vosper, J. *The Good Housekeeping Baby Book*, 14th (revised) edn. (Ebury

Press, London, 1974)

Young, M. and Willmott, P. *Family and Kinship in East London* (Routledge and Kegan Paul, London, 1957)

5 CARE OR CUSTODY? THE EXPERIENCES OF WOMEN PATIENTS IN LONG-STAY GERIATRIC WARDS

Helen Evers

Introduction

This chapter argues that women patients present the health-care system with distinctive, gender-related needs, strengths and problems. It is particularly important to recognise these in the context of geriatric wards, where a majority of patients are female. In geriatric wards the gender order emerges as a key factor in understanding how care work is organised and carried out. Yet neither in its policy nor in its professional practice does the health-care system take any explicit account of the distinctive characteristics of women geriatric patients. This has adverse consequences both for women patients and for nurses. The women patients tend to be subjected to particular forms of oppression: the nurses — also women, on the whole — tend to label women patients as more 'difficult' than men. This labelling goes hand in hand with various conflicts for the nurses, who are socialised into a female-dominated 'caring' profession, yet at the same time are subject to administrative pressures towards efficient control of work, by routinising the running of the ward. In the context of these conflicts, the 'difficult' patient represents both a care problem and a control problem for the nurse. Analysis of the experiences of women geriatric patients and their carers, the nurses, is necessary if the lot of both groups is to be better understood and improved through changes in health-care practice and organisation.

The sociological research into the patterns of work organisation in geriatric wards which this chapter draws upon relied largely on non-participant observational methods. The careers of a sample of 86 geriatric patients — of whom 62 were women — in eight wards, each in a different hospital, were analysed. A particular interest was taken in how patients' careers were created and controlled within the structure of social relations in the ward setting, and in how this affected patients' well-being or, more precisely, various indices of ill-being, these being easier to define and observe.

The first section discusses some of the contrasts between men and women as patients and the second examines how these apply to geriatric patients. Features of geriatric nursing work and its organisation are then discussed. A summary of pervasive patterns of work organisation in geriatric wards is followed by a discussion of nurse-patient interaction, focusing on three stereotypes of women patients. Their experiences, in terms of care and custody or control, are contrasted with those of men patients. It is suggested that the gender order may render women patients uniquely threatening to women nurses, especially in geriatrics. It is not necessarily the case that care experiences of the men patients are 'better' than those of the women. They are, however, different; women tend to be depersonalised in a fashion not generally applied to the men. This seems to be because the identity of women, particularly of the current generation of elderly, is often grounded in 'women's work' of the home and family, the 'private domain', as Stacey (1980a) has described it, whereas the identity of men derives from the world of work in the market place, the 'public domain'. The final section of the chapter looks at the implications of the analysis for the organisation of work in geriatric wards, and identifies various key questions for future research.

Women Patients and Men Patients

It is not the purpose of this chapter to discuss studies of the 'sick' role, becoming a patient or patient-professional interaction. However, one particular feature of patienthood which is relevant here is that it involves the individual in surrendering, whether voluntarily or involuntarily, a lesser or greater part of his or her autonomy and/or competence to the scrutiny, judgement and control of the 'experts'. For the adult hospital patient, this means becoming dependent upon, and subject to control by health workers and, most directly and obviously, by nurses. The nurses are the perpetrators of doctors' orders, guardians of wards 24 hours a day, and surrogate performers of the individual's activities of daily living. Thus McFarlane's (1976) definition of the functions of nursing stresses the concern with performing for individuals those functions which they would otherwise perform for themselves unaided.

Thus dependency is a feature of patienthood, and subordination, caring and control are features of the structure of the social relations within which patienthood is experienced. The experience of dependence on others for the performance of some or many of the basic functions of life can be expected to give rise to different experiences for men and for women patients. Particularly within the family, women are the carers, preparers of food, nurturers and servants. Men are the beneficiaries of such work as this. Thus for men patients, dependency upon the care work of nurses can be seen as an extension of their conventional relationship to women in the family. For women patients, things are very different. Patienthood and attendant dependency requires surrender of part or the whole of the woman's ownership of care work to other women: professional carers, the nurses. Generally speaking, only upper-class women tend to have any experience of being waited on by other women. Thus, for most women, dependency in patienthood conflicts with the social arrangements for care work in the wider society, whereas for men there is no such conflict. Patienthood for women is therefore inherently different from patienthood for men. (It is recognised that this generalisation is an oversimplification, and requires many qualifications to take account of the range of social and individual contingencies influencing patienthood, for instance, the disabling or life-threatening characteristics of the illness which has led to patienthood, and the person's habitual structure of social relations.)

Geriatric Patients in Hospital

How does this general proposition fit the specialty of geriatrics? In western society the elderly are a low-status social category. Labelling and stigmatisation becomes a self-fulfilling prophecy: old people tend to have low expectations of their health-care rights and their health status, and to be easily satisfied with what little benefits they have or services they receive. Thus dependency through patienthood reinforces the stigma of old age as a non-productive, thus socially burdensome, phase of the lifespan. Dependency for women in old age also reinforces their loss of their central life role as care givers and as supporters of economically productive or potentially productive (children) kin. Thus for old women, the analysis of the experience of patienthood is in part parallel to that for younger women: they become dependent, and surrender to others responsibility for aspects of their autonomy of functioning in the day-to-day business of living, including the performance of their 'womanly' work of caring for self and perhaps others. They may, of course, have experienced dependency prior to entering hospital. The likelihood of this is greater for old rather than younger women. Old women may have suffered the humiliation of becoming dependent upon, typically, their daughters. But dependency increases and takes on a qualitatively different form through the process of entry to, and sojourn in, hospital. It reinforces the loss of their role as care giver, which an old woman may well already be experiencing through failing health, increasing disability or loss of the recipients of her care, in particular, her spouse. Old women thus become, through patienthood, not only incompetent, but doubly incompetent.

For old men, many of whom have retired from full-time work, dependency as a patient can be seen as a continuation of reliance on female nurturance, perhaps including dependence upon a daughter, particularly for the current generation of elderly. The state of retirement creates the likelihood of a diminished sense of worth in terms of economically and socially valued roles, but the legitimation of retirement by the attachment of this rite of passage to the magic age of 65, common to the majority of employed people, leaves the former experience of work intact as a socially meaningful and valuable role which has been responsibly discharged. Thus for an old man the relationship of dependency to the level of integrity of the self and self-esteem differs from that for an old woman.

What of the professional carers' views of elderly patients? If it is the case that the past identity of old men patients tends to remain intact, whereas that of old women patients tends to disintegrate with the passage of time and attendant role loss as care giver, then we may expect men and women patients to be seen differently by their carers. Women patients are likely to be less highly esteemed than men patients because, through becoming dependent, the validity and completeness of their social identity as care givers and as people is threatened.

To understand the range of patients' experiences in geriatric wards in the context of the gender order, we need to focus on the structure and process of social relationships within the geriatric ward and in particular on the nurse-patient relationship, since it is the nurse with whom the vast majority of interactions are sustained. Before doing so it is necessary to look briefly at the position of nurses in the wider hospital organisation and, in particular, the position of geriatric nurses, as part of the argument is that geriatrics, as an arena for experiencing patienthood and for doing nursing work, has various unique characteristics.

Hospital Nursing and Geriatrics

The subordination of nursing to medicine is a central feature of the structure of social relations of the nursing profession in the health-care system. The relationship is not only one of professional subordination, but also one of gender subordination, as has been pointed out by a number of writers (for example, Dingwall, 1980; Gamarnikow, 1978). The medical-dominated ethos of the hospital is associated with a set of values within the nursing profession which reflect those of medicine, in particular, a disease-cure-oriented rather than a person-oriented conception of illness and health care. This is associated with an emphasis on curative and therapeutic interventions aimed towards arresting or reversing disease processes and restoring health. Curative work in nursing tends to be more prestigious than caring work, because of its more obvious links with medicine.[1]

Care work in nursing has often been labelled as 'basic' nursing (for example, Goddard, 1953; Rhys-Hearn, 1973) in contradistinction to 'technical' work. As McFarlane (1976) has pointed out, the label 'basic' work has too often been taken as a synonym for straightforward, less important aspects of nursing work, for which professional skills and experience are not required. As such, it is work to be routinised on a task-defined basis, to be 'got through' as rapidly as possible (Clarke, 1978; Wells, 1980) in order, among other things, to free the nurse to participate in the more highly prized, scarcer, 'technical' and curative work.

As Gamarnikow (1978) points out, the lower status of care work arises not only from the professional relationship of domination and subordination between medicine and nursing, but also from a sexual division of labour in which male-dominated, technological, interventionist, curative work takes precedence over female-dominated care work. Indeed, in hospital, the medical prescription of 'tender loving care' has come to have connotations of a negative, last-resort, passive strategy to be applied by nurses to the 'hopeless cases' of medicine.

Geriatric nursing is a low-status specialty within nursing. Apparent shortage of staff is the norm; the environment, equipment and facilities are often poor (Wells, 1980) and untrained nursing auxiliaries form, perhaps, a more substantial proportion of the regular workforce than in any other specialty. Geriatric nursing is among the cinderella areas when it comes to attracting resources within the health service, partly because geriatrics is also a cinderella medical specialty: the miracle of medical cure and rapid discharge from hospital is far more elusive than in many other specialties. As with medicine, so nursing too derives much of its fulfilment and satisfaction from cure. Another reason for the low status of geriatric nursing is that 'basic' nursing work predominates to a greater extent than in other specialties. 'Basic' work tends to be seen as mundane, humdrum work, and not 'real' nursing, which is equated with dressings, drips and drama. Further, geriatric work tends to be extremely heavy: most geriatric wards serve a substantial proportion of patients who are very dependent physically or psychologically or both.

The position of the ward nurse, whether trained, in training or un-trained, is also crucially influenced by the rigid hierarchical arrange-ment of authority and control within the nursing profession itself (Davies, 1976, 1977; Carpenter, 1977). Nurses in training are workers first and learners second (Fretwell, 1980) and a strong culture demands unquestioning obedience from the lower participants (Mechanic, 1962). In geriatrics, 'basic' nursing work predominates. Such work is eminently routinisable; 'basic' nursing has come to represent the non-problematic, straightforward set of maintenance tasks surrounding the performance of physical activities of daily living. Because the focus is on the physical, the observable and the commonplace, task routines tend to become the stuff of life on geriatric wards (Baker, 1978; Wells, 1980). Treating individual patients as work objects (Hughes, 1971), or subsuming constellations of tasks into a series of work routines, renders them subject to hierarchical control in the same way that their carers, the nurses, are subject. This is not to suggest that routinisation is peculiar to geriatric nursing, far from it, but in geriatric nursing a greater proportion of the work has come to acquire the label 'basic', and has hence become more open to extensive routinisation and hierarchical control.

Thus the two features of the female-dominated nursing profession which are particularly relevant here are, first, its subordination to medicine which is both male-dominated and technologically oriented, and second, its rigid hierarchical control structure. It must also be noted that geriatric nursing features inherent contradictions. For example, although Clarke (1978) shows how, in psychogeriatric nursing, the nurses' strategies were geared to 'getting through the (routine) work', Baker (1978) points out that several leading pro-fessional writers (for example, Norton, 1965) have argued that, in an ideal conception, geriatric nursing is the very essence of the art of nursing, requiring a central emphasis on the 'caring' role of the nurse.

In my own research, those ward nurses, of all categories, who expressed preference for, or satisfaction with, geriatric nursing argued that their satisfaction derived from getting to know patients and their relatives as people, over a long period of time, and caring for the 'whole person' rather than an impaired organ. Yet despite these expressions by nurses of a person-centred approach to geriatric care, task-centred routinisation and the depersonalisation of patients to the status of work objects prevailed. Baker (1978) and Wells (1980) made parallel findings.

Geriatric nurses have to deal with a number of inherent conflicts. Such conflicts have been documented in other settings (for example, Menzies, 1960; Jacobs, 1979), but in geriatrics they take on particular forms. First, the care/cure conflict: the rewards deriving from cure and discharge are far scarcer in geriatrics than in other specialties, yet to derive rewards from care rather than cure requires quite a different attitude towards nursing work (Brown, 1973). Second, conflicts arise from the simultaneous pressures to treat patients as people, and to treat them as work objects, the former deriving from a particular ideology of nursing, the latter from the routinisable nature of what has come to be seen as work, and from the hierarchical control structure within which that work is carried out. Although work routinisation and treatment of patients as work objects too often prevails, particularly in long-stay geriatric wards, the conflict remains unresolved. The nurse faces persistent dilemmas; for example, the geriatric patient is often seen as equivalent to a grandparent or a parent. As such, both the professional-caring and humanitarian urge to help combine in a personal goal of doing good care work. At the same time, the thought of a parent or grandparent requiring feeding or, worse and commonly, changing and toiletting — akin to the needs of a child yet in an old person unacceptable, undignified and often irremediable — is abhorrent.

Worse, for predominantly female nurses caring for predominantly female patients, there is a dilemma arising from the patient as an image of the nurse's future self, engendering conflicting responses of total rejection and provision of care to the best of the nurse's ability. Personal and professional attitudes may evoke such conflicts for nurses *vis-à-vis* old men, too, but these take on a different form; the prevailing sex difference precludes such close identification with the patient. Also, the probability of women surviving into extreme old age, and suffering the attendant disabilities, is so much greater than for men; thus the reality of the future self is presented more starkly.

Strategies employed by nurses, albeit unconsciously, to handle these

sorts of conflicts and maintain control of their work arena with as
little stress as possible, have been documented by Menzies (1960),
Coser (1963) and, in the context of old people's homes, by Paterson
(1977). These strategies include categorising individual patients within
a range of more general labels or stereotypes, which derive from
cultural notions about old age and practices towards the elderly, a
'professional' stance towards illness and dependency, professional
socialisation regarding care of the elderly, socialisation into a 'people-
work' setting where the elderly are accorded low status and value,
despite official pronouncements to the contrary (for example,
Department of Health and Social Security, 1976, 1978), and gender
divisions in society.

Having looked at some of the issues relating to the position of the
nurse in the wider setting of the health-care arena, and some of the
inherent tensions of geriatric nursing in particular, we can now consider nurse-patient relationships and, thereby, some of the range of
patients' experiences.

Experiences of Patients in Geriatric Wards

I have discussed elsewhere (Evers, 1980 and forthcoming) some of the
factors influencing the creation of patient careers in geriatric wards, and
described some different career patterns within an 'acute dischargeable'
category, and a 'long-stay' category. Looking at the care outcomes for
patients of these two categories, the study hospitals were, by various
criteria, including patient morale, rather successful in creating 'good'
careers for 'acute dischargeable' patients. However, the career patterns
of long-stay patients did not match official or professional policy nor,
indeed, the aspirations of the staff themselves. There was much
evidence, from observation, of patients, both men and women, under-
going unnecessary suffering. Overtones of custodial care were un-
mistakeable.

For the purposes of the discussion in this chapter I will describe
typical patterns of work organisation for long-stay patients. Common
to all, across the different wards, was the extent of routinisation.
Each day, and each phase of each day, tended to be the same, its
events structured almost exclusively by the operation of the routine
by the nurses. The day started very early, often around 6.30 a.m.
Tea, breakfast and ablutions of varying superficiality were followed
by getting the patients up. The last patients to be got up were usually

finished with just before lunch, which in most of the hospitals was
served around midday. The process of putting patients back to bed
began early in some wards, after the afternoon cup of tea, at around
3.30 p.m., although in other wards some patients were able to stay
up as long as they wished. The order of putting to bed usually took
no account of the order of getting up, thus those that were up last
might well find themselves the first back, having been up, perhaps,
no more than two to three hours. The afternoon nurses were often
different people from the morning nurses, and heavy reliance on part-
timers meant that there were often problems of continuity and com-
munications as to what had been done, and what remained to be done.
The last meal of the day was served around 5.0 p.m. on most wards
though, on one ward, the staff had managed to negotiate with the
kitchen for the meal to arrive at 6.0 p.m. During the patients' daytime
hours there was, typically, little for them to do. Most patients spent
their time sitting in a day room with the television on, and sometimes
the radio as well. Two hospitals had quite a number of regular
volunteers who spent time with the patients and for some patients
there were various therapeutic activities and, occasionally, diversional
activities laid on by the occupational therapists. Most wards carried
out routine toilet rounds, which were sometimes most undignified
affairs. If patients wanted to go to the toilet between rounds, it was
often difficult for them to get the necessary attention. Only those
patients who were independent enough, either in a wheelchair or by
walking, were able to go to the toilet when they chose. There was
little privacy in many of the wards; patients could seldom escape one-
another's company.

The routine was pervasive in all eight study wards, especially for
patients who were neither acutely ill nor subject to intensive rehabilitation. However, there were differences among the wards in the
type of patient career created for patients by nurses, which I have
described elsewhere (Evers, 1980) as 'minimal warehousing'
and 'personalised warehousing'. The former featured sketchy basic
care — patients' cleanliness and toileting needs attended to sporadically
on a somewhat hit-and-miss basis, and almost no attention at all to
patients' individuality and idiosyncracies, and to their emotional needs.
Patient contact was almost exclusively with nursing staff, and restricted
entirely to task-centred interactions initiated by the nurses. Patients
had virtually no personal possessions, not even clothes, and the
hospital clothes picked out for them by the nurses were often ill-fitting,
and left patients looking ridiculous or even indecent. This was custodial

care in the tradition described by many social researchers (for example, Stanton and Schwartz, 1954; Goffman, 1961; Baker, 1978; Wells, 1980; Evers, 1980 and forthcoming). Personalised warehousing, although strongly coloured by the operation of 'the routine', differed in various ways. Patients had the opportunity to have more personal possessions. They sometimes had their own clothes and, where they did not, attention was paid to the suitability of available clothes for particular patients by the nurses. There was some room for negotiation about patients' preferences regarding, for example, where to sit, whether to have a doze on the bed during the afternoon, when to go to the toilet. Patients' physical care was, typically, attended to scrupulously. There was some contact between nurses and patients which was not solely task-oriented. Social talk might take place while nurses were carrying out tasks for a particular patients, and occasionally interaction between a nurse and a patient would be centred solely around some social activity such as talk or a game of Scrabble. The outcomes of the typical career patterns of long-stay patients included various kinds of suffering: boredom, very often; loneliness; discomfort or pain caused or exacerbated by inability to attract a nurse's attention to some felt need or other; low morale or even depression engendered by lack of privacy, feelings of worthlessness and bleak future prospects. There was evidence that on wards where personalised warehousing careers predominated, fewer negative, and some positive, outcomes accrued for patients. The positive ones included enjoyment of a wide range of social relationships. It appeared that positive outcomes were more often related to the personal characteristics of the patients concerned than to the experiences they underwent in the hospital ward. On many of the study wards, positive outcomes were far less in evidence than negative ones.

These two patterns of patient care did not appear to be contingent upon gender-order factors. However, within both patterns, the experiences of individual patients was apparently shaped in part by gender-order factors.

Women Patients in Geriatric Wards: Three Stereotypes

Three illustrative stereotypes of the experiences of some of the women patients will be described. The stereotypes are strategic ones, chosen because of the importance of the gender order in influencing the kind of patient career that is created by the nurses in each case. My research indicated that men have, in general, subtly different experiences as patients in geriatric wards from those of women. Nurses often say that they prefer to look after men patients. Doubtless part of this alleged preference derives from sexuality. But there was no evidence in the research discussed here of a general preference for nursing men. This accords with the social labelling of old age as a sexless phase of the life-span for both men and women. The differences between women and men patients will not be discussed in any detail here. Rather I wish to explore something of the variety of the experiences of the women, and the implications of this kind of analysis both for a better understanding of the role of the gender order in shaping the social relationships sustained by geriatric patients in hospital, and for the organisation of geriatric care work for women patients.

Type One: Dear Old Gran

A minority of patients fitted this category. All were popular patients, in terms of nurses expressing positive feelings about caring for them. As in Stockwell's (1972) study, all tended to be cheerful much, though not all, of the time. They enjoyed social chit-chat with the nurses on various topics, and they were explicit and liberal in their praise of the nurses, both to the nurses themselves and in conversation with the researcher and others. All of them either fitted in with the routines established by the nurses or had succeeded in negotiating minor points of idiosyncracy within aspects of the routine. For example, Ann G. had established a mutual understanding that she was always one of the first patients to be helped to the bathroom in the mornings, when the nurses were getting the patients up. Some of these patients were virtually independent; others needed considerable help with basic living activities and were even, on occasion, incontinent. Most of these patients were mentally oriented and alert most of the time. Some had spells of mild or even severe confusion, and two, both labelled 'senile', were disoriented mentally most of the time, but were still cheerful and able to engage in animated, positive conversations having internal, if not external, validity. Another common feature of Grans was that they never criticised the nurses, nor complained.

Within the general pattern of warehousing, Gran's career stood out in various ways from that of other women patients. Patients who fitted this category were often the recipients of any 'treats' which might be available, for example, clothes arriving on the ward which were judged to be particularly nice by the nurses or perhaps a cake brought in by voluntary workers. Their idiosyncracies became widely known and treated with indulgence; thus one patient liked to study the racing form, and it had become customary that nobody looked at the papers delivered each day to the ward until she had finished with them.

They interacted more with the nurses and some of these interactions appeared to be purely social rather than being structured around some identifiable task being performed by a nurse. They were generally more successful at attracting a nurse's attention if they wanted something they were unable to see to for themselves, and they were usually apologetic about disturbing such busy people – the nurses – and very grateful if their request was met. Where they were left waiting for some time, as did happen from time to time, they did not complain, but waited patiently, perhaps making tentative attempts to speed the nurses' response to them. This was always done in a pleasant, even deferential, way and, if not successful, did not usually attract the irritation of the nurses, as happened with patients of the Awkward Alice type, to be described below. Such patients tended to have a higher morale and to experience less suffering than many of the other patients. On wards where minimal warehousing was the prevailing pattern, dear old Gran was exceptional in that her experience took on the appearance of a personalised warehousing career.

What can be noted about the articulation between the patient and the nurse-created ward 'routine'? First, Gran 'fitted in'. She was not a control problem for the nurses, cheerfully surrendered her autonomy to them, and posed no threat to their meeting the bureaucratic requirements of a tidy ward and clean, fed and watered patients. Thus they could treat her as they might an indulged child, and relax aspects of the routine as they affected her, as part of a process of mutual rewards. The nurses rewarded these 'good' patients, and the patients rewarded the nurses for those small privileges they managed to obtain, and thereby also invested in the continuation of these privileges. These patients did not criticise the nurses' work behaviour. Where they did comment on it, they rather praised them, and condemned other patients who were 'a nuisance to the nurses', 'ungrateful old things, who don't appreciate all that is done for them'. Patients of the Gran type had adjusted to the pressure to surrender their autonomy and their own former roles as care givers, by doing just that – becoming dependent upon the nurses as professional carers, while 'making the best of it' in such a way as to ease the implied indignity and incompetence for themselves, and surrendering their potential to challenge the professional and hierarchical requirements of the nurse to standardise and routinise.

When speaking of patients of this category, and sometimes also when speaking to them, the nurses would implicitly ascribe child-like qualities to patients, or treat them like children. Paterson (1977) quoted a nursing auxiliary as saying that the best way to gain the co-operation of residents in an old people's home was to humour them, to treat them like children. Staff other than nurses and ancillary workers played little part in the careers of patients of this category, as indeed was the case with most long-stay patients. There was implicit, or sometimes explicit, understanding that, although the doctor remained officially accountable for Grans, in practice they were virtually entirely the nurses' responsibility. Thus, care and control requirements were in effect defined and put into practice by the nursing staff. Since the control requirements were easily fulfilled, there remained some space to allow and attend to personal care requirements. The relationship with such patients was rewarding for nurses in various ways, and the rewards sustained and strengthened the particular form of the relationship as it has been outlined above.

What of the men? Did Gran have her male counterpart? What was unique about the experiences of Gran and her ilk, if anything? Gran's equivalent certainly existed, and can be called 'Pop'. Pop's career was in virtually all respects equivalent to Gran's, and at least some of the Pops were spoken of and related to by the nurses as an indulged child might have been. However, there was an important difference, which subtly coloured the nurse-patient relationship, and 'assigned' Pop rather more legitimate adult status than Gran. Pop tended to be a person, with his individuality grounded in his own past life and contributions. Many of the nurses knew quite a bit about Pop's biography, in particular his occupation and standing in the community and his family relationships. When talking of such patients, there would often be reference to the status ascribed to Pop in the light of knowledge of his biography. In contrast, Gran was either divorced from her past or her past simply was not known by the nurses; it was not important to them to gather information about Gran's biography. Gran was more obviously regarded and treated as a non-adult or even a non-person. This distinction between men and women patients recurs repeatedly, and will be discussed below, after the other two types of women patients have been described.

Type Two: Poor Old Nellie

Patients of this category were more common in the study wards than
were Grans. They shared a number of personal characteristics. All were
'senile', though not all 'senile' patients were Nellies — for example
some were Grans, if they were cheerful, grateful and capable of conversations with the nurses which the nurses enjoyed. All were deemed
to be fairly (or heavily) dependent on the nursing staff to facilitate performance of daily living activities even when they were mobile and
physically largely intact, for example by a nurse supervising a patient
washing herself, without which she would forget to do so entirely.
Many were incontinent, at least intermittently. Some were incapable
of conversation, and a proportion of these were apparently incapable
of any kind of meaningful communication at all. Such patients tended
to be neither especially popular, nor especially unpopular with the
nurses. Poor Old Nellies were at the centre of the routine of both
minimal warehousing and personalised warehousing. All members of
this category of patient fitted, or were fitted into, the ward routine.
They were mechanically processed through it by the nurses, with
minimal evidence of any attempt to individualise or to vary the routine
from one day to the next so as to take account of idiosyncracies of
any particular patient. Patients' requests for attention were often
ignored, and practically all interaction between nurses and these
patients was initiated by the nurses and centred around the performance of a task as defined and decided on by the nurses, and virtually
never by the patient. Some of the dirtiest of the nursing work came
from these patients; some faecally incontinent and restless patients
would need showering or bathing frequently. Although the nurses did
not like this work, nor the burden of physical work generally, which
was associated with many of these patients, it was tolerated fairly
cheerfully. Nellies were regarded not as sweet children as with the
Grans, but as unfortunate, helpless children. In the main, they presented
the nurses with care problems in the form of an immense burden of
work, much of which was distasteful, but which could be tolerated
because patients were not on the whole to be held responsible for their
parlous state. Usually they did not present the nurses with control
problems. When they did, these took the form of wandering around
or out of the ward, noisiness, interfering with other patients or their
belongings, agitated and sometimes even aggressive behaviour. Control
strategies seen by the nurses as straightforward and effective were used,
including restraining patients in geriatric chairs, and some form of
sedation.

Care outcomes for these patients varied from one ward to another. On wards where personalised warehousing predominated, physical care activities were carried out in a less serendipitous fashion than on minimal warehousing wards. Occasionally a patient's little whims would be indulged. For example Fanny A. was known to become extremely agitated if she was without her hat, thus she wore this faded and battered blue straw creation at all times, including in bed.

In common with the Grans, the Nellies were in effect handed over by the doctors to the nurses. Although the control requirements were not usually a problem for the nurses, little room was created for attending to care requirements over and above the —often extremely demanding and heavy — physical requirements. Poor Old Nellie lacked the characteristics and personal resources to confer any kind of reward on the nurses; nurses' activities in caring for her had to be their own reward, in terms of the nurses' commitment as professional carers and/ or concerned human beings. The human reciprocity in the nurses' relationships with these patients was often tenuous, because of the patients' senility. Thus the nurses could only respond to them as professional carers. These patients were completely dependent upon the professionals, physically or psychologically, or both.

What of the men? There were indeed men patients having parallel characteristics to those of poor old Nellie, and their careers had much in common. The distinguishing feature, as between Gran and Pop, was that the men tended to be 'non-persons' less often than the women.

Type Three: Awkward Alice

A minority of patients fitted this category. They shared a number of characteristics. Importantly, they were mentally alert all or most of the time. They were fairly, or very, articulate, and tended to assert their individuality in various ways when this was challenged by the operation of 'the routine'. They expressed gratitude to the nurses on occasions, depending upon the nurses' behaviour. Gratitude was not expressed in a general, indiscriminate fashion. Some of the time they were cheerful and 'good company', but when suffering, or experiencing a particular need which they were unable to meet for themselves, they would not hesitate to make their requirements known and, although sometimes patient if asked to wait, they would usually press their requests where no 'reasonable' cause for delay was evident or explained to them. They were at times critical of staff, particularly nurses, and of the way they went about their work, not only as it affected them, but also in its effects on other patients. The kinds of criticism included the nurses' attitudes; the way they did basic care-work (helping patients with washing, dressing, feeding, getting to the toilet); the lack of freedom of choice allowed by staff (thus patients had little choice but to spend their time in the day room, unless judged by staff to be too unwell to get up); constant TV and radio; the grind of the daily routine; the services provided, notably the food; difficulty of access to doctors and sometimes remedial therapists; lack of provision for privacy or for activities outside the basic routine of ward life. Awkward Alices shared these kinds of characteristics, but differed from each other with respect to the extent of their physical dependence on the nurses. Some were almost completely dependent, whereas others could do almost everything for themselves and were able to get about the ward without help.

As for their ward careers, these could be described as a running battle, which was sometimes overt, and sometimes featured a truce. All were seen by the nurses as 'difficult' patients, understandable since not only did some such patients present the nurses with care problems (some of the more dependent, ill patients) but they also presented control problems. The nurses' goals were to process the patients through the routine, and to attend to their needs as they, the professionals and their helpers, defined them. The patients' implicit goals were, on one level, to avail themselves of the care they felt themselves to require, which in part reflected their own understanding and judgement of the professionals' opinion. So to some extent the patients submitted themselves to the judgement and practices of the professionals, the experts. But on another level, the patients resisted the pressure to hand over their autonomy to the nurses, and to 'fit in' to the routine and the ward community. Some patients consciously resisted hierarchical control, others challenged it unwittingly, through their attempts at self-preservation. Awkward Alices made such comments as:

I shouldn't really be in a geriatric ward at all, it's only that there wasn't a bed for me in a proper hospital. This ward is really run for all these poor old things . . . I've got nothing in common with them . . . they're unable to do anything else but watch the TV, and I hate the TV . . . and of course the nurses have that dreadful radio on all day long, well you can't really blame them, having to look after this lot, but it does ruin my nerves, and there's no escape from it.

or: 'It's humiliating, some of the things they do to you here. They treat you as if you were senile'.

Straightforward control strategies, as used by nurses in relation to Nellie-type patients, were less effective with Awkward Alices. Their mental alertness and articulateness precluded the use of physical restraint and made it difficult to justify pharmacological restraint. Thus nurses' control strategies included avoidance, such as locating patients in parts of the ward which could be traversed seldom, such as single side wards; ignoring patients' requests by always being occupied with something more pressing; publicly rebuking patients for being demanding; and leaving patients till last — and making sure that the patients understood this — on 'rounds' such as back rounds, bed rounds, dressing rounds. In their talk about such patients, nurses tended to emphasise the difficulties they presented. Patients were blamed for their difficult behaviour in discussions amongst nurses, such as report sessions, and generally a priority for the nurses was to identify ways of getting the patient to 'fit in'. Their strategies often incorporated a 'punishment' ethos.

Career outcomes for patients varied in relation to which party — nurses or patient — gained the advantage, whether through tactics or chance, in the running battle, or whether a truce was in progress. On the whole, though, the nurses had the upper hand, and patients manifested various forms of suffering over and above whatever physical suffering they experienced. Once a patient had become labelled as an Awkward Alice, there was little she could do to change the definition even when she realised this. One or two such patients became aware that their relationships with the nurses were a problem, and actively sought ways to improve things by suppressing requests, offering to help or expressing their gratitude. More often than not, when such a change was noticed by the nurses, it was regarded with extreme suspicion: 'Mrs X has only complained once this afternoon, I can't believe it . . . she must be up to something or other.'

Awkward Alice has been stripped of her competence to make judgements about the appropriateness of the care provided for her in her enforced dependency, and her persistence in offering such judgement verbally and behaviourally presented a threat to the nurses' professional caring role and to their control and custody role. This threat was dealt with through punishment.

Like the Grans and the Nellies, the Alices were on the whole assigned by the machinations of the hospital system to the management of the nurses, although, of course, the doctors remained officially accountable for their care. The nurses made use of this as part of their control repertoire: 'If you don't eat something/help yourself more/ stop complaining about x, y, z, then Dr A won't be at *all* pleased with you when he does his round.'

What of the men? Awkward Alice, like Gran and Nellie, had her male equivalent, Churlish Charlie. But he offered a qualitatively different critique of nursing work from the women, which was more global and less detailed. The experiences of the men differed in two ways. First, the strategy for controlling them by ignoring 'excessive' demands was less successful. The men would enlist other patients to do their bidding or physically go and fetch a nurse, or they would simply shout. This was quite effective on the whole. Shouting could be heard outside the ward and thus posed a threat to the nurses' competence to retain both professional and hierarchical control. The nurses' strategy of last resort was to attempt to engineer a transfer of the patient to another ward. Thus the men were sometimes more successful and occasionally less successful than the women in sabotaging aspects of the routine where these were seen to threaten their individuality and autonomy in a way they found unacceptable. It may be that nurses' implicit expectation is that women will normally submit to hierarchical control. When they do not, whether wittingly or unwittingly, this is unacceptable and they must be put down. In contrast, when men, ascribed the dominant gender role, do not submit to the hierarchy, this is more acceptable. 'Resisters' can either be contained, by giving in to these men, or utterly rejected by engineering their transfer.[2]

The second difference between Churlish Charlie and Awkward Alice was, as with the male equivalents of Gran and Nellie, that these men were far from being non-persons; they maintained their identity, deriving from their former roles in the market place.

The Three Stereotypes Compared

Three stereotypical examples of long-stay women patients have been described, and their experiences of being in hospital recounted, so as to illustrate the main ethos of care and control in each case. For all three types, a major distinguishing feature from the circumstances of equivalent men patients was that the women tended to be depersonalised; their identities, grounded in their former and indeed current social roles were seldom more explicitly known by nurses than at the level of extremely vague ascription of family responsibilities and roles. Most of the women patients in this study had indeed devoted their lives to caring work in the home, but the details of their family relationships were seldom discovered by nurses. A tiny minority owned a known biography and, without exception, all of these had fulfilled roles in the world of paid work or public life, or had been 'deviant' in some way, for example, alcoholics. This is a direct reflection of prevailing gender divisions in the wider society: 'men's work' is public, visible and important; 'women's work' in the home remains unremarkable and unremarked, an activity of the 'private domain' (Stacey, 1980a). We can suggest that the experience of dependency for patients who are mentally alert becomes more demeaning when they are divested of their biographical identities. For the nurses, who are professional, paid performers of 'women's work', 'basic' caring, there is pressure to reaffirm the legitimacy of the appropriation of the work of the private domain by the public domain. Where this work is being performed in relation to people who may themselves be qualified to offer an expert analysis by virtue of their own experience of caring work — that is, women patients — the nurse's status is threatened. Denial of the woman patient's expertise is possible through devaluing the expertise of the old generally, in line with the low status of elderly people in Western society, by precluding the possibilities for old women to continue their skills in 'women's work' while in hospital, and by separating the patients from their own feminine biographies. Stacey (1980b), for example, describes how the expertise of older women in relation to their daughters' child-rearing concerns is systematically devalued by the professionals.

Nursing men patients does not pose a challenge to the nurses' ownership of caring work but reinforces it. There is no discontinuity, for the patients or the nurses, between dependency of men patients on women nurses, and the dependency of men upon women in, for example, the family. Male patients neither need to be separated by the nurses from their own biographies, nor can they be so easily stripped of their identities, deriving as they do, in the main, from the performance of 'men's work', and male roles in a male-dominated society. The male equivalents of the three stereotypes retained some identity as people. Even the male equivalents of Nellie, despite senility, retained their biographies in most cases. Churlish Charlie not only retained his biography, but was able to resist hierarchical control by the nurses in a forthright fashion. Sometimes this was successful, and although he was unpopular and labelled as 'difficult', Charlie got his

way. However, he risked being undermined through the nurses' sometimes successful attempts to implement their ultimate sanction:
expulsion.

The Grans, the Nellies and the Awkward Alices were all divorced
from their own biographies in a way that their male equivalents were
not. It can be argued that this resolved various conflicts for the nurses,
and assured their success in organisational bureaucratic terms as care
givers to, and controllers of, Grans and Nellies. However, for the
Awkward Alices this strategy was inadequate, since Awkward Alice
was insistent about her claims of competence to offer 'expert' and
detailed criticisms of the nurses' basic care work and to organise at
least part of her own life while in the ward. The nurse-patient relationship here characteristically featured latent conflict which, not infrequently, became manifest.[3] The relationship and repertoire of
control strategies of the nurses, so far as Awkward Alice's male
equivalent went, were qualitatively different. The men's complaints
were more general and global than the detailed criticisms volunteered
by the women. Their more aggressive tactics, of sabotaging the
routine, called forth different responses from the nurses.

Conclusions

What of the practical and theoretical implications of the analysis
developed in this chapter? First, it must be acknowledged that the
analysis may well be peculiar to the current generation of elderly. If,
as has been argued here, past work roles and the gender order are
important in establishing an identity for the elderly sick, then the
changing pattern of labour-market participation may influence the
form taken by stereotyping of old people in the future and hence the
social relationships of old people in hospital. However, it is not only
changes in patterns of labour market participation which are important.
Notions of the nature of 'work', whether in the market place or the
home, and the gender division of labour, may be changing, and various
feminist analyses draw explicit attention to some of the issues here.

Stacey (1980a) has argued that the understanding of the relationship
between the public domain, the world of paid work and the market
place, and the private domain, the world of domestic work and the
home, may call for a reconceptualisation of the nature of 'work', and
a theoretically innovative analysis of the division of labour in the
private domain.

As for the current lot of women geriatric patients, the analysis developed here calls for a consideration of changes in organisation of hospital geriatric services which might reduce the suffering of patients, which is compounded by gender divisions. Thus, for example, hospital buildings, the physical geography, furnishing and equipment of wards, as well as ward regimes, might be reorganised so as to create opportunities for women patients to maintain their identity and their competence in 'women's work'. Seldom is it possible for patients even to be able to make themselves a cup of tea on a geriatric ward, let alone anything more ambitious. However, such changes do not offer a real solution. Awkward Alices would still be exposed to the oppression of hierarchical control, although their autonomy might be increased. For the nurses, such changes would offer a threat in the form of diminishing the scope of their professional and hierarchical control of women patients, and would thereby call into question, theoretically and empirically, aspects of the appropriation of care-work by paid, professional workers. A change in the relative status of women patients and nurses would, in turn, create new tensions and conflicts in the wider organisation of health-care services. Thus the implications of seeking to address the problems of women geriatric patients through organisational change would be far-reaching and fraught with new problems.

Finally, it must be stressed that the analysis offered in this chapter is both tentative and partial. In the context of available commentaries on geriatric care, it needs no defence: in this country, research as well as public and professional policy and practice has yet to give serious consideration to the implications of the fact that a majority of old people, including geriatric patients in hospital, are women. The modest aim of this contribution has been to expose some of the issues, and to try to develop a basis for their analysis. Further research might address a range of issues, including the relevance of the gender order to the professionals' perceptions of 'need' among dependent elderly people, and the kinds of intervention strategies and goals which are perceived to be available or precluded in response to perceptions of need.

Notes

This chapter derives from research funded by a Social Science Research Council project grant. I am grateful to the patients and staff of the wards I studied, for their kind co-operation. Thanks are also due to Margaret Stacey, Celia Davies and

Mary Hope for their constructive comments on an earlier draft of this chapter.
1.   See, for example, Fretwell (1980) on learner nurses' views of what types of work they regarded as useful experience and valuable for their education.
2.   Rosenthal *et al.* (1980), too, observe that demands by male patients may be more likely to be perceived as legitimate behaviour by the nurses than demands by female patients. This, they say, reflects a stereotyped view of men as 'naturally' assertive. They also note that, 'Nurses as females are socialised to be subservient to males and to meet their demands' (p. 130).
3.   Tagliacozzo and Mauksch (1972) report a study of hospital patients' expectations and roles. They found that 'Women were considerably more critical of nursing care than were men' (p. 178). They observe that (p. 179):

It is compatible with the male role to receive care and to have someone else maintain the physical surroundings. Women, however, are typically the managers of the home and the performers of major house-keeping tasks. They 'know' from experience the standards of personal care and housekeeping, and thus tend to apply them to their judgement of the nursing team.

Lorber (1975) notes that staff tended to label as 'problem patients' those who were seen to disrupt work routines without 'good' reason. Men as well as women patients fell into this category. This was also the case in my own study. However, Rosenthal *et al.* (1980) found that, of a patient population having 52 per cent women, two-and-a-half times as many women as men were defined by nurses as 'problems'.

Bibliography

Baker, D. 'Attitudes of Nurses to Care of the Elderly in Hospital' (unpublished PhD thesis, University of Manchester, 1978)
Brown, G. 'The Mental Hospital as an Institution', *Social Science and Medicine*, vol. 7 (1973), pp. 407–24
Carpenter, M. 'The New Managerialism and Professionalism in Nursing', in M. Stacey, M. Reid, C. Heath and R. Dingwall (eds.), *Health and the Division of Labour* (Croom Helm, London, 1977)
Clarke, M. 'Getting Through the Work', in R. Dingwall and J. McIntosh (eds.), *Readings in the Sociology of Nursing* (Churchill Livingstone, Edinburgh, 1978)
Coser, R.L. 'Alienation and the Social Structure: Case Analysis of a Hospital', in E. Freidson (ed.), *The Hospital in Modern Society* (Collier-Macmillan, London, 1963)
Davies, C. 'Experience of Dependency and Control in Work: the Case of Nurses', *Journal of Advanced Nursing*, vol. 1 (1976), pp. 273–82
——— 'Continuities in the Development of Hospital Nursing in Britain', *Journal of Advanced Nursing*, vol. 2 (1977), pp. 479–93
Department of Health and Social Security *Priorities for Health and Personal Social Services in England* (HMSO, London, 1976)
——— Welsh Office *A Happier Old Age* (HMSO, London, 1978)
Dingwall, Robert 'Problems of Teamwork in Primary Care', in S. Lonsdale, A.L. Webb and T.L. Briggs (eds.), *Teamwork in the Personal Social Services and Health Care* (Croom Helm, London, 1980)
Evers, H.K. 'The Creation of Patient Careers in Geriatric Wards: Aspects of Policy

and Practice' (unpublished paper, University of Warwick, 1980)
————— ' "Tender Loving Care"? Patients and Nurses in Geriatric Wards', in
L.A. Copp (ed.), *Advances in Care of the Elderly* (Churchill Livingstone,
Edinburgh, forthcoming)
Fretwell, Joan 'An Inquiry into the Ward Learning Environment', *Nursing Times
Occasional Papers*, vol. 76, no. 16 (1980), pp. 69–76
Gamarnikow, Eva 'Sexual Division of Labour: the Case of Nursing', in A. Kuhn
and A. Wolpe (eds.), *Feminism and Materialism* (Routledge and Kegan Paul,
London, 1978)
Goddard, H. *The Work of Nurses in Hospital Wards* (Nuffield Provincial
Hospitals Trust, Oxford, 1953)
Goffman, E. *Asylums* (Anchor Books, Doubleday, New York, 1961)
Hughes, E. 'Social Role and the Division of Labour', in E. Hughes (ed.),
The Sociological Eye (Aldine-Atherton, Chicago, 1971)
Jacobs, Ruth 'The Meaning of Hospital: Denial of Emotions', in D. Hall and
M. Stacey (eds.), *Beyond Separation Further Studies of Children in
Hospital* (Routledge and Kegan Paul, London, 1979)
Lorber, J. 'Women and Medical Sociology: Invisible Professionals and
Ubiquitous Patients', in M. Millman and R.M. Kanter (eds.), *Another Voice*
(Anchor Books, New York, 1975)
McFarlane, Jean 'A Charter for Caring', *Journal of Advanced Nursing*, vol. 1
(1976), pp. 187–96
Mechanic, D. 'Sources of Power of Lower Participants in Complex Organisations',
Administrative Science Quarterly, vol. 7 (1962), pp. 349–64
Menzies, I. 'A Case Study in the Functioning of Social Systems as a Defence
against Anxiety', *Human Relations*, vol. 13 (1960), pp. 95–121
Norton, D. 'Nursing in Geriatrics', *Gerontologia Clinica*, vol. 7 (1965),
pp. 59–60
Paterson, E. 'Social Organisation of Old People's Homes' (unpublished PhD
thesis, University of Aberdeen, 1977)
Rhys-Hearn, C. 'Evaluation of Patients' Nursing Needs: Prediction of Staffing',
in G. McLachlan (ed.), *The Future – and Present Indicatives* (Oxford
University Press, Oxford, 1973)
Rosenthal, C.J., Marshall, V.W., Macpherson, A.S. and French, S.E. *Nurses,
Patients and Families* (Croom Helm, London, 1980)
Stacey, Margaret 'The Division of Labour Revisited or Overcoming the Two
Adams' (Paper given at British Sociological Association Annual Conference,
1980a; to be published by Allen and Unwin)
————— 'Women as Unpaid Health Workers' (seminar paper, Oxford Women's
Committee, 1980b)
Stanton, A.H. and Schwartz, M.S. *The Mental Hospital* (Basic Books, New York,
1954)
Stockwell, Felicity 'The Unpopular Patient' (London Royal College of Nursing.
The Study of Nursing Care Project Report Series,1, no. 1, 1972)
Tagliacozzo, D.L. and Mauksch, H.O. 'The Patient's View of the Patient's Role',
in E. Gartly Jaco (ed.), *Patients, Physicians and Illness*, 2nd edn (The Free
Press, New York, 1972)
Wells, T. *Problems in Geriatric Nursing Care* (Churchill Livingstone, Edinburgh,
1980)

6 WOMEN AND BROADMOOR: TREATMENT AND CONTROL IN A SPECIAL HOSPITAL

Colin Rowett and Phillip J. Vaughan

Crime is a predominantly male activity, or at least that is the picture given by the official statistics. For England and Wales, Home Office figures show that, of all those found guilty of indictable offences in 1978, little over 15 per cent were women (Home Office, 1979a). Further, it is generally stated that women are comparatively rarely involved in violent situations and that, when they are, the acts of violence are normally situation-specific, which is taken to mean that they occur largely in the home; that the victims are generally weaker, usually children; and that the offence is precipitated by a state of physical and mental exhaustion in the assailant (Scott, 1977). Only 5 per cent of female offenders who are detected and prosecuted are involved in crimes of violence against the person. The great bulk of convictions (79 per cent) are for theft, particularly the so-called female offence of shoplifting, and handling stolen goods. Thus, crime committed by women is usually considered trivial and of little threat to society, with serious violence a particular rarity.

One way to interpret the official statistics of female crime in general, and crimes of violence in particular, is to assume pathology in the women concerned. And one way to do this is to compare the general behaviour of these women with a socially acceptable sex stereotype. Thus Levin (1979) points out that female offenders contradict the stereotype of the 'normal' female personality in that they do not embody the specific feminine qualities of docility, gentleness and frailty. The narrow dividing line between deviation from arbitrary norms and mental illness is perhaps hinted at in the following comment made by the governor and staff of Holloway Prison to the Butler Committee (Home Office/DHSS, 1975):

The ratio of disturbed against non-disturbed offenders is much higher for females than males. There are very few mentally ill women in Holloway, but, there are many who may be considered 'mentally abnormal' according to our definition (below), in that there is a great deviance from sociological and psychological norms. The term 'mentally abnormal' made here applies to:

a) people with a defined psychiatric diagnosis, e.g. schizophrenia, which can be treated psychiatrically or medically;
b) those people with the broad psychiatric diagnosis of 'personality disorder' or 'behavioural disorder', which might be helped with medical, psychiatric, psychological or sociological methods;
c) those people who are classified as 'psychopaths' or 'sociopaths' whose condition cannot be treated medically or psychiatrically, but might be more appropriately treated by psychological or sociological methods.
The majority of our population would come under categories (b) and (c) described above.

This would seem to be a fairly clear statement that Holloway considers most of its inmates mentally abnormal, if not mentally ill. This reflects a more general view that female prison populations are more 'unstable' than male ones (Woodside, 1974). However, the 'diagnostic' terms used — 'personality disorder', 'behavioural disorder', 'psychopath' and 'sociopath' — are notorious catch-all terms, which do not have an agreed definition, even among the psychiatric profession.

Most female offenders do not, however, go to prison. In 1978 only 2.7 per cent of women found guilty of indictable offences were sentenced to immediate imprisonment, as opposed to 10 per cent of the men. Furthermore, the average length of sentence for women is in general shorter than for men, with 89 per cent serving a sentence of under 18 months and over one-third serving their sentence in an open prison. Overall, in 1978, females accounted for just over 3 per cent of the average daily prison population of 41,796 in England and Wales (Home Office, 1979b).

It is often argued that at least part of the explanation for this sentencing policy lies in the desire of the preponderantly male judiciary to avoid separating a wife and/or mother from her family whenever possible. Thus only the more disturbed or disordered women or those who have committed the more serious crimes find their way into prison. If this is true then it would indicate that the judiciary has a rather different set of social values to the similarly male-dominated psychiatric profession.

In direct contrast, women constitute some 57 per cent of the resident population of psychiatric hospitals (DHSS, 1978). Forty-four per cent of female patients have been in hospital for five years and over. The continued residence of these long-stay patients is, however, often related to isolation from the family, the absence of alternative

forms of accommodation in the community and the general despair
that surrounds the organic dementias of old age, rather than the
severity of the illness itself and the consequent need for hospital care.
In 1975 the great majority of psychiatric patients (87 per cent)
entered hospital on a voluntary basis and comparatively few required
compulsory detention for their own safety or that of others (DHSS,
1978). Of those who were legally detained under the 1959 Mental
Health Act, 53 per cent were compulsorily detained for up to 72 hours
(Section 29) and a further 40 per cent for up to 28 days (Section 25).
This leaves a small proportion of patients who were detained on a
yearly basis (Section 26) because of their persistent difficult or disruptive behaviour, and those who were detained under a hospital order
imposed by a court (Section 60). This latter group will have committed
an offence but because of their obvious need for psychiatric care were,
following a medical recommendation, sent to hospital for treatment
rather than to prison as a punishment. Nevertheless, four-fifths of the
hospital-order group, although sometimes disruptive and difficult, are
not considered to need care and treatment in conditions of maximum
security and are catered for in conventional psychiatric hospitals. It is
only the remaining one-fifth of hospital-order cases and a few Section
26 patients who are considered dangerous enough to need treatment
in conditions of special security. It is this group that makes up the
bulk of the population in the Special Hospitals of Broadmoor, Rampton,
Moss Side and Park Lane. These Special Hospitals exist for people who,
in terms of the 1959 Mental Health Act, 'require treatment under
conditions of special security on account of their dangerous, violent
or criminal propensities'. They are not part of the NHS regional framework but are administered by the DHSS and are the direct responsibility
of the Secretary of State. Broadmoor, the first state asylum of any
size built specifically for the mentally abnormal offender, is sited just
outside the village of Crowthorne in Berkshire, and houses some 600
male and 120 female patients. Rampton Hospital, the largest in the
group, contains 635 men and 200 women on a remote site at Retford
in Nottinghamshire. The remaining two hospitals, Moss Side and Park
Lane, are situated on adjacent sites at Maghull, near Liverpool. Moss
Side has about 300 male patients and 80 female patients, and Park
Lane, when completed, will have a maximum bed quota for 400 males,
largely overspill from Broadmoor which is chronically overcrowded.
Together, the Special Hospitals account for only 0.6 per cent of the
mental-illness beds and somewhat less than two per cent of the mental-
handicap beds in England and Wales. Of the Special Hospital population

of about 2,160 in 1978, one-fifth were women (Locke, 1978).

The History of Control

The range of models, notions and beliefs which address themselves to 'mental illness' are numerous, competitive and have an alarming tendency to be mutually exclusive. For example, Szasz (1971) argues that asylums are devices used by dominant social groups to control and regulate the behaviour of unacceptable marginals. Jones (1972, p. xi), on the other hand, says that:

Some time in the first half of the eighteenth century, in a quieter but harsher England, the idea began to develop that there was a group of people who needed special protection because of their mental condition. The idea grew under its own momentum. Influential men in the larger cities compared notes, discovered a state of quite appalling misery, and began to plan reforms.

In this brief precis of the history of the control of the mentally abnormal offender it will be assumed that such a thing as mental illness does exist, that it has always existed, but that the definitions it receives and the social responses it merits vary with time and place. Two further points need to be made. Firstly, the bulk of the material on the history of the mentally abnormal offender is contained in tracts on the all-embracing topic of mental illness, and tends in them to receive only a cursory coverage. Secondly, virtually nothing of any substance has been written specifically on the female mentally abnormal offender.

In 1377 The Priory of the Order of St Mary of Bethlehem was converted into Bethlem, a six-bedded hospital for Londoners who experienced the more acute forms of mental disorder. Bethlem remained the only specialised institution until the seventeenth century, slowly increasing in size so that by 1642 it had 44 beds. The vast majority of the mentally ill were either left to their own devices to wander the countryside, or were contained within the family, or were lodged in the ecclesiastical hospitals along with the 'sick, aged, bedridden, diseased, wayfaring men, diseased soldiers and honest folk fallen into poverty' (Scull, 1979, p. 19). If they were violent or criminal they were locked in the local gaol. The Poor Law Act of 1601 transferred responsibility for the insane from religious to secular authority, though did not result in any appreciable change in their fate, other than placement in almshouses rather than church hospitals. From 1555 the spread of Bridewells or houses of correction for vagrants and beggars or petty criminals became an additional available disposal for the unmanageable lunatic.

This situation changed little until the middle of the eighteenth century, when there were two significant developments in the social response to lunacy — the creation of the private-madhouse trade for paying patients and the development and rapid use of public asylums on a wide scale. Although neither form of institution had achieved any great size by the turn of the century — probably averaging 20–30 beds, though some of them exceeded 200 beds — they were to become the major growth areas in the nineteenth century in the control and care of the mentally ill, and constituted two important additional disposals for the criminal lunatic. The Act of 1784 attempted to influence the fate of inmates in gaols and institutions with the recommendation that women be separated from men, felons from petty criminals, witnesses from accused and the convicted from the unconvicted. Prior to this, as Walker and McCabe (1973) put it, 'Sometimes two inconvenient minorities were combined, the lunatics being put into the women's room'.

The years between the mid-eighteenth and mid-nineteenth centuries are usually said to contain the age of reform as far as the mentally ill are concerned. Abuses in the private-madhouse trade, the acceptance of county asylums as an economic proposition, public awareness of the supposed insanity of George III and the initially favourable results of the moral-treatment programme provided by the Tuke family at the York Retreat led to a substantial change in provision for the mentally ill.

The 1808 County Asylum Act recommended that each county should provide an asylum with 'separate and distinct Wards for Male and Female Lunatics, and also for the Convalescents and Incurables, and also separate and distinct Day Rooms and Airing Grounds for the Male and Female Convalescents' (Sections 16 and 26). Women seem to have been no longer just another inconvenient minority but now merited a more delicate consideration. Certainly there was no doubt about the appropriate activities for its patients: 'Every attempt was made to occupy the patients suitably. Some cared for the animals, some helped in the garden, the women knitted or sewed' (Jones, 1972, p. 49). This, however, was the exception. The asylums that were built were large, understaffed, isolated and functioned more as warehouses than hospitals. It is perhaps interesting that slightly more women than men were admitted to these asylums (ratio 5:4), and that there were a third more pauper lunatic women in the workhouses than there were men.

The expansion in county asylums continued until the 1950s and was ended only by the 1959 Mental Health Act and its recommendations for the development of community resources as an alternative disposal for the majority of the mentally ill, or rather for those whose mental stability could be supported by the recently developed psychotropic medication. The average size of hospitals built during this time increased rapidly, from 542 beds in 1870 to 961 beds in 1900 and 1,221 beds in 1930.

The fate of the criminal lunatic reflected this overall trend. Although an attempt had been made in 1723 to deal in legal terms with the problems of the insane criminal, with the introduction by Mr Justice Tracey of the so-called Wild Beast Test which was an attempt to substitute life imprisonment for death as the punishment for chronically disturbed lunatics who had committed major crimes, it was not until the 1800 Criminal Lunatics Act that insanity came to be used as a defence on any scale. The Act allowed for insanity as a defence in cases of treason, murder and felony; if the accused was insane at the time of the offence, or insane on arraignment or insane when about to commit a crime. A national survey in 1837 identified 178 such criminal lunatics — 55 were in Bethlem, 48 were in seventeen county asylums, 35 were in private madhouses and the remainder were in various gaols. As the demand for beds increased so did the reluctance of asylums and madhouses to cater for particularly difficult patients, particularly if they were to adopt the liberal regimes advocated by the supporters of moral treatment.

In 1845 the Metropolitan Commissioners, a licensing and inspection body which had access to only a few of the numerous institutions where the mentally ill were detained, was replaced by the Lunacy Commissioners, a full-time inspectorate with access to any institution where the insane were detained, except for Bethlem. They revived a suggestion made by the Select Committee responsible for the 1808 County Asylums Act that a State Asylum should be built to contain as many criminal lunatics as possible. This proposal received government approval in 1856, and following upon the 1860 Criminal Lunatics Act, gave the Home Secretary control over all criminal lunatics and placed all asylums under his jurisdiction. Broadmoor Asylum admitted its first inmates in 1863.

Built on a ridge in the middle of a Berkshire pine forest, Broadmoor was designed by Sir Joshua Webb, the military engineer who had been responsible for the building of Pentonville Prison some twenty years earlier. It consists of two separate enclosures surrounded by high walls: the larger enclosure, some 14 acres, contains seven three-storey blocks, each designed to hold some 60 male patients, together with various offices and workshops; the smaller enclosure contains two female blocks, each designed for some 50 patients. The first admissions to Broadmoor were 85 women. Maximum numbers — 400 men and 100 women — were reached in 1865, and Broadmoor has remained largely at, or well over, capacity ever since. It currently houses some 600 men and 120 women. Additional asylums specifically for mentally ill or mentally handicapped offenders were opened in 1912 (Rampton), 1933 (Moss Side) and 1975 (Park Lane).

The history of Broadmoor from 1863 to 1952 has been chronicled by Partridge (1953), in what seems to have been quite close collaboration with the then Physician Superintendent, Dr Stanley Hopwood. The book devotes five pages specifically to women, which provide a useful insight into some of the notions which may well have surrounded female criminal lunatics (Partridge, 1953, pp. 150–2):

> females have less natural aggressive instinct than the male, and any homicidal impulse they develop under the influence of insanity is commonly grafted on to the maternal instinct and directed towards children, generally their own.

> insanity is often brought on by child rearing.

> Women are just as prone to insanity as men; but as they are less homicidal and aggressive in that state, less accommodation need be found.

> individual pride in her personal appearance seems to be the requisite to a recovery of a woman's sanity.

Current visitors to the female wing of Broadmoor are often shown the room of one woman patient as an example of what can be achieved in a difficult setting. The room, decorated in pale yellows and pinks, with shelves of vanity goods and cosmetics, contains a sizeable collection of elaborately dressed dolls. Perhaps the room symbolises what is still sometimes seen as a significant factor in 'recovery' — pride in one's 'feminine' appearance and ability to fulfil a stereotype. The irony of this situation for the majority of the women perhaps becomes apparent when their backgrounds are examined in more detail.

Today's Women

Both Rampton and Moss Side have always specialised in the cure and treatment of the dangerous mentally handicapped or psychopathic patient, though in recent years Rampton has begun to accept a higher number of mentally ill patients of normal intelligence. Broadmoor, on the other hand, accepts only those mentally ill or psychopathic patients of average intelligence or above (Tennent *et al.*, 1976). Tennent's profile of a statistically typical female admission to Broadmoor was:

> in her early thirties and came to the hospital by way of the 'criminal system'. She may show some evidence of disturbance in her early upbringing and environment, is probably single (or has been married and is now a widow or divorced). There is a high probability that she would have been employed in a social class III or IV occupation, and that her admission to hospital will have been precipitated by an episode of violence. She will almost certainly have had a number of previous admissions to psychiatric hospitals, most commonly will be diagnosed as having a schizophrenia or psychopathic disorder. She will probably be of at least average intelligence, and is likely to be discharged from the hospital within five years of her admission.

The Rampton female patient is likely to be younger, in her early twenties, with a disturbed early life; almost certainly single and with little work experience; of low intelligence and admitted to Rampton from a subnormality hospital because of an attack on a member of staff; and she is unlikely to be discharged within five years. The typical Moss Side female patient is described as being similar to the Rampton patient though of higher intelligence; there is likely to have been some confusion over the diagnosis and she will consequently have spent time in both psychiatric and subnormality hospitals. She is more likely to have been employed than the Rampton patient and stands an even chance of being discharged within five years of admission.

In general, women in this country rarely kill. Those who do are

Table 6.1: All Convictions, Current and Previous, Committed by Women Admitted to Broadmoor, 1972–4

Type of Offence	No. (N=61)	Percentage of women
Homicide*	16	26
Other violence	13	21
Thefts, burglary	19	31
Arson	13	21
Criminal or wilful damage, etc.	13	21

*Including attempted murder, threat or conspiracy to murder.
Source: Special Hospitals Case Register Triennial Statistics (1972–4); Dell and Parker (1979).

largely diagnosed as experiencing some form of mental disorder. Their victims are commonly their own children. Indeed, amongst the Broadmoor population, twice the proportion of female patients have committed offences against children as have the male patients. However, although Broadmoor women have committed more offences of violence than Rampton and Moss Side women, Table 6.1 shows that the majority of Broadmoor female patients will not have been convicted of assault on others.

Those Broadmoor women who are violent tend to have committed their offences within the context of a severe psychotic breakdown; typically they remember experiencing persecution delusions, bizzare phantasies and emotional turmoil. Nor surprisingly the psychiatric conditions most likely to produce such florid symptoms, such as the schizophrenias, affective disorders and general personality disorders, feature highly in the diagnostic categories of new admissions, as shown in Table 6.2. There is little divergence in the percentage of male and female patients in each diagnostic category. Furthermore, Broadmoor females differ significantly from female patients in conventional psychiatric hospitals, where the most prominent diagnostic categories are the psychoneuroses, other psychoses not listed below and senile and pre-senile dementia.

Most patients, however, commit lesser acts of violence and some commit no actual offence at all. Nevertheless, these patients will have been considered sufficiently seriously disturbed as to be dangerous to others and to themselves and in need of treatment in conditions of security. Self-mutilation or annihilation seems to be more common in women than men and a study of mental hospital

Table 6.2: Diagnoses of All Women Admitted to Broadmoor, 1972–4

	No. (N=61)	Percentage of women
Depression (affective disorder)	7	12
Mania (affective disorder)	2	3
Schizophrenia	41	67
Epilepsy	2	3
Other organic disorder	1	2
Personality disorder	25	41
Neurosis	1	2
Paranoid state	14	23
Subnormality	4	7
More than one diagnosis	34	56
More than two diagnoses	7	11

Source: Special Hospitals Case Register Triennial Statistics (1972–4); Dell and Parker (1979)

patients by Chesler (1974) asserted that women are more often self-deprecating, depressed, perplexed and have more suicidal thoughts or attempts than do men. Nurses at Broadmoor report a much higher incidence of suicidal gestures and self-inflicted wounds among the female patients than among the male patients. Similarly, Brooks and Mitchell (1975) assert that 66 per cent of female patients at Carstairs State Hospital, near Glasgow, the only Scottish Special Hospital, have a history of a previous suicide attempt or gesture.

It is clear from Table 6.3 that a far greater proportion of female patients are non-offenders than men. Altogether, 36 per cent were admitted under civil law, that is, transfers from other hospitals under Section 26 of the Mental Health Act 1959, although a number may

Table 6.3: Civil and Criminal Admissions to Broadmoor, 1972–4

	Male		Female	
	N	%	N	%
Civil	22	7	22	36
Criminal (non-court)	75	22	8	13
Court	240	71	31	51
Total	337	100	61	100

Source: Special Hospitals Case Register Triennial Statistics (1972–4); Dell and Parker (1979).

have committed offences at an earlier stage in their career. Once admitted to Broadmoor, the patient's stay is likely to be a prolonged one. Whereas most prisoners have a fixed sentence, Broadmoor patients all face an indeterminate period of detention and treatment. The rationalisation for this is that it is impossible to forecast accurately how long it will take to control or eliminate dangerousness or to treat a particular mental disorder.

The length of stay of each patient therefore depends upon her response to treatment and/or management and her readiness to cope in a less secure setting without reproducing the behaviour that led to her admission. The average length of stay for all newly admitted female patients is between four and a half and five years, and for the 42 per cent who stay for more than five years the mean is 14.3 years (Dell, 1979). This more closely reflects the situation of women in psychiatric hospitals, where some 44 per cent have been there for over five years, than of those in prison. Of the 1,200 female prisoners in England and Wales in 1975, only 29 were serving sentences of between four and ten years and only 28 were lifers (Short, 1979).

Thus, very few female prisoners are detained long enough to experience the more chronic forms of institutionalisation such as apathy, withdrawal and rigid adherence to institution norms. Even long-term female psychiatric patients have benefitted from the comparatively recent national adherence to an open-door policy, emphasising freedom of movement in and around the hospital and encouraging contact with the community through outside visits and home leaves. The majority of female patients in Broadmoor, however, spend very long periods of time almost entirely cut off from the outside world. Although some women, for a variety of reasons, actively encourage alienation from their previous family and friends, the majority desire continued contact, though very few manage to retain significant relationships for the length of their stay in Broadmoor.

Those friends and relatives who do remain in contact with the patient are often faced with the practical difficulty of having to travel considerable distances to get to Broadmoor, whose catchment area is the whole of England and Wales. Martin and Webster (1971) found that, in cases when an offender's family lived more than 150 miles from the prison where he was detained, his chances of being visited were almost negligible. A survey by Vaughan (1980a) of 62 male and 70 female Broadmoor patients detained for over two years, revealed that, in general, the patients are a very isolated and neglected group, although the women did have significantly more outside contact than the men. Over half the men, but only a quarter of the women, had only one or two visits a year, or none at all.

For some families, admission to Broadmoor is a relief following a long period of difficult and disruptive behaviour by the patient, and visits are seen as being an act of duty to be performed as infrequently as is respectable. For others, particularly where the patient has experienced a fairly rapid breakdown, presenting the family with a series of rapid and incomprehensible events culminating in admission to Broadmoor, regular visits are undertaken at considerable financial and emotional cost even, at times, in the face of rejection or lack of interest from the patient. Conversely, families with an insidiously destructive influence on the patient, and family members who are the focus of a patient's pathological jealousy, may have to be encouraged to terminate their relationships in order to further the patient's progress and advance the prospects of discharge.

Women patients were significantly more concerned than the men with maintaining contact with outsiders, and more adept at carrying this out in practice. They wrote more letters and received more letters and had more visits from the wider family and personal friends. Contact with family and friends therefore seems to be more important and feasible for the women than for the men. Maintaining contact with the family is, perhaps, the closest the Broadmoor women came to exhibiting an example of the stereotypical feminine role.

Life Inside

Admission to Broadmoor is a traumatic event for most new patients. Young single women face the prospect of watching their youth pass them by, and those who are married forfeit their role as wife and possibly mother. A change in self-image is likely. Jarvis (1978), in discussing the institutional care of female offenders, comments that most women are still oriented towards the family and home, and accordingly their loss has a tremendous impact, creating psychological and emotional injuries not unlike grief on the death of a family member. Additionally, for the women in Broadmoor who have killed their children while psychotic, response to treatment can bring a painful return to reality, with consequent feelings of guilt and depression.

These women enter a total institution — a segregated world of isolation and regimentation – of the kind described by Goffman (1961). Broadmoor is a maximum-security hospital and its regime is bounded by the needs of security. Although some of the women do require close care and supervision, there are many who are not security risks or particularly dangerous within the closed-hospital setting (women who have killed their children typically fall into this category), but all live within the strict security arrangements necessary for the potentially dangerous minority. The hospital is bounded by a high perimeter wall; all doors are locked; staff carry keys; the handling of money is not allowed; heads are frequently counted; and patients are escorted whenever they move from one part of the hospital to another.

All new patients are assessed by members of a multi-disciplinary team within four to five weeks of admission. The team consists of a clinical psychologist, a medical officer, a psychiatrist, members of the nursing staff, an occupational therapist, a teacher and a social worker. The social worker visits significant relatives and liaises with relevant outside agencies in order to compile a chronological social-background report. The case conference is used to try and formulate a diagnosis and prognosis, and to decide upon an appropriate form of treatment and a suitable occupation during the day. Subsequently, the patient stays on a 30-bedded ward, where she will remain until she either shows progress and is moved 'up' to a ward with slightly more privileges and less restrictions, or deteriorates and is moved 'down' to the 20-bedded intensive-care ward where security is most intense. An additional ward with some 15 beds is used for chronic schizo-phrenic and highly institutionalised patients, where they are encouraged to improve their personal appearance, awareness of current affairs and social skills. Patients thought suitable for internal parole, that is, free movement within the hospital perimeter, or for possible discharge or transfer, are placed on the rehabilitation ward, where they are allowed the greatest personal freedom anywhere in the hospital.

The absence of any effective treatment for schizophrenia, and the acknowledged difficulty in satisfactorily changing the behaviour of the 'psychopath', leaves Broadmoor largely dependent on its own milieu to change behaviour, although conventional psychiatric treatments are comprehensively used, from psychotropic medication and electro-convulsive therapy to group psychotherapy and social skills training. A highly conservative organisation, Broadmoor is not inclined to adopt untested 'radical' approaches in the treatment of patients, preferring to use treatments which the consultant psychiatrists are familiar with, and which, it is believed, achieve results consistent with Broadmoor's purpose, which is to control difficult, dangerous or criminal behaviour and not necessarily to eradicate the associated mental disorder.

Broadmoor is overcrowded: designed for 500 patients, it currently houses some 720. In some dormitories on the male wing, mattresses are only some 18 inches apart. However, the female wing is not as overcrowded as the male side and living conditions are significantly more comfortable. Furniture is domestic rather than institutional; one ward has a grand piano and ward cat. However, although living conditions are better for women, work opportunities are far more restricted. Despite having some of the best workshops of any psychiatric hospital in the country, women are denied access to most of them because of the hospital policy of segregating the sexes in all wards and most work areas. Most women are therefore assigned to areas having a stereotypically feminine ring to them — sewing room, occupational therapy (where they knit, sew or make soft toys for example), laundry, kitchen and dining room.

Broadmoor is severely understaffed, and patients' activities are therefore influenced by the need to maintain adequate staffing levels in key areas. The majority of nursing staff on the women's wing are women though, in response to the high incidence of injury to staff in recent years, on some of the female wards there has been the introduction of male staff, who, it is felt, are physically better able to handle physical violence. This small number of men is supplemented by three or four male doctors and social workers, though does little to 'normalise' the social relationships of the patients. The situation on the male side is even more artificial, with only one female nurse supplemented by a number of women from other disciplines. Male and female patients tend to mix freely only at socials, though staff are always present. Homosexual behaviour is fairly commonplace among both female and male patients, but is not seen in itself as a problem unless difficult emotional triangles are created.

In general, Broadmoor has a surprisingly calm and relaxed atmosphere, punctuated only occasionally by violent incidents, most frequently in the intensive-care wards, where higher staffing ratios are designed to facilitate fast and efficient control.

Day-to-day routine differs little for the women and the men. A typical day starts at 7.0 a.m., when the patient is awakened by nursing staff. Most women sleep in single rooms, the remainder in small dormitories. By contrast, most men sleep in large dormitories, and single rooms are either a privilege or a therapeutic tool in promoting desirable behaviour. Apart from a few privileged patients, there is no access to normal toilet facilities during the night, and for many patients, the day therefore begins with the antiquated and degrading 'slopping-out' process. Breakfast, like all meals, is communal for all patients except those on parole or those too ill or disturbed to tolerate company. The patients work from 9.0 a.m. until 4.0 p.m., with a two-hour lunch-break. This may be broken up by attendance at the hospital school, participation in a treatment programme, interviews with staff or the receipt of visitors in the central visiting hall. Evenings are for recreation, with optional attendance at dances, socials or various interest clubs such as chess, drama, film and choral. Female presence on social occasions tends to consist of a small group of particularly sociable women who attend most functions, while the majority remain in the female wing. Activities cease at 8.30 p.m., and patients are locked in for the night thirty minutes later.

Those They Leave Behind

Admission to any institution, but perhaps particularly to a special hospital, with its dual stigma of insanity and criminality, has emotional and practical repercussions for the inmate's family as well as the inmate herself. Although work has been done on the family structure of prisoners and psychiatric patients before and after admission of the relative (Doniger, 1962; Morris, 1965; Fasman *et al.*, 1967; Spitzer, 1971; Merriman, 1979), little has ever been published specifically on the families of Special-Hospital patients.

Table 6.4: **Marital Status before Offence: All Admissions to Special Hospitals, 1972–4**

Marital status	Males	Females
Single	509	121
Married	76	18
Widowed	6	–
Divorced/separated	58	16
Not known	66	58
	715	213

Source: Special Hospital Research Unit Report no. 15, p. 16; Dell and Parker, 1979.

As Table 6.4 shows, most inmates to Special Hospitals have not been married. Of course, marital status is probably a poor indicator of the existence of a stable relationship prior to admission, and tells us nothing of any children.

In an attempt to shed a little light on the implications of admission on one particular family member, the child of the Broadmoor patient, Rowett (forthcoming) carried out a survey of 78 male patients and 86 female patients detained in Broadmoor in October 1979, matched for age (mean 40 years) and the legislation which officially detained them. Their marital status prior to the offence was slightly different from the overall pattern for Special-Hospital patients described above. Over 20 per cent of the women and 14 per cent of the men had been married.

It was also found that 16 of the male patients had been fathers, of a total of 28 children, and 36 of the women had been mothers, of 77 children in all (Table 6.5).

Table 6.5: Broadmoor Patients Who Were Parents

Marital status	Male	Female
Single	3	12
Married	9	15
Separated	1	2
Divorced	2	6
Widowed	1	1
Total	16	36

Almost all the children of male patients were living at home prior to the offence. After the offence the majority remained at home. In this sample, six of the men had killed their wives and their children were subsequently cared for by relatives. Only one child was moved away. For the children of female patients, the situation is rather different, as shown by Table 6.6. It is evident that a substantial number of female patients' children were already living away from home prior to the offence: ten had been adopted shortly after birth, 14 had been fostered or placed in care and five were independent. Following the offence, perhaps surprisingly, the majority continue to be looked after at home.

Admission to a Special Hospital would not seem to involve major changes of placement for the children of male or female patients. The children of male patients largely continue to be looked after by the

Table 6.6: Placement of Children of Male and Female Patients

	Male Patients		Female Patients	
	Before offence	After twelve months	Before offence	After twelve months
At home	27	19	45	26*
With relatives	0	7	3	5
Away	1	2	29	35
Total	28	28	77	66

*Eleven killed by mothers.

Table 6.7: Offences

	Male patients		Female patients	
	Without children	Who were fathers	Without children	Who were mothers
Homicide	18	6	10	18
Wounding/assault	29	7	26	13
Sexual offence	6	2	0	0
Arson	5	1	12	5
Theft/burglary	1	0	0	0
Other	3	0	2	0
Total	62	16	50	36

Table 6.8: Victims

	Male patients		Female patients	
	Without children	Who were fathers	Without children	Who were mothers
Relative	12	9	8	15
Other	42	6	29	16
No victim	8	1	13	5
Total	62	16	50	36

remaining spouse or, if she was the victim, are placed with relatives. The placement of the children of female patients also remains fairly stable. However, for a large number of these children, disruption to their life may have occurred much earlier. The majority who remain in contact with their mother prior to the offence continue to be cared for at home subsequently. Tables 6.7 and 6.8 give information on the offences and victims of the patients in the sample. It is apparent that most parents were violent: the fathers were likely to have attacked members of the family, typically the partner; a fairly equal proportion of mothers had attacked relatives, normally the child, or others, normally nurses in previous hospitals.

Since most patients receive little outside contact, Broadmoor is deprived of the major resources available to conventional psychiatric hospitals when the time comes to consider discharge — the patients' families. This renders somewhat superfluous the advice of the Aarvold Committee (1973), who reviewed procedures for releasing Special-Hospital patients: '"only if there are strong arguments for doing so should a patient be discharged direct from a secure special hospital to his family or to casual lodgings'. In practice, therefore, most patients are effectively only moved from one institution to another on 'release'. This raises a number of issues about the most appropriate form of preparation for discharge.

Their Future

There are five possible ways in which a patient can leave Broadmoor — discharge by a Mental Health Review Tribunal if the patient is not subject to Home Office restrictions; transfer back to a prison; conditional or absolute discharge to hostels, lodgings or family; transfer to an NHS hospital; or repatriation to the country of origin.

General agreement that it is necessary to prepare patients for release has only been reached among Broadmoor staff in recent years. Previously it was argued that Broadmoor's role was purely to treat the 'criminal, violent or dangerous' elements of the patient's behaviour, and that rehabilitation was the role of the next institutional link in the chain, be that a county hospital or some form of hostel. In the last few years, however, various attempts have been made to increase the patients' ability to survive after release. There is still no overall policy; any preparation individual patients receive on the male wing depends on the interests, enthusiasm and abilities of the staff attached to a particular house. On the female wing, however, preparation for release is seen rather differently.

Women on the 'rehabilitation' ward, for example, take part in a fairly comprehensive programme designed to improve their level of functioning in areas considered essential for their continued progress. The full programme is set out below.

Women's Rehabilitation Programme
Part A
1. Accident prevention: (a) fire; (b) kitchen; (c) garden; (d) falls; (e) road safety.
2. Simple first aid: (a) burns; (b) cuts; (c) sprains; (d) bandaging.
3. Personal hygiene: (a) home; (b) body/clothes; (c) beauty care; (d) kitchen.
4. Home management: (a) housekeeping; (b) shopping.
5. Diet: (a) good food; (b) food value; (c) changing eating habits; (d) feeding a family.
6. Dependence: (i) alcohol: (a) uses and abuses; (b) social aspects; (c) costs; (ii) cigarettes: (a) dependence; (b) medical aspects; (c) giving it up.
Part B
1. Sex education: (a) family planning; (b) conception; (c) birth; (d) contraception.
2. Venereal disease: (a) forms; (b) causes; (c) cures.
3. Prevention: (a) breasts; (b) cytology.
Part C
1. Living in society: (a) finding a job; (b) visits to job centres, dole offices.
2. Social skills: (a) returning damaged goods; (b) assertive behaviour.

In addition to this, a scheme described by Vaughan (1980b) has recently been established whereby a senior management consultant is involved with social workers, nurses and psychologists in providing advice and experience in the selection of a job, how to make an application and, by using video feedback techniques in role-play situations, how to deal with the various types of job interviews.

Thus, in the last few years at least, female patients awaiting release have had the opportunity for some form of preparation for the outside world, preparation that ranges from the old notion of the importance of beauty care to the newer interest in assertive training. However, the usefulness or effectiveness of this programme remains a matter for speculation, since neither male nor female releases receive follow-up from Broadmoor staff, and the vast majority of the women are in fact transferred to another psychiatric hospital rather than to hostels or families.

Suzanne Dell (1980), looking at transfers and discharges from all Special Hospitals in 1976 ($N = 190$) found that Broadmoor recommended 45 men and five women for transfer to another psychiatric hospital; and 17 men, but no women, for conditional discharge to a hostel or family or directly into the community. The difficulty in arranging transfers to county hospitals is comprehensively outlined by Dell, who recommends that patients suffering delayed transfers of anything up to five years because of the unwillingness or apparent inability of local hospitals to make a bed available should be considered for discharge into the community as an alternative. If waiting lists for transfer become even longer, then pressure may be exerted to increase the number of discharges into the community, and thereby create a new sort of future for some of the Broadmoor women. Most of such women would be 'restricted patients' in terms either of Section 65 of the 1959 Mental Health Act or of the Criminal Procedures (Insanity) Act 1964, with release into the community conditional upon consent from the Home Office, who insist on patients being placed in 'suitable' accommodation, with an appointed supervising psychiatrist and probation officer or social worker, together with any other restrictions considered appropriate. Dr Margaret Norris of the University of Surrey is examining how successful this policy has been for male discharges from 1974 to date.

Final Comments

Special Hospitals have been used to control and treat the most 'unmanageable' mentally abnormal offenders since the middle of the nineteenth century. They are designed primarily to detain, and are built on lines similar to some prisons, though they also show their origins in the growth of the large asylum warehouses with segregated male and female wings and sex-appropriate division of work areas. Patients are detained for indefinite periods of time, normally with little or no outside contact with either family or friends, and live a regimented existence based on the sometimes conflicting demands of security, treatment, care and management.

There is little public awareness that one fifth of all Special-Hospital patients are women. These women are in some ways in a most curious situation. The 120 women detained in Broadmoor are considered to be of violent, dangerous or criminal propensities — although, in fact, many of them have not been convicted of any offence — and accordingly, to merit disposal in a maximum-security total institution. They have simultaneously been diagnosed as suffering some form of mental disorder, a comparatively frequent occurrence for women, but find themselves outnumbered 5:1 by men. Compared to some parts of the male wing their surroundings are fairly pleasant and, since some importance is attached to the cultivation of stereotypically feminine attributes such as the ability to make a home in difficult surroundings, the female wing feels less like an institution. Unlike the men, the women receive a systematic rehabilitation programme preparing them for life in the community but, again unlike the men, they are largely transferred to another psychiatric hospital, where they receive no formal follow-up.

Thus, present social response to female mentally abnormal offenders has resulted in a series of anomalies that perhaps reflect more deep-seated conflicts about the control of deviant women in our society — conflicts that focus on the boundaries between mental illness and criminality, detention and rehabilitation, isolation and sociability, stereotypes and realities, inmate and controller, sexuality and sex roles. These boundaries sometimes shift, depending on whether we are talking about men or women. The purpose of the present chapter is not to attempt a theoretical analysis of these issues. Rather, it is a first attempt to gather together a number of facts about a particular group of women, facts that require a theory; and to express the feelings we have about the fate of these women, feelings in search of a synthesis. We leave it to others to provide what we, as practitioners, have not.

Notes

The views expressed are solely those of the authors, and do not necessarily represent the view of the Department of Health and Social Security.

Bibliography

Aarvold, C. *Report on the Review of Procedures for the Discharge and Supervision of Psychiatric Patients Subject to Special Restrictions*, Cmnd 5191

(HMSO, London, 1973)

Brooks, P.W. and Mitchell, G. 'A Fifteen Year Review of Female Admissions to Carstairs State Hospital', *British Journal of Psychiatry*, vol. 127 (1975), pp. 448–55

Chesler, P. *Women and Madness* (Allen Lane, London, 1974)

Dell, S. '1976 Census of Special Hospital Patients with a Five Year Length of Stay', in *Special Hospitals Case Register* (Special Hospitals Research Unit, London, 1979)

—— *The Transfer of Special Hospital Patients to National Health Service Hospitals*, Special Hospitals Research Report no. 16 (Special Hospitals Research Unit, London, 1980)

Dell, S. and Parker, E. 'Special Hospitals Case Register – Triennial Statistics 1972–74', in *Special Hospitals Case Register: The First Five Years*, Research Report no. 15 (Special Hospitals Research Unit, London, 1979)

DHSS *In-patient Statistics for the Mental Health Enquiry for England 1975*, Statistics and Research Report Series 20 (HMSO, London, 1978)

Doniger, C. 'Children Whose Mothers Are in a Mental Hospital', *Journal of Child Psychology and Psychiatry*, vol. 3 (1962), pp. 165–73

Fasman, J., Grunebaum, H.U. and Weiss, J.L. 'Who Cares for Children of Psychotic Mothers', *British Journal of Psychiatric Social Work*, vol. 2 (1967), pp. 84–9

Goffman, E. *Asylums* (Penguin, Harmondsworth, 1961)

Home Office/DHSS *Report of the Committee on Mentally Abnormal Offenders*, Cmnd 6244 (HMSO, London, 1975)

Home Office *Criminal Statistics England and Wales 1978*, Cmnd 7670 (HMSO, London, 1979a)

—— *Prison Statistics England and Wales 1978*, Cmnd 7626 (HMSO, London, 1979b)

Jarvis, D.C. *Institutional Treatment of the Offender* (McGraw-Hill, New York, 1978)

Jones, K. *A History of the Mental Health Services* (Routledge and Kegan Paul, London, 1972)

Levin, R. 'Women and Crime Today', *Prison Service Journal*, no. 35 (New Series, 1979), pp. 1–3

Locke, J. 'The Special Hospitals', *Social Work Service*, no. 15 (1978), pp. 22–6

Martin, J.P. and Webster, D. *Social Consequences of Conviction* (Heinemann, London, 1971)

Merriman, P. 'The Families of Long-term Prisoners', *Probation Journal*, vol. 26, no. 4 (1979), pp. 114–20

Morris, P. *Prisoners and Their Families* (Allen and Unwin, London, 1965)

Partridge, R. *Broadmoor: A History of Criminal Lunacy and Its Problems* (Chatto and Windus, 1953); reprint (Greenwood Press, 1975)

Rowett, C. 'What Happens to the Children of Broadmoor Patients?' (forthcoming)

Scott, P.D. 'Assessing Dangerousness in Criminals', *British Journal of Psychiatry*, vol. 131 (1977), pp. 127–42

Scull, A.T. *Museums of Madness: The Social Organisation of Insanity in 19th Century England* (Allen Lane, London, 1979)

Short, R. *The Care of Long-term Prisoners* (Macmillan, London, 1979)

Spitzer, S.P., Morgan, P.A. and Swanson, R.M. 'Determinants of the Psychiatric Patient's Career: Family Reaction Patterns and Social Work Intervention', *Social Service Review*, no. 45 (1971)

Szasz, T. *The Manufacture of Madness* (Routledge and Kegan Paul, London, 1971)

Tennent, G., Parker, E., McGrath, P., McDougal, J. and Street, D. 'Female

Patients in the Three English Special Hospitals: A Demographic Survey of Admissions 1961–1965', *Medicine, Science and the Law*, vol. 16, no. 3 (1976), pp. 200–7

Vaughan, P.J. 'Letters and Visits to Long-Stay Broadmoor Patients', *British Journal of Social Work* (1980a)

―――― 'Interview Training with the Mentally Abnormal Offender', *Apex News*, vol. 2, no. 3 (1980b), pp. 22–3

Walker, N. and McCabe, S. *Crime and Insanity in England*, vol. 2 (Edinburgh University Press, Edinburgh, 1973)

Woodside, M. 'Women Offenders and Psychiatric Reports', *Social Work Today*, vol. 5, no. 11 (1974), pp. 341–2

Zalba, S.R. *Women Prisoners and Their Families* (Delmar Publishing, Los Angeles, 1964)

7   WOMEN, ALCOHOL AND SOCIAL CONTROL

Shirley Otto

It is worth taking the time to reflect on the theme of women, alcohol and social control for two reasons: first, what is now being revealed about the nature of female drinking problems has much to teach us about the alcoholic condition; and secondly, a lot can be understood about women's situations, both past and present, through their use of such a widely available drug.

It has been for very good reasons that alcohol consumption — whether in moderation or in excess — has been considered to be primarily a male activity. Men drink much more than women (Shaw, 1980), and can physically tolerate the imbibing of greater amounts (Ghodse and Tregenza, 1980). Certain male-dominated occupations (such as mining) and geographical areas (such as the Scottish Highlands and rural Ireland) are characterised by social norms which allow, if not encourage, heavy drinking amongst men (Plant, 1979).

Hand in hand with the tolerance of male drinking is a widespread social acceptance of drunkenness. It is not at all unusual for drunkenness to be sought by male drinkers, and for it to be regarded as desirable in terms of appropriate masculine behaviour. Heavy drinking is not uncommonly thought to be glamorous or, at the very least, as in some way natural to the behaviour of men, especially young men. It would not be at all surprising to find that a man who does not drink has greater difficulties socially than one who gets drunk regularly — that is, unless he happens to be a member of a group or a religious sect which adheres to a principle of abstinence.

The general tolerance of male drinking and drunkenness, whether it occurs in mixed sex company, with or without food, in private or in public, has no parallel for women. Despite the lack of any comprehensive coverage of historical attitudes to drinking patterns, it is clear that only in recent years has it been acceptable for women to drink in pubs or at home, although in no way has it become acceptable for women to be drunk. There are a few historical examples of heavy drinking amongst groups of women, and these are the exceptions that prove the rule. Hogarth's prints vividly illustrate excessive public drinking amongst female members of the 'dangerous classes' (one rung lower than the working classes). It is significant that gin, then so

154

cheap and easily obtained, was nicknamed 'mother's ruin'.

The reasons why male and female drinking are viewed so differently have not been thoroughly clarified; however, recent research suggests some of the factors that appear to contribute to the different patterns of drinking of the two sexes and of attitudes towards these behaviours. Alcohol, contrary to popular belief, acts predominantly as a depressant or sedative. With increasing blood alcohol levels, various functions of the brain become depressed, leading ultimately to stupor and coma. The most highly integrated functions are affected first, with the impairment of concentration, memory, perception and motor function. Alcohol consumption also has psychological consequences which vary in their manifestation across different cultures, and which are most commonly understood in western societies. In such societies, psychological effects are associated with the freeing of inhibitions, so that drinkers behave in ways that they would not allow themselves when sober. Sexual promiscuity is often associated with drunken behaviour – particularly in women. Cartwright *et al.* (1975), in a study of attitudes of lay and professional people towards drunkenness and drinking problems, found drunkenness to be associated with sexual licence in women and aggression in men. Those interviewed said the aggressive behaviour of men was *more* acceptable than promiscuity in women. Given these findings, it is worth noting that no studies of women with drinking problems have shown them to be any more or less sexually promiscuous than any other women – and no comment can be made of equivalent male behaviour, as few studies exist on this topic.

A revealing illustration of differences in attitudes to male and female drunkenness is provided in a speech made in 1978 by the Secretary of State for Health and Social Security of the day, David Ennals, during a public-health campaign in North East England: 'drunkenness amongst men is disgusting', he said, 'and amongst women it is absolutely sickening'.

A number of writers (Saunders, 1980; Curlee, 1968) have suggested that female drunkenness is so very unacceptable because drunken behaviour conflicts with a woman's capacity to carry out primary roles as wife and mother. Curlee (1968) writes:

> Because the role of women has been equated with the stabilising functions of wife and mother, the drunken woman has seemed to be a special threat: no one likes to believe that the hand that rocks the cradle might be a shaky one. Even amongst alcoholic women

themselves, it is not unusual to hear the statement, 'There is nothing so disgusting as a drunken woman'. According to the stereotype, a woman who has deserted her feminine roles sufficiently to be an alcoholic has deserted respectability in all areas, especially the sexual ones.

Hence, the notion of 'loss of control' inherent in heavy drinking behaviour simply has no place in our society's concept of motherhood. Nor is it assumed that women, in fulfilling such roles, need the release from tension and frustration that are regarded as the rationale for much of male heavy drinking and drunkenness. Hence, as with sexuality, there exists a double standard which allows both men and women to drink but only men to become drunk.

A further consideration is that, usually, regular heavy drinking requires a degree of financial flexibility in terms of the amount of money a person has available after expenditure on essential items such as housing, heating and food. It is men who mainly work outside the home, for a wage, and it is only recently that women's average income has come anywhere close to that of the men. Hence, women have been restricted because they have had less access to any marginal expenditure to spend on 'non-essentials' such as alcohol.

Finally, it is only in recent years that women, in any numbers, have begun to work in high-risk occupations, that is, occupations where drinking problems are likely either because of the availability of drink (for example, in employment where alcohol is made or sold) or where there is a norm of heavy drinking within a profession (for example, in journalism and sales promotion).

Hence, from the studies that are available it appears clear that male and female patterns of drinking are rooted in cultural assumptions about appropriate male and female behaviour *per se* and by more specific factors such as exposure to drink in drink-related working environments and the amount of income available to a person for expenditure on alcohol.

Present Trends in Female Drinking Patterns

What statistics are available indicate that quite significant changes have gradually taken place in female drinking patterns since the last war (Shaw, 1980; Otto, 1977). In particular, there has been an increase in the incidence of alcoholism amongst women, in comparison with men.

As it is not possible literally to count the number of alcoholics in an area, it is common practice to rely on certain key indicators of the prevalence of drinking problems: drunkenness offences, admissions to hospital and/or community-based counselling services for alcoholics, rates of liver damage and records of alcoholic mortality.

Offences of Drunkenness

Male drunkenness offenders heavily outnumber female offenders. However, female drunkenness has increased at a greater rate than male drunkenness. Between 1975 and 1976 there was an increase of three per cent for offences of drunkenness amongst men compared with 14 per cent amongst women (Home Office, 1977). Far fewer women than men have been convicted of offences for drinking and driving; the trend is now for the number of men to be slowly decreasing and for the number of women to increase (Brewers' Society, 1978).

Admissions to Hospital/Community-based Agencies for Alcoholics

Between 1964 and 1975 the number of men admitted to hospitals for alcoholism doubled, while the number of women trebled. In 1964, 4,030 men and 1,043 women were admitted to hospital for the diagnosis of alcoholism or alcoholism psychosis, compared with 8,144 men and 3,028 women in 1975 (Wilson, 1976).

A major community-based agency for alcoholics, Alcoholics Anonymous, publishes no annual figures; however, there have been a number of studies of AA from which useful information can be drawn. In 1964 there was one woman for every four men attending AA (Edwards *et al.*, 1967), while in 1976 there was one woman for every two men (Robinson, 1979). Furthermore, the study by Robinson showed that for new attenders of AA, in Britain and the USA, the ratio of women to men is one to one. It is not without significance that there are now women-only AA groups in England.

Other forms of community-based services for alcoholics tend to vary in kind and geographical distribution. The most prominent type of service are the Councils on Alcoholism. Figures published by the national body for the co-ordination of councils on alcoholism — The National Council on Alcoholism — showed that, for 1977, there were on average 2.7 men for every one woman coming forward to these services (National Council on Alcoholism, 1979). The annual reports for some of these councils show that the ratio is now one woman to every man.

Cirrhosis of the Liver

Cirrhosis of the liver is now regarded as a direct consequence of damage through alcohol consumption. Statistics on the rates of cirrhosis of the liver show that women are as likely as men to suffer this form of damage (Office of Population Census and Surveys, 1976). It would appear that the rates are so high for women (that is, women under 55 years of age) because they are physiologically more vulnerable to damage from alcohol consumption than men, for reasons that are not yet clear but may have something to do with their pattern of drinking (that is, drinking regularly as opposed to in bouts) and to physical factors related to the particular way in which females absorb and metabolise alcohol (Ghodse and Tregenza, 1980).

Records of Death

In 1973, 103 men and 49 women were recorded as having died from alcoholism or alcoholic psychosis compared with 118 men and 81 women in 1975 (Office of Population Census and Surveys, 1976). Hence, between 1973 and 1975 the ratio of men to women had dropped from 2:1 to 1.5:1. What is surprising, given doctors' reluctance to diagnose alcoholism in women because of the stigma attached to it, is that the ratio is so small.

The figures quoted above demonstrate that there has been an increase, across all indicators, in problems related to alcoholism, and that this increase is proportionally greater for women than for men.

Reasons for Increased Prevalence

Influence of Public-health Campaigns

The last few years have seen an increase in the number of health-education campaigns about alcohol and alcohol problems. The goals of these campaigns have been two-fold; to inform people about the nature and causes of drinking problems and to reduce the stigma attached to alcoholism. The emphasis of such campaigns has been to instruct people on the physical, emotional and social effects of problem drinking and to challenge the stereotype of the alcoholic as a 'meths drinker'. Methods used range from posters (showing enlarged livers or alternatively, the distraught and crying face of an alcoholic's child) and television ads to day conferences and seminars. Hopefully, the effect of these campaigns has been to make it easier for both lay and professional people to detect alcohol problems and encourage those with drinking problems to feel more secure about coming forward for help. Hence, the increase in the number of alcoholics in recent statistics could be accounted for by otherwise unknown alcoholics coming forward and therefore being identified as such. Unfortunately, although increased public awareness and improved rates of detection should accrue from public-health campaigns, there is no evidence to suggest that these factors explain the total increase in the prevalence of drinking problems amongst women. For women in particular, the stigma attached to alcoholism still exists (Cartwright *et al.*, 1975; Saunders, 1980).

Lessening of Social Constraints

As has been already mentioned, it is now acceptable for women to be seen drinking in mixed-sex company, in private and in public, although the experience of many women is that it is not as easy for them to drink *alone* in pubs as it is for men. However, compared with the attitudes held by the majority in society prior to the last war the social constraints on women drinking have eased considerably – even if drunkenness remains taboo. One example of the decrease in social constraints is the number of male-only bars that have now admitted women.

Increased Availability

The 1961 Licensing Act allowed off-licences to open during normal shopping hours and in 1966/7 retail-price maintenance on alcohol drinks was abolished, with the effect that grocery-store chains and supermarkets were encouraged to open drinks departments on their existing premises. By 1977 approximately half of Britain's super-markets had licences to sell alcohol (Shaw, 1980). In the view of Shaw (1980, p. 16), 'it has become much easier, more impersonal and more "respectable" for women to obtain alcohol at a supermarket than it has been in pubs and in off-licences'.

A survey in 1975 by Gordon Simmons Research (Otto, 1977) found that licensed stores accounted for 42 per cent of all take-home alcohol sales, and off-licences for 40 per cent and that as many women as men were buying alcohol from stores with licences. All the indicators suggest that women have now become more important than men for the bulk of purchases of alcohol from such stores. In 1976, IPC's *Women's Market* magazine stated: 'With grocery outlets accounting for almost half the current £860 million drinks trade, it is clear women have become the big spenders in the alcoholic drinks market' (Shaw, 1980, p. 17).

Alcohol Advertising

Alcohol advertising is increasingly being aimed at women. Women are being encouraged to drink beer (traditionally a male drink) by manufacturers such as Guinness who have increased their advertising in women's magazines. Consistent with this there has been an increase in advertising in women's magazines by manufacturers of liqueurs, sherry and aperitifs — the traditional women's drinks.

Financial Flexibility

Between 1972 and 1977 the average weekly earnings of men rose by 104 per cent while women's rose by 147 per cent, which in effect meant that the typical or average wage of women actually doubled during this period (Department of Employment, 1978). The influence of rising income amongst women has meant a greater disposable income for women as a group, and therefore the availability of money to buy such 'inessential' items as alcohol. This becomes particularly significant when considered in the light of studies that have shown that the consumption of alcohol is almost exactly related to its price as a proportion of real disposable income. Whenever the price of alcohol falls as a proportion of real disposable income, then alcohol consumption rises (De Lint and Schmidt, 1971). As the real price of alcohol has declined at the same time as women's disposable income has been increasing it is therefore to be expected that they would increase their consumption as a group (Shaw, 1980).

Employment

It would appear that not only have women's average weekly earnings been increasing faster than men's but the disposable income of women as a group has increased still further because more of them have been coming into employment. In fact, the number of women entering employment has been increasing while the number of males in employment has been decreasing (Department of Employment, 1978). An increasing number of women are also entering traditional 'high-risk' occupations, such as journalism, the media, serving in pubs and executive or middle-management positions. In occupations where heavy drinking is the norm, women are as much at risk as men of developing alcohol problems, although women must also contend with the double standard — unlike men.

It would appear that middle-class women are the group most affected. It is the view of Shaw (1980, p. 141) that the

influence of rising income may be especially important in the case
of women, since American surveys have shown that the percentage
of men who drink is higher amongst lower income than among
higher income groups, but the opposite is true of women. The
higher the income bracket, the less women abstain from drinking.

Role Ambiguity

Changing social norms and expectations about women's roles have
created a situation where women are increasingly uncertain about their
identity as individuals and as a group. Women at home face conflicts
as to whether they should or could work outside the home and/or with
any dissatisfaction or lack of fulfilment they experience in their roles
as wife and mother. Women working outside the home must come to
terms with competition with men, the inherent pressure in any
particular type of employment and also conflict over the extent to
which they should perform their traditional roles as mothers and
home makers. In the view of Shaw (1980, p. 21), 'the dual pressure
of holding down a job and maintaining a home and family can create
intolerable pressures for some women, and the tranquillising and
relieving effects of alcohol is one recourse they may take'. Keil
(1978), in a recent American survey, found that women in non-
traditional or multiple roles were likely to drink more than women
with purely domestic responsibilities. Unfortunately, there is little
research in the UK as yet on alcohol problems amongst women
working either in or outside the home from which to draw more
precise conclusions.

In summary, women have a greater opportunity to both buy and
consume alcohol. There are fewer social constraints about drinking
to contend with and more encouragement to drink by advertising,
greater availability through supermarkets, etc., and more money for
this kind of expenditure. Some women are vulnerable because they
work in high-risk occupations; more generally, there is the stress felt
by many women due to uncertainty about appropriate behaviour
and expectations. In the view of Shaw (1980, pp. 21—2):

women drink more to experience the sense of escape from difficult
situations and if there is amongst women a greater feeling that
there is more to escape from, then given the increasing availability
of alcohol, it is not surprising that more women should be
drinking and getting into problems as a result. The similarity can

be traced here with the massive increase amongst women in the usage of other legal tranquillisers and sleeping aids such as mogadon, valium and librium.

The Double Standard

Although social constraints have lessened such that women can drink alcohol without social disapproval, there is no sign that they are therefore now able also to become drunk. It is important to understand the reason for society's rejection of the women who become drunk, if we are to understand the importance of gender in drinking behaviour and in society *per se*.

Litman *et al.* (1976) found that women alcoholics were not only held in low esteem, but they were conceptualised as devoid of gender and personality characteristics — they were virtually seen as non-entities. Such findings are consistent with the work reported by Cartwright *et al.* (1975), wherein women drinkers were seen as more likely to experience loss of personal esteem and respect than men, and were thought to be sexually promiscuous.

In a recent study of representation of women alcoholics in the cinema (Harwin and Otto, 1979), it was found that only one film could be identified as presenting a woman alcoholic in a positive light — that is, as in any way heroic. This is in contrast to many more positive representations of men alcoholics in the cinema. It is noticeable that this one positive representation in *Key Largo* (1948, directed by John Hudson, and starring Humphrey Bogart and Lauren Bacall) was made in the 1940s, when the cinema was perhaps at its most positive in the way in which women were presented, in terms of relationships with men and as workers (Rosen, 1973; Haskel, 1974).

The typical representation of women alcoholics reflects two stereotypes: they are shown either as sluts, totally devoid of any self-respect, or as pathetic homeless women. The most immediate example of this latter stereotype can be seen in *Edna, the Inebriate*, a film about a homeless woman who developed a drinking problem. It is interesting to note that Edna is portrayed with some sympathy, albeit heavily tinged with patronage, but without any of the sexual connotations of being a woman.

There are indeed few films about women with drinking problems *per se*, and these few provoked considerable disgust in film critics when first screened. In a contemporary *Daily Mail* film review of

Too Much, Too Soon (1958), Fred Majdalany (Harwin and Otto, 1979) wrote:

> in one field I think women would do well to avoid equality with men. I have in mind alcoholism. There is something formidable and tragic about any alcoholic but the female variety is really terrible. Nothing more fatally draws attention to this than a film having as its heroine a lush — as the Americans describe a lady afflicted with this malady — unless it is animated by a spirit of compassionate enquiry, intelligent analysis or art.

In the same vein, a review (Otto, 1980) of both scientific and fictional literature on the homeless alcoholic has shown there to be no female equivalent of the 'noble-savage' portrayal of the male homeless alcoholic seen most vividly in the novels of Anderson (1923), Orwell (1933) and Kerouac (1962). Almost no films or books romanticise the female tramp or hobo; such women really do not excite anyone's fantasies or envy.

Social Control

The previous sections illustrate something of the nature of the social controls that have long been employed to constrain women's drinking behaviour. The nature of the controls and the way in which they are employed reveal both the power and complexity of attitudes towards women and alcohol.

The common picture drawn in research and social-work literature is that, when a woman alcoholic is first diagnosed as such by her family, relatives or general practitioner, the common response is to 'protect' her. The woman is likely to be diagnosed as depressed or suffering from 'nerves' rather than given the more appropriate, but stigmatising label of alcoholism. Various means are likely to be employed to influence the woman's drinking, ranging from informal social pressure — to behave in a more lady-like fashion — to actual removal of the woman's children into her husband's custody.

The prevailing assumption is that women alcoholics are essentially emotional, immature, manipulative and child-like and yet at the same time they are seen as deviant in terms of appropriate female behaviour — in other words, as sad or mad but never bad, for this would be to regard the woman as being responsible for her own behaviour. The case histories of women alcoholics show them to have many more hospital admissions for psychiatric treatment than is found with male alcoholics (Saunders, 1980).

It must be concluded that society's response to such women is determined by the women's drinking behaviour. Little validity is attributed to what the women do as the actions of members of an oppressed social group, who therefore reflect issues far greater than the sum of their drinking behaviour. Male alcoholics, however, particularly the homeless, have at times (Archard, 1976) been ascribed a political role in that their life-style is seen to comment on the nature of society and the values of the majority. They too are represented as retaining not only self-control but a sense of responsibility for themselves, as is associated with adult behaviour.

Should a woman alcoholic become a public drunk, she is very likely to experience very direct social control, for she will be seen as having violated the numerous norms about acceptable female behaviour (Otto, 1980). Such women are not only drunk in public but exist outside a family network. They are assumed to be more aggressive, intractable and hopeless than their male counterparts, and are much more likely to be apprehended, arrested and convicted. This is despite normal police reluctance to put women through the penal process (Steele, 1978). Walker (1965) found that female habitual-drunkenness offenders made up 13—18 per cent of the annual admissions to Holloway Prison (which takes the majority of female drunkenness offenders), which was twice the rate of habitual-drunkenness offenders amongst male prisoners. Many homeless female habitual-drunkenness offenders spend more time in prison than at liberty, with up to 100 drunkenness offences each (Woodside, 1961; D'Orban, 1969).

Reports of the experience of male social workers and police suggest that what may underline this discrimination against homeless alcoholic women is their gender. As one worker put it during an interview, 'you can't manhandle a woman in the same way as a man'. It appears, from discussions with male workers, that fear of accusations of rape and of manipulation through feminine wiles are the reasons for the threat felt by men in working with homeless alcoholic women.

There are, as yet, fewer homeless women alcoholics than men — that is, as far as we know; no systematic surveys have yet been done. Nevertheless, it is commonly assumed that there is one homeless alcoholic woman for every six to eight men. Consequently, there are many more men than women in residential facilities for alcoholics, to the extent that there are likely to be ten men and two women in a facility of twelve beds. This can have the effect of making the women's behaviour stand out and of provoking women to act as 'prima-donnas', thereby making their behaviour more memorable and more commented on (Otto, 1980).

We can as yet only speculate as to whether homeless alcoholic women are indeed more violent, intractable, etc., than men or, if they are, whether this behaviour is inherent in their condition or provoked by the unease their presence creates. Either way it could be argued that the homeless alcoholic woman has every reason for being angry, since it would appear they are given little respect or right to self-determination. In the words of Adrian Jones (1977, p. 5) in an article on his work at a Cyrenian house in Leeds: 'it's all there in that statement — the utter reasonableness of saying "it's not what you want, but what we say you need" '. In his view, this attitude effectively puts women off, for he goes on to comment:

it is not surprising then that even at our house — a liberal institution . . . 39 people wandered: it is not surprising that 45 out of a 100 we knew wandered from hostel to hostel, and town to town on the roundabout of homelessness.

From this perspective, it could be argued that the women's 'difficult' behaviour would be better understood as an assertion of independence, arising out of a desire for self-determination — none too clearly communicated. To quote Adrian Jones (1977, p. 5) again:

They have overwhelmingly shunned hostels and Cyrenian houses as in any way being an acceptable, permanent life style. They have elected, rather, for privacy and independence. Some 60 out of a 100 people who lived at our house in its first year wanted to live in flats, bedsits, and private houses. But the referring agencies are not geared to helping homeless women in this way: so that the women are denied the opportunity, money and practical help to live how they want.

In Conclusion

The increase of alcohol problems amongst women over the last few decades is of sufficient proportion to require serious consideration, even at this time of economic austerity and cuts in health and social services. There is to date no evidence that the numbers of such women problem drinkers are beginning to decline or stabilise.

The acute lack of appropriate facilities for women alcoholics, and particularly for those who are homeless, further aggravates an already serious social problem. Clearly, more resources are required to develop the kind of agencies and institutions that will help women, particularly in the early stages of their problem. However, as this chapter suggests, the creation of more facilities is not enough. It is a question of not only the right facilities but of a fundamental change in attitudes towards women — encompassing their appropriate roles and the values and assumptions associated with them. Women face problems not only of role ambiguity but of actual contradiction in the messages they receive about appropriate drinking behaviour. To put it simply, the availability of alcohol, etc., encourages women to drink more, while at the same time powerful social pressures exist to punish them if they are seen to drink to excess. Women as yet have little freedom of choice or opportunities to determine their own destiny when confronted by such economic and social forces.

Bibliography

Anderson, N. *The Hobo. The Sociology of the Homeless Man* (University of Chicago Press, Chicago, 1923)

Archard, P. *The Bottle Won't Leave You* (Alcoholics Recovery Project, London, 1976)

Brewers' Society *UK Statistical Handbook* (Brewing Publications Ltd, London, 1978)

Camberwell Council on Alcoholism (eds.) *Women and Alcohol* (Tavistock, London, 1980)

Cartwright, A., Shaw, S. and Spratley, T. *Designing a Comprehensive Community Response to Problems of Alcohol Abuse*, Reports to the Department of Health and Social Security (Maudsley Alcohol Pilot Project, London, 1975)

Curlee, J. 'Women Alcoholics', *Federal Probation*, vol. 32 (1968), pp. 16–20

De Lint, J. and Schmidt, W. 'Consumption Averages and Alcoholism Prevalence. A Brief Review of Epidemiological Investigations', *British Journal of Addictions*, vol. 72 (1971), pp. 237–46

Department of Employment Condensed from *Annual Abstract of Statistics* (HMSO, London, 1978)

Edwards, G., Hensman, C., Hawker, A. and Williamson, B. 'Alcoholics Anonymous. The Anatomy of a Self Help Group', *Social Psychiatry*, vol. 1, no. 4 (1967), pp. 195–204

Ghodse, H. and Tregenza, G.S. 'The Physical Effects and Metabolism of Alcohol', in Camberwell Council on Alcoholism (1980)

Harwin, J. and Otto, S.J. 'Women, Alcohol and the Screen', in J. Cook and

M. Lewington (eds.), *Images of Alcoholism* (Tavistock, London, 1979)
Haskel, M. *From Reverence to Rape. The Treatment of Women in the Movies* (Penguin, USA, 1974)
Home Office *Offences of Drunkenness 1976 in England and\Wales*, Cmnd 6952 (HMSO, London, 1977)
Jones, A. 'These Women Want Houses. Yes, But What Do They Need?', *National Cyrenians News Letter* (February 1977)
Keil, J.T. 'Sex Role Variations and Women's Drinking. Results from a Household Survey in Pennsylvania', *Quarterly Journal of Studies on Alcoholism*, vol. 39 (1978), pp. 859–67
Kerouac, J. *Lonesome Traveller* (Panther, St Albans, 1962)
Litman, G.K., Stewart, R. and Powell, G. 'Evaluation of the Female Alcoholic. A Study of Person Perception', in *Proceedings of the Annual Conference of the British Psychological Society* (1976)
National Council on Alcoholism *News*, vol. 5 (1979)
Office of Population Census and Surveys, Reproduced in *Annual Abstract of Statistics* (HMSO, London, 1976)
D'Orban, P.T. 'Habitual Drunkenness Offenders in Holloway Prison', in T. Cook, D. Gath and C. Hensmen (eds.), *The Drunkenness Offence* (Pergamon, London, 1969)
Orwell, G. *Down and Out in Paris and London* (Gallancz, London, 1933; Penguin, Harmondsworth, 1970)
Otto, S.J. 'Women, Alcohol and Work', in M. Grant and W.H. Kenyon (eds.), *Alcoholism and Industry* (Alcohol Education Centre Publications, London, 1977)
────── 'Single Homeless Women and Alcohol', in Camberwell Council on Alcoholism (1980)
Plant, M. *Drinking Careers* (Tavistock, London, 1979)
Robinson, D. *Talking Out of Alcoholism* (Croom Helm, London, 1979)
Rosen, M. *Popcorn Venus. Women, Movies and the American Dream* (Avon, New York, 1973)
Saunders, B. 'Psychological Aspects of Women and Alcohol', in Camberwell Council on Alcoholism (1980)
Shaw, S. 'Causes of Increase in Drinking Problems', in Camberwell Council on Alcoholism (1980)
Steele, D. 'Feminism and Social Policies' (thesis submitted for MA in deviance social policy, Middlesex Polytechnic, 1978)
Walker, N. *Crime and Punishment in Britain* (Edinburgh University Press, Edinburgh, 1965)
Wilson, C. 'Women and Alcohol'. Paper presented at USA Airforce in Europe School (Camberwell Council on Alcoholism, London, 1976)
Woodside, N. 'Women Drinkers Admitted to Holloway Prison during February 1960. A Pilot Survey', *British Journal of Criminology*, vol. 1 (1961), pp. 221–35

8 ABORTION: THE MYTH OF THE GOLDEN AGE

Madeleine Simms

Abortion in Britain has always been so widespread that it is difficult to understand why it should ever have been associated with the concept of 'deviance'. What can be deviant about doing what so many women do and have always done? Perhaps part of the answer to this question is that women have not always done it openly. As long as abortion was a surreptitious activity it was possible to pretend that it was very rare and engaged in only by the immoral. But why should anyone want to pretend this? The evidence of the widespread practice of abortion was all around. To ignore it meant deliberately averting one's eyes from reality. In whose interest was it to pretend that abortion was not taking place when it obviously was?

It is a curious fact that, even now, many MPs, priests, leader writers, doctors and others who might be supposed to know better talk as if abortion only came into existence on any scale with the passing of the Abortion Act in 1967. Before that, in that hazy golden age that prevailed before our present irreligious era of permissiveness and licentiousness, women cheerfully had all the babies God sent them, and did not complain. Indeed, far from complaining they recognised that this was what a woman's life was essentially about. Any woman who did complain was by definition unnatural, and so could be ignored with a clear conscience.

As recently as 7 February 1980, Ronald Butt wrote in *The Times* about how the 1967 Abortion Act had resulted in what he called 'a huge rise in the number of abortions (by some 400 per cent) and the shattering of the old conviction that defenceless human life must be protected'. Mr Butt failed to reveal how he had arrived at this particular figure, though various earnest readers, including myself, wrote letters to *The Times* to try to find out. But they were not published.

On the same day Professor Hugh McLaren, the most militant of the medical anti-abortion campaigners, is quoted in the *Listener* as resisting the coming of the 1967 Abortion Act with the words: 'There'll be nobody murdering little babies in Birmingham'. Birmingham was a notable criminal abortion centre in the inter-war period. Women even travelled there from the capital to obtain their cheap, backstreet abortions. Sometimes, unfortunately, they died as a result of the conditions in which these abortions were carried out, and then Dr Donald Teare, the eminent pathologist, or a colleague would be sent scuttling up to Birmingham to pronounce upon the cause of death (Simms, 1978). Not surprisingly, their more affluent middle-class sisters preferred to have their abortions carried out in more civilised conditions in Harley Street. Professor McLaren's notable predecessor at Birmingham University, Sir Beckwith Whitehouse, rather crossly informed the Birkett Committee on Abortion in 1937 (Simms, 1974a, p. 49): 'Patients for whom I have refused to evacuate the uterus have had the operation performed in London without difficulty.'

On 16 February 1980, at the height of the debate on the Corrie anti-abortion bill, the *British Medical Journal* (I, pp. 477–9) carried three pages of angry correspondence from doctors, dedicated by the proposition that 'the clock of civilisation was turned back by the 1967 Abortion Act'. If only this clock could be reversed, then we might be able to reduce 'the continuing toll of suicides, murders, rapings and physical and mental morbidity arising from our over-sexed society.'

It may therefore be salutary to look more closely at this golden age before the Abortion Act corrupted British womanhood and gave it ideas about abortion that it had apparently never had before.

Abortion in the Twenties

Women denied surgical abortion experimented on themselves with all kinds of drugs. During World War I, lead-based abortifacient drugs became so popular and widespread, especially in the Midlands, that there had been outbreaks of lead poisoning among women in the child-bearing age groups. Lead poisoning showed itself in stains across the gums; it was therefore simple to detect the condition. On 7 February 1920, the *British Medical Journal* (I, p. 192) reported that: 'In the outpatient rooms of the Nottingham and Sheffield hospitals it became routine practice to examine the gums of the women patients'. Marie Stopes recorded in her book, *The First Five Thousand* (1925, pp. 16–17), that when she opened her first birth-control clinic in Holloway in 1921 she made all her staff sign a 'Statutory Declaration' in which they had solemnly to swear not in any circumstances to 'impart any information or lend any assistance whatever to any person calculated to lead to the destruction *in utero* of the products of conception'. She insisted on this seemingly eccentric step for a good reason. She recognised that the pressure for abortion was overwhelming. In order to safeguard her already controversial birth-control activities, she needed to be able to demonstrate that she was 'holier than thou'. Despite this, she was bound to confess: 'We have had many sad cases coming to us praying for operations for abortion, either for themselves or on behalf of some near relative, and trying to bribe our staff to perform abortions'. In another part of London, an enterprising Anglican clergyman augmented his meagre stipend by exploiting this market. The curiously named Rev. Francis Bacon, aged 70 years and vicar of All Saints', Spitalfields, carried on a thriving business under an assumed name 'which advertised and supplied varieties of treatment to pregnant women with the object of procuring abortion' (*Lancet*, 1928, I, p. 412). The manageress of his business, Annie Bolton, the daughter of a local chimney sweep, sold three types of 'female remedies' on his behalf, priced at 5 shillings, 2 guineas and 5 guineas, respectively. The actual cost of these preparations was estimated in the *Lancet* (1928) to be but a shilling or two. A letter was routinely sent to all potential customers pointedly stating that the treatments were 'NOT for women who were pregnant'. In due course, Annie Bolton received a six-month sentence, and the clergyman fifteen months and a good deal of moralising from the bench.

Throughout this period, the popular papers were full of thinly disguised advertisements for abortifacient drugs. Even the religious press carried such advertisements. A number of public bodies came together to attack the symptom while ignoring the cause. The National Birth Rate Commission, the Pharmaceutical Society, the London Council for Public Morality and the British Medical Association urged the Home Secretary to amend the Indecent Advertisements Act to render such advertising illegal. But depriving the press of advertising revenue was too serious a step to contemplate: in the event, no action resulted and the abortion-drug trade continued to flourish.

In 1937, The Midwives' Institute, in its evidence to the Birkett Committee on Abortion, pointed out that barbers, hairdressers, tobacconists and herbalists sold abortifacient drugs as a matter of course, One drug cost as much as £9 a bottle. Ordinary working-class women could not afford such luxury drugs. They had to make do with 'silver coated quinine pills'. Even these cost 7s 6d for 50. A 12-oz bottle of the poison ergot cost 12s 6d. Since entire families had to subsist on incomes of £2 or £3 a week, even these cheaper abortifacients had to be purchased at the expense of food for the family. And though they often made the mother very ill, they rarely caused the desired abortion. As late as 1965 a survey of abortifacient drugs on sale in chemist, herbalist and rubber goods shops in Birmingham and London found that of 40 retail outlets investigated, no less than 31 sold preparations 'designed to facilitate abortion' (Cole *et al.*, 1965). The researchers concluded that, while most of these preparations had 'no effective abortifacient function', there was some risk that the drugs taken by the mother would damage the foetus in addition to the risk of poisoning the mother. So not much had changed in this respect during thirty years, except perhaps the price. The most-expensive drug in Cole's study cost £3; most cost less than £1. Had popular abortifacients in fact become cheaper during that period?

In its evidence to Birkett (1937—9), the Midwives Institute pointed out that some women preferred vaginal douches to drugs. Seventeen of these were known to be in common use. These included iodine, carbolic soap, vinegar, Lysol and turpentine. If these too failed, then the next resort was 'foreign bodies'. The midwives had had experience of crochet hooks, wax tapers, goose quills, meat skewers and even a hairpin attached to an electric battery. One midwife stated that in her presence a patient 'removed a piece of elm bark five inches long'. The patient told the midwife that it took a fortnight to insert the bark, commencing with one inch, and increasing every few days, until she was able to insert five inches (Simms, 1974b). The midwives noted many reasons for the widespread practice of abortion: poverty, the stress of constant child-bearing, the better education of women and fear of another war in which their children might have to be sacrificed: 'Above all, the midwives noted a strong desire to give children a better time and better opportunities than the parents had enjoyed. The revolution of rising expectations had arrived' (Simms, 1974b).

Women Speak Out

Women within the Labour Party had long been battling to bring birth-control services within reach of working-class women. In 1936, the Abortion Law Reform Association was formed, and here again many of the women involved were members of the Labour Party. But some of the most outspoken women politicians on these issues were also Conservatives, a striking contrast with the present period. Lady Astor made a series of speeches in the House of Commons on both birth control and abortion, and even managed to introduce the subject into a debate on the Civil Estimates on 17 July 1935, when she informed her fellow MPs (*Hansard*, 1935, col. 1135): 'A high percentage of maternal mortality is due to attempted abortion . . . We, as a House of Commons and as a Nation, must face up to the fact today'. The male MPs of the period had little enthusiasm for facing up to any such facts. She therefore quoted to them the Report of the Commission on Maternal Mortality, which stated that, out of just over 3,000 maternal deaths investigated, more than 400 were found to be due to abortion.

Mr David Logan, the devout Roman Catholic Labour MP for the Scotland division of Liverpool, later to become 'father' of the House of Commons, was outraged by Lady Astor's speech. If she was taken seriously, he said, there would be no soldiers to fight future wars on Britain's behalf. He described birth-control information as 'the knowledge of the prostitute' (*Hansard*, 1935, col. 1139).

Mrs Mavis Tate, the Conservative MP for Frome, was also closely associated with this cause, and in the debate on the Medicines (Advertisement) Bill on 27 March 1936 she denounced the hypocrisy of those who thought that by simply banning advertisements for abortifacient drugs or birth control they had somehow improved the position of women (*Hansard*, 1936, col. 1595):

Supposing this bill did away with all those advertisements altogether, are women going to be one whit safer? Of course they are not. It is a very unpleasant subject to discuss in this House but it is quite time that the House did realise what the position is. If we take away these drugs which I realise are a danger, because I know full well the harm they do, what are the women going to do? Simply to go in increasing numbers to the little woman of the street who uses some sort of instrument, an unsterilised knitting needle or something of that kind? We all know that these things are done. We know, or hon. Members ought to know, that the people who are in most real danger today, in that respect, are the poor women who cannot afford to pay. It is perfectly possible for a woman in the West End of London, with sufficient knowledge and with sufficient money, to have a miscarriage brought about at any moment she wants, through doctors of the recognised medical profession. It is happening every day. I am not condemning those doctors. I think in many instances they are doing very useful work, but do not let us pretend that it is not done because it does not happen to be legal or that it is not done by men with every possible medical qualification. It is time that the awful hypocrisy that goes on should be recognised, that people should be honest and realise that in many cases there is need for this help for women. We are not going to do away with malpractice and we are not going to safeguard women from very dangerous methods of terminating pregnancy in the very least by prohibiting these undesirable advertisements. The Bill will do nothing to safeguard women but it may make their position very much more dangerous than it is today.

Nowadays, in sad contrast, Conservative women politicians seem to have quite lost their concern for the social welfare and personal freedom of women. The torch is now carried by Labour women in Parliament. Mrs Sheila Faith, a new MP from a marginal seat, has been the only woman to speak out positively on this issue from the Conservative benches. Why Conservative women politicians should have become so anti-feminist during the past half century is a question sociologists may want to ponder.

Questions of birth control and abortion continued to occupy the House of Commons at intervals right up to the outbreak of World War II. It could hardly have been otherwise, given the lurid abortion cases that were so gleefully reported in the press during those years. In one well-publicised case in the Midlands, a woman police officer had disguised herself as an abortion client and had purchased 45 lead-based pills from the local back-street abortionist, whom the police were anxious to trap because a previous client had been temporarily blinded as a result of taking these pills. The Chief Detective Inspector on the case observed how common this type of offence was (*Wolverhampton Star and Express*, 26 July 1939). In the course of one of these debates in the House of Commons, Mr Richard Acland, a Liberal MP, mentioned in passing that Higginson's syringes were openly displayed for purchase along the Charing Cross Road alongside abortifacients of all kinds, flanked by books with such titles as *Flagellation through the Ages* and *The History of Corporal Punishment*.

On the 11 December 1938, under the banner headline, '25,000 Women Visited Doctor the Law Couldn't Trap', the *Sunday Referee* recorded the death and funeral of Dr Daniel Powell of High Street, Tooting. The paper reported that 'women from all parts of the

country were journeying to London to see him laid to rest'. These
were his grateful clients whom he had aborted in the course of a long
professional lifetime. On two occasions, he had accidentally killed
his patients. When the police tried to run him in for illegal abortion,
his patients collected £1,700 to pay for his defence — a sizeable
sum of money in the thirties in a working-class practice. One
detective who had been on his trail for many years said ruefully:
'He was a great hearted and fearless man whose work was directed
by the highest motives'.

Illegal abortionists were in fact widely tolerated, provided they
were not too grasping and not too dangerous — so much so, that law
officers were becoming less and less enthusiastic about pursuing their
duties against abortionists, and doctors were increasingly reluctant to
testify against them. 'I wish to protest against giving evidence in this
case', Dr Violet Glover is reported as saying in the *Daily Mail* of 4
February 1939. 'I will refuse to give evidence unless I am forced to
do so.' She was forced, by an embarrassed magistrate, who
apologetically explained that he had no option in the matter with the
law as it stood: 'I shall be very glad to see the law altered'.

Maternal Mortality

Meanwhile, without benefit of modern contraception, births fell
relentlessly. In the period immediately after World War I, about
800,000 babies were born each year. This declined to 700,000 in the
mid-twenties, to 650,000 in 1930 and to 580,000 in 1933. The birth
rate in this period fell from over 18 per 1,000 population to 14.4 —
the lowest figure ever recorded in England and Wales till that time.

The maternal-mortality statistics caused dismay. They obstinately
refused to improve, unlike the other health statistics of the period,
notably infant mortality. This had declined from 90 to 64 per 1,000
between the end of the war and 1933. But, in 1933, the deaths of
2,600 women were attributed to 'pregnancy and child-bearing' and
the deaths of another 800 were returned as 'associated' therewith. In
his Annual Report (1933, pp. 213–17), the Chief Medical Officer
observed: 'There is also, it is to be feared, a substantial increase in
abortion, and in the habit of abortion . . . which is now materially
affecting maternal mortality'.

The total number of deaths directly attributed to abortion in
1933 was 463 (compared with twelve in 1973 and five in 1978) but,

as the Chief Medical Officer admitted, 'The figures so provided are far from complete, as from the nature of the case no mention is made of the condition in a certain number of death certificates in which abortion has, or may have, played a part'. The social stigma then attached to the subject ensured its systematic under-reporting. An estimate quoted in the 1933 Annual Report was that 'about one in seven pregnancies terminates in abortion' but it was recognised that this estimate was a conservative one: 'the figures on which this estimate is based cannot be assumed to furnish a true index of its frequency throughout the country'. In 1935, Parish published his celebrated paper on 1,000 abortion cases treated at his hospital at St Giles, Camberwell. Of these patients, 485 admitted illegal inter-ference, 374 of them with instruments. In only 246 cases of the 1,000 was Parish (1935, p. 1120) certain there had been no illegal inter-ference. In all, 18 patients died. He concluded:

> Abortion is increasing in frequency, and the chief factor responsible for subsequent morbidity and mortality is illegal interference with pregnancy, the interference being usually determined by poverty. The law has failed to prevent the self-induction of abortion, and the problem, which is one of preventive medicine, must be reviewed from this aspect, consideration being given to the changed economic and social conditions of the present day.

The BMA Investigates

Public and professional concern about this issue grew so much that in 1935 the British Medical Association set up a committee on the medical aspects of abortion under the chairmanship of Professor James Young of Edinburgh University. Young was a radical figure in medicine, and the conclusions arrived at in the Report probably owed much to him. In 1933 in a lecture to the British Medical Association, Young had drawn attention to the recent League of Nations Epidemiological Report which had stated that, 'for Europe generally, abortion causes more maternal deaths than full-time childbirth, the main cause of fatality being sepsis'. He went on to point out that abortion not only caused death but also 'chronic invalidity', which he referred to as a 'widespread menace'. He concluded (Young, 1933, p. 215):

The only two suggestions so far made to deal with the problem which exhibit a realistic grasp of the facts are, in the first place, legalization of abortion under controlled conditions for other than medical reasons, by which it is hoped that the dangers to life and health would be largely removed, and, in the second place, the diffusion of a knowledge of birth control.

The conclusions of the 1935 BMA Report proved so startling to conventional opinion that internal efforts were made by one faction within the Association to prevent its publication. Eventually, these efforts were successfully resisted, and the Report was published in July, 1936. It recommended that abortion should be legalised on grounds of the physical or mental health of the mother. It also recommended that consideration be given to legalising abortion in cases of rape under the age of consent (16 years), where there was 'reasonable certainty that serious disease will be transmitted to the child' and on social grounds, about which the Report had this to say (British Medical Association, 1936, p. 237):

> While the Committee has no doubt that the legalisation of abortion for social and economic reasons would go far to solve the problem of the secret operation, it realises that this is a matter for consideration by the community as a whole, and not by the medical profession alone.

The Birkett Committee

Thus challenged by the medical profession, the Government in 1937 appointed an inter-departmental committee of the Ministry of Health and the Home Office under Mr Norman Birkett KC, later a Lord Justice of Appeal, to examine the abortion question from a wider, community point of view. The Committee immediately recognised that the number of prosecutions for abortion bore no relation to its incidence (Birkett, 1939, p. 139): 'If the impression of the prevalence of criminal abortion which we have formed is at all accurate, the number of cases coming to the knowledge of the police represents only a fraction of the total number of offences committed'.

It also accepted that reliable health statistics on this matter were 'almost non-existent'. It concluded rather tentatively that there were possibly up to 150,000 abortions each year, of which perhaps 40 per cent were due to 'illegal interference'. In a notable Minority Report, however, Mrs Dorothy Thurtle, the only member of the Labour Party on the Birkett Committee, disputed these figures (Birkett, 1939, p. 139):

> I wish to express the opinion that it is possible that many abortions classed as spontaneous may be the result of illegal interference in an early stage. When, for example, a woman's condition of health gives her a natural predisposition to abortion, and she succeeds in terminating pregnancy by taking pills or drugs, there is frequently no reason to suppose that abortion is not spontaneous, although in truth it is an illegal abortion.

During the preceding few years, between 400 and 500 deaths following abortion had been notified each year. The Registrar General expressed the view that the abortion deaths were probably under-reported by some ten per cent. Often the general practitioner involved would contrive to ascribe the death to some more acceptable condition in order to spare the feelings of the family. The Birkett Committee examined several abortion studies. These showed wide variations in the statistics produced. The Committee could not be sure whether these variations were due to regional differences or to the reluctance of women in some of these studies 'to reveal the occurrence of past abortions'. The number of abortion cases being admitted to hospitals was now rising rapidly, but this might simply be due to changes in hospital-admission policies. In the event, the Birkett Committee came down on the side of limited reform of the abortion laws. Mrs Thurtle's Minority Report made more radical suggestions. She recommended that 'scientific contraceptive advice' be made available to all women, that all women who had had four pregnancies should be eligible for legal abortion, and that abortion should be legal in all cases where a sexual offence had been committed.

Mrs Thurtle's view that the proportion of induced abortions had been underestimated was supported in a paper published in the *British Medical Journal* by a London gynaecologist, Albert Davis. He described a series of 2,665 cases of abortion dealt with in his two hospitals and observed (Davis, 1950, p. 124):

> my own impression is that the great majority — perhaps 90% — of all abortions are induced in one way or another. The testimony of ward sisters, who are in the closest personal contact with the

patients, bears this out; for most of them, when asked their opinion, will corroborate this impression. The methods employed to procure abortion vary widely. The great majority were self-induced, either medicinally or by douching. Purgatives, 'female pills', quinine, and herbal preparations comprised most of the former, but a curious specialty of the district was a tablespoon of powdered ergot taken in a wineglassful of hot port.

In a lecture delivered to the Abortion Law Reform Association, Dr Eustace Chesser (1949), another London gynaecologist, had estimated on the basis of his own practice, and long clinical experience, that the real number of illegal abortions each year was in the region of 250,000. Also in 1949, Dr Keith Simpson, then Reader and later Professor of Forensic Medicine at Guy's Hospital, described the Birkett Committee's calculations as 'conservative'. In a paper in the *Lancet* (Simpson, 1949, p. 47), he said:

A mere 500 or so deaths from these causes appear annually in the Registrar General's returns for deaths in England and Wales. This is no true reflection of the actual incidence. The figure gives no indication of the ill health and sterility which result from procured abortion. Though the mortality may be very low, the morbidity is very high indeed.

He came to the conclusion that:

The principal dangers of abortion will remain unchanged so long as it is unlawful to induce it for mere social and economic reasons, for it will be done secretly with limited skill, under conditions which encourage infection and without the advantages of skilled care or modern protective chemotherapy. (p. 48)

Letter from a Back-street Abortionist

In 1963, Dr Moya Woodside published an article on women abortionists imprisoned in Holloway Prison. She interviewed 44 such women between 1959 and 1962. All were or had been married, most had children, and 13 were grandmothers. 'It was unexpected', she observed, 'to find grandmothers making such a large contribution to crime'. Half of all the women were in fact over 60 years of age. They came from working-class backgrounds. Half were housewives and ten were doing domestic work. However, 17 of the women had previously had some nursing or midwifery experience. Three had been State Enrolled Assistant Nurses, two had been uncertified midwives and two had worked as midwives' assistants. One was a fully qualified midwife. Others had had VAD[1] training or worked in hospitals as probationers. Five women were foreign born. Three-quarters described themselves as Church of England, and five as Roman Catholics. The preferred method used was the Higginson's syringe. There were ten deaths in this series, but several abortionists had previously performed many operations without any complications. Their sentences ranged from two months to four years, the majority being nine, twelve or 18 months. Nine women had previous abortion convictions. In three cases, their offences were discovered as a result of an alleged 'plant' by women police officers which was felt to be very 'unfair'. One woman told Dr Woodside: 'Sixty per cent of women use Higginson's syringe regular every month, just to be sure they bring the period on'. Another remarked: 'I didn't see no harm in it. I used to syringe myself'.

Dr Woodside concluded:

Except in a few cases, financial gain was not the main motive in these women's activities. Had large fees been the rule, it was unlikely that so many would have been living in the poor circumstances described in police reports . . . There is no doubt that compassion and feminine solidarity were strongly motivating factors among women who had acquired this skill.

Blackmail was a recognised hazard of the profession: 'once it gets known that you can help people in this way, you become exposed to blackmail . . . So you can't escape. You're caught. You're in a trap' (p. 101). The other great problem was that clients often lied about gestational age. Eight of the ten deaths in the series occurred with women over 16 weeks.

In 1966, while the Abortion Act was painfully coming into being, I received a letter of some 30 pages from a woman who had once been imprisoned in Holloway Gaol on an abortion charge. She may even, for all I know, have been one of Dr Woodside's sample. She was a soldier's wife with seven children of her own. When she found herself pregnant for the eighth time, she managed to obtain an illegal abortion, and was so grateful to be able to obtain one that she learnt how to do them herself. She became good at carrying them out and her reputation spread. Before long friends of friends started arriving on her doorstep. She never had a death or a serious accident, though the possibility of this was a constant preoccupation. She eventually got caught as a result of a police raid on a working man's club, and was sentenced to six months in Holloway. There she met several dozen other abortionists, a few of whom were 'professionals', and realised she could have made a fortune had she been in it for cash:

> when I went to prison and met people in there for the same thing, and hear the amount of money they have got out of it, and houses, and been abroad for holidays, out of what they have charged, and they tell you straight they don't mind getting a few months worth, and there was me in, and got nothing − still, what I done I done with a good heart, and was only too glad to help out and see them happy and free from worry.

When she emerged from Holloway, she obtained a job, and decided to try not to become involved with abortion again:

> I had a good job, and good money, but it wasn't long before I was being asked to help again; people I never knew. But they soon got to know about me and where I worked, even to wait outside the works for me to go home. But I made a promise I'd never go through that again, but I lost count of the number of people that stopped me to see if I would help them . . . they were working class people struggling to get on and how can you get on if you have a large family . . . but I got asked by a close friend to help a friend of hers out . . . I said alright, just this once . . . I know I've made lots of friends, and all I've ever got out of this is the joy of seeing people happy and free from worry.

By mischance, she got caught a second time. But this was post-war when illegal abortion was no longer taken so seriously, and she was given probation, despite her previous sentence. Her account of her life as a young girl growing up in the poverty of Britain in the twenties, her life as a young wife and mother, grandmother and 'criminal' abortionist is a revealing piece of social history, spanning as it does both pre-war and post-war Britain. Her account is written on cheap, lined paper of varying sizes, the spelling is dreadful, but the message comes through loud and clear. The working classes who were ambitious and wanted to improve the quality of their own and their children's lives could only do so if they limited their families. To do this successfully, they needed to have recourse to abortion when birth control was unknown to them or had failed them. This social, economic and personal need existed irrespective of the state of the abortion law. If abortion happened to be illegal, then the abortions were carried out illegally. Every working-class estate and every army barracks, which were working-class estates by another name, had its own abortionist. Some were quite skilled and honest. Others were less skilled and mercenary. Who can blame them for this? The middle classes who made the abortion laws forced them to take those risks, while their own wives and daughters obtained their more expensive and much safer abortions from respectable but hypocritical doctors in and around Harley Street. One law for the rich and another for the poor — a phrase that recurs constantly throughout the abortion literature of the period and provided the title for the book of that name, *Law for the Rich*, by Alice Jenkins (1960), the first Secretary of the Abortion Law Reform Association.

Middle-class Abortion

The middle classes, as I have suggested, had it easier. But even they needed to be well-informed as well as well-off, or it was possible that they might end up at the mercy of someone like the Manchester psychiatrist who wrote to the *British Medical Journal* (II, p. 179) on 16 July 1949 to describe how he dealt with tiresome women who were so desperate about their unwanted pregnancies that they became hysterical in the surgery and threatened suicide or madness. He was, he said, 'not infrequently being faced with this problem':

> Ask the patient if she is willing to undergo treatment for the mental illness as a 'voluntary' patient in a mental hospital . . .
> The hysterics (and they are many) . . . will usually not be willing
> . . . The Lunacy and Mental Treatment Acts are designed to safe-
> guard the interests of the mentally ill. I think a good deal of
> trouble and anxiety would be saved if doctors would apply them
> in these cases.

Even the more fortunate middle-class patients were sometimes appallingly delayed by the necessity for doctors to cover themselves legally by subjecting their patients to endless examinations at various hands. A case was reported in the *British Medical Journal* (1949) in which a 21-year-old doctor's daughter had died after abortion in a private nursing home in Slough. She had had to have no less than three psychiatric consultations and did not make it to the clinic until she was at seven months' gestation. She was charged £150 — possibly £1,000 or more by present-day prices — and the Matron of the nursing home, it transpired, had 'no certificates'. Her knowledge of nursing 'had been acquired by experience'. The jury returned a verdict of mis-adventure, and the gynaecologist had the grace to return the fee to the dead girl's parents. So even the Law for the Rich was pretty shoddy and corrupt, as such a law is bound to be.

In the context of social class differences, it is worth noting the figures Karen Dunnell (1979) presented in a table headed 'Outcome of Pre-maritally Conceived Pregnancies to Women in Different Social Classes'. This shows that before the Abortion Act, in the years 1960—4, about eight times as many middle-class as working-class women had a pre-maritally conceived 'wasted pregnancy' (that is, miscarriage, abortion or stillbirth) despite their better environment, nutrition and health. By 1970—4, after the Abortion Act, this difference had shrunk to little over two times. So the gap between the classes in relation to choice over childbirth was clearly narrowing fast.

The Present

During the past decade there have been no less than seven attempts to destroy the Abortion Act. There will be further attempts during the lifetime of Conservative governments since anti-feminists recognise that their best chances of restricting the Act are in periods when they can count on discreet government support. If a restrictive abortion bill were to pass, its main effect would be to recreate the social class differences in access to legal and safe abortion that are now rapidly being eliminated. In these circumstances, a proportion of the 100,000 or more British women who obtained such abortions in 1980 might not be able to do so in the years following 1981. Working-class women would once more be forced to seek out the names of back-street abortionists through their grapevines in working-class districts and housing estates.

If they were lucky, they would find criminal abortionists who were reasonably skilled and reasonably unmercenary. If they were unlucky in their quest, they would find only death, injury or an unwanted child. As the historical evidence suggests, this group would include the poorest, the youngest, the most ignorant and the least resourceful. The Sanctity of Life lobby would regard this outcome as a triumph, though not a total triumph. It would constitute a step forward on the road it has been travelling since the Abortion Act was passed in 1967. Meanwhile the private Harley Street abortionists would grow rich once more, grabbing back the business taken from them in the intervening years by the non-profit abortion charities. The numbers of abortion deaths would slowly creep up from the single figures they have now reached. More important, as Professor Keith Simpson pointed out, would be the dramatic but concealed increase in the 'ill-health and sterility that result from procured abortion' in such conditions.

The truth is that no Golden Age ever existed when there was little or no abortion in Britain, and women cheerfully and obediently had all the babies they happened to conceive. There is vast evidence to the contrary, and it has been available to anyone who was more interested in truth than propaganda for very many years. In an advanced democratic society the state of the abortion law can only marginally affect the numbers of abortions performed, since the penalties can never be made savage enough to deter all illegal abortionists, or to deter women from seeking abortion abroad. The state of the abortion law can, however, greatly affect the safety with which a country's abortions are performed.

Abortion has come to be seen not only as a crucial issue in preventive medicine, but also as a critical indicator of women's status in society. In our own time we have come to recognise that no true state of equality can exist for women in a society that denies them freedom and privacy in respect of fertility control. Increased expenditure on contraceptive services and research, and innovative ideas about how to diffuse contraceptive knowledge more widely, will be needed if we are ever to reach a genuine Golden Age, in place of the mythical one, in which induced abortion becomes a genuinely rare occurrence. Perhaps we might start by spending as much on contraceptive advertising as the tobacco manufacturers spend on cigarette advertising. The results might be startling and overcome many of the problems in the birth-control field at present thought to be incapable of solution.

184   *Abortion: The Myth of the Golden Age*

Notes

1.   Voluntary Aid Detachment: nurses with war-time training.

Bibliography

Birkett, N. *Report of the Inter-departmental Committee on Abortion* (HMSO, London, 1939)
Birkett, N. Evidence to the Birkett Committee (Public Records Office, 1937–9, cited Simms (1974a, 1974b))
British Medical Association 'Report of the Committee on the Medical Aspects of Abortion', *British Medical Journal* (Suppl.) (1936) I, pp. 230–8
British Medical Journal (7 May, 4 June, 1949) I, pp. 825, 1004
Butt, R. 'Abortion: The False Charges', *The Times* (7 February 1980)
Chesser, E. *Society and Abortion* (Abortion Law Reform Association, London, 1949)
Cole, M. *et al. Survey of Abortifacient Drugs* (Abortion Law Reform Association, London, 1965)
Davis, A. '2,665 Cases of Abortion', *British Medical Journal*, vol. 2 (1950), pp. 123–30
Dunnell, K. *Family Formation, 1976* (HMSO, London, 1979)
Hansard, vol. 304, cols. 1131–40 (Commons) (1935)
——— vol. 310, cols. 1595 (Commons) (1936)
Jenkins, A. *Law for the Rich* (Gollancz, London, 1960)
Ministry of Health *On the State of the Public Health*, Annual Report of the Chief Medical Officer (HMSO, London, 1933)
Parish, T.N. 'A 1,000 Cases of Abortion', *Journal of Obstetrics and Gynaecology of the British Empire*, vol. 42, no. 6 (1935), pp. 1107–21
Simms, M. 'Gynaecologists, Contraception and Abortion – From Birkett to Lane', *World Medicine*, vol. 10, no. 1 (1974a), pp. 49–60
——— 'Midwives and Abortion in the Nineteen Thirties', *Midwife and Health Visitor*, vol. 10, no. 5 (1974b), pp. 114–16
——— 'Forty Years On – Abortion in the Press', in *Abortion Ten Years On* (Birth Control Trust, London, 1978)
Simpson, K. 'Dangers of Criminal Instrumental Abortion', *Lancet*, vol. 1 (1949), pp. 47–8
Stopes, M. *The First Five Thousand* (John Bale and Danielsson, London, 1925)
Woodside, M. 'Attitudes of Women Abortionists', *Howard Journal*, vol. 11, no. 2 (1963), pp. 93–112
Young, J. 'The Medical Profession and Birth Control', *British Medical Journal*, vol. 1 (1933), pp. 213–7

9 WOMEN IN LATER LIFE: PATTERNS OF CONTROL AND SUBORDINATION

Chris Phillipson

One of the less publicised developments of the past ten years has been the politicisation of groups of older women, and corresponding interest in women in later life as a field of study. Carol Hollingshead (1977) has documented an impressive list of studies and films — nearly 300 in all — entirely devoted to the theme of the older woman. Pauline Bart (1975) in one of the first conferences devoted to older women (held at Ann Arbor, Michigan) documented the spread of activities in which older women in America were engaged: classes for older women, older women's liberation groups, menopause discussion groups. American older women now have their own newsletter, *Prime Time*, which proclaims on its masthead that it is 'for the liberation of women in the prime of life'. It has a readers' service for the sole purpose of answering inquiries, and there are advertisements offering services, such as workshops for women over 40, courses, and so on[1] (Bart, 1975, p. 19).

There are also now some particularly fine novels dealing with the theme of women in later life, most notably: Barbara Pym's *Quartet in Autumn* (1977), a novel which presents a bleak portrait of the lives of a group of retirees — including two single women; and June Arnold's *Sister Gin* (1979), whose central character is a 77-year-old grandmother whose Tuesday afternoon bridge club doubles as an efficient vigilante gang dealing out suitable punishment to local rapists.

The spread of interest in older women, in America at least, reflects three developments. First, the growth of women's health groups led to alternative perspectives on areas such as mid-life change, with some of the critiques of existing medical practice leading to a new view of the psychological and sexual needs of older women (Phillips and Rakusen, 1978). Secondly, there was sociological concern about the experiences of isolated, older women, particularly widows, which has increased with recognition both of the demographic trends (the increase in the number of elderly women) and the changes in household composition (the increase in the number of single household units).[2] Thirdly, there has been the involvement of older women in politics (for example, Maggie Kuhn of the Grey Panthers; see Hessell, 1979) an engagement which has contrasted sharply with the quiescence of older age groups in the past.

Impressive though these developments in the United States may be, the situation in Britain is less satisfactory. The theme of older women has been a discussion point at National Women's Liberation Conferences. However, debates have too often been couched in terms of older people's problems being a form of 'extra-conditioning' — a problem of their perceptions rather than ours. If we take *Spare Rib*, the only monthly radical magazine on a national basis for women, we find that, apart from some notable exceptions (Long, 1979), the magazine is dominated by articles and photographs concerning younger women. Certainly, if in its philosophy the magazine is critical of the presentation of 'ageless' women in the mass female weeklies, it does very little to depart from that tradition.

It is not only a relatively 'popular' magazine such as *Spare Rib* which may be criticised. If we move to a more academic context, the 'invisibility' of older women is an underlying feature of most British feminist texts. Elizabeth Wilson's *Women in the Welfare State* (1977) is almost entirely devoted to women with families. There is no mention of the army of single women (without family support) caring for elderly relatives; and no mention either of what happens to women when children leave home and husbands die. Does a benign welfare state take over, or is there a more protracted struggle for resources? The book does little to inform us. Another example is Marjorie Mayo's *Women in the Community* (1977). Here again, virtually all the chapters are devoted to women with children or women caring for children. Significant though the problems of these groups are, do we have no 'women in the community' without children? Are women in the community uninvolved in any caring role but that *vis-à-vis* children? Once again, there appears to be silence on these issues.

I am aware that there is an objection to the points put forward here, and it might be useful to deal with this from the outset. The argument would be that there is simply no need for women in later life to be a specific field of study. The problems faced by women are roughly the same for all age groups and older women do not need special consideration. They experience economic dependence upon men; sexual assault by men; and sex-role segregation in common with other groups of women. All this is familiar. How far, therefore, does membership of a specific age group radically change the analysis made of a woman's position?

The point I want to make here is that there are now three very com-pelling reasons for developing work on the question of women in later life:

(1) By studying what happens both to older, single women and to women when children leave home, we learn a considerable amount about how sexual divisions are maintained across the life span. How, for example, the caring role which is allocated to women moves from caring for her own children to caring for her parents (or her husband's parents) and back to her grand-children. Even in her 60s and 70s, a woman may find her life predominantly shaped by an image of her as a caring and mothering figure.

(2) We are now moving (and have been for some time) towards an ageing population. People aged 60 or more consitute nearly 20 per cent of the total population of Great Britain. In this age group, women outnumber men by almost 50 per cent; and amongst the 'old' elderly (those aged 75+), women make up nearly 70 per cent of the total. Moreover, there is a sharp contrast between the sexes in living arrangements. Nearly four-fifths of the men aged 60 are married and living with a spouse. Amongst women, however, even among the relatively young (60–64), only two-thirds are married, and among the 3.2 million aged 70 or more as many as three out of four are widowed, single or divorced (four-fifths of these are widowed).[3] So women are surviving men and learning to live alone, with all the accompanying problems of possible isolation and loneliness. The emergence of large numbers of single, elderly women poses important issues for the women's movement — in particular, their involvement and integration within the movement's network of self-help groups and their identification with the broad political aspirations of women's liberation.

(3) The main areas of social control experienced by women provide powerful undercurrents to the lives of older women. Patterns of sub-ordination, which in earlier years may have been experienced singly, surface as a complex, interlocking web in later life. Sexism, which is experienced throughout the life cycle, is joined by ageism, defined here as the stereotyping of and discrimination against people on the basis of their age. Economic dependence and exploitation at home and work produce poverty and reliance on state benefits in the final years of the woman's life.

The combination of these three factors produces new demands and new forms of control on the daily lives of women. Before discussing the political implications which this raises, I shall present a detailed analysis of these three areas.

Women as 'Mothers' — Supporting the Elderly

In her major study *The Second Sex*, Simone de Beauvoir (1949) presents us with a bitter, sardonic portrait of the ageing woman. The description is of a woman no longer dominated by her husband or by the demands of her children. Rid of her duties and her obeisance to the conventions of dieting or the rigours of the beautician, she at last finds freedom. However, according to de Beauvoir (1949, pp. 595—6):

> Unfortunately, in every woman's story recurs the fact we have verified throughout the history of woman: she finds this freedom at the very time when she can make no use of it. This recurrence is in no wise due to chance: patriarchal society gave all the feminine functions the aspect of a service, and woman escapes slavery only at times when she loses all effectiveness. Towards 50 she is in full possession of her powers; she feels she is rich in experience; that is the age at which men attain the highest positions, their most important posts; as for her, she is put into retirement. She has been taught only to devote herself to someone, and nobody wants her devotion anymore. Useless, unjustified, she mutters: 'no one needs me'.

There is much that is powerful and accurate in this argument, particularly when applied to women in their 70s and 80s, that is, when they are alone and widowed. But regarding the women to whom de Beauvoir is referring, women in middle-age and the so-called young elderly (60—75), there are important objections to her thesis. The argument presented is that women are released from the caring system as children grow up and leave home. This viewpoint is relatively common, leading to assertions about the so-called 'empty-nest' syndrome (Treas, 1975). But this notion of a reduction in activity ignores an important aspect of female labour, namely, the role of older women both in paid work and in the social and physical support of an ageing population. In short, we need to recognise the 'double burden' occurring in the middle and upper stages of the life cycle; a double burden which, in the context of the present climate of social expenditure cuts, presents major dilemmas for many women. I now want to trace this phenomenon across three fronts: caring for ageing parents; caring for male partners; older women in paid work.

Caring for Ageing Parents

The withdrawal of children from the home does not necessarily produce a vacuum of inactivity. The ending of this phase in the family may coincide with new demands being made from one or more elderly parents; in some instances, of course, these may occur much earlier, when children are some years away from independence. In almost all cases it will inevitably be the woman who will respond to the needs of ageing parents. Isaacs *et al.* (1977), in a study of geriatric patients in Glasgow in 1972, showed a disturbing picture of daughters struggling alone to provide support for an elderly relative. Quite often, the researchers reported, one daughter took on the care of the patient whilst other members of the family quietly disappeared from the scene.

The point to underline here is the feminisation of the labour involved in the care of older people. Three times as many old people live with married daughters as with married sons and, even when living separately, daughters are the most likely relatives to be called upon for help. The Equal Opportunities Commission, in a comment on this trend, argued (1979, pp. 7–8): 'By curtailing her activities outside the home in order to care for her elderly relative, a woman may risk her job, financial difficulty, social isolation and deteriorating health. The burden of caring can be heavy indeed!'[4]

Nowhere is this more the case than for the 300,000 single women looking after an elderly parent. A survey published in 1979 (National Council for the Single Woman and her Dependents, 1979) found that caring not only takes up many years of the carer's life but much of her time on a day-to-day basis. Eight hours or more per day may be spent meeting the needs and demands of the dependent; during the night, sleep may be interrupted by a dependent who needs care and attention.

Despite the intense demands made upon these women, it is notable that two-thirds of the survey respondents were not receiving any help from friends or relatives. Thus, the type of situation described by Isaacs *et al.* in their study is certainly not uncommon; they report (Isaacs *et al.*, 1977, p. 6) the case of a woman who had given up work three years previously to look after her mother who had become helpless as a result of multiple sclerosis. 'It wasn't so bad at first', she said. 'My friends used to come round and sit with me, and occasionally my cousin or my married sister would let me out, to go to the pictures or a dance. But gradually they stopped coming one by one, and my mother had a row with my cousin, so she stopped coming too. My mother doesn't like me to go out, and I suppose I have just got used to it. But at times I could scream'. This girl refused the offer of holiday admission for the patient. 'What would be the use?' she said, 'I've no one to go away with'.

Even where the woman maintains friendships the condition of the elderly relative may strictly curtail social activities. Toynbee (1979) reports on the case of a 47-year-old woman who had been looking after her parents for 20 years:

She has not been away from her mother for a single night in the last 17 years. She has only very occasionally been out for an evening alone. Her mother is now too crippled to manage expeditions. 'The most we can do on Saturday now is to hobble down the road to a bench, sit on it, and come back again,' she says. She talks regretfully of friends who beg her to go and see them, but she feels she can't leave her mother alone in the evenings or weekends as she is alone and lonely all day in the week while she is at work.

This isolation strongly parallels the situation faced by women at the other end of the life cycle in the very early stages of family building (Oakley, 1974a, b; Hughes *et al.*, 1980). In addition, both are equally affected by expenditure cuts which leave the young mother without nursery facilities and the single woman without the offer of facilities such as a holiday home for an elderly parent.[5]

Caring for Male Partners

It is women rather than men who face the major agony of seeing a life-long partner sicken and eventually die. And it is women, often with scant community support, who have to re-construct their lives in the aftermath of their partner's death. Of course, if the relationship was an oppressive one, then the loss of a partner can be a 'liberating' event. Butler and Lewis (1973) have noted that many women who were forced into marriage by cultural and family pressures might have been happier single, as career or professional women. Other older women, they suggest, may be lesbians who have been hiding as hetero-sexual for a lifetime and who might be willing to 'come out' if the climate were favourable. These possibilities, however real, are not at issue here. What is at issue is the position of women in the final years of their marriage, and this position may be far removed from any form of liberation.

For many men, retirement, although welcomed as a source of release from strenuous work, may be marred by ill-health and a drastically reduced income. Social class is an important factor determining the degree of ill-health experienced.[6] Class differences in mortality still persist — they may in fact have widened — and similar differences occur in rates of sickness. In 1971, in England and Wales nearly two and a half times as many unskilled as professional men reported absence from work due to illness or injury during a two-week period, and they lost on average four and a half times as many days from work in the year. (For recent discussions on class differences, see Doyal, 1979; Townsend, 1979; Walters, 1980).

It might be concluded that for many working-class wives the death of their husbands will not only come earlier as compared with their middle-class counterparts, but may also be accompanied by work-related illnesses which provide an additional burden to the task of caring. Puner (1978) has suggested that the stresses provoked by this care may haunt the survivor because of compassion for the sufferer, or because of guilt feelings over not having done enough to help. All of this will be exacerbated where the support system is undermined through geographical and social mobility and through cuts in basic services.

It could be argued that women have a direct interest in reducing the huge volume of disease and injury still affecting the industrial worker. In 1975, 203,000 former workers were receiving an industrial disablement pension, while 31,000 widows were in receipt of industrial death benefit (Doyal, 1979, p. 67). It is they who, if not themselves suffering from a work-related illness, will almost certainly play a central role in the care of the disabled worker.

Women in Paid Work

All the various activities sketched above need to be placed within the context of the increased importance of paid work to older women — the other side of the 'double burden'. While in the post-war period economic activity rates for men over pensionable age have been halved, for women there has been a three-fold increase (from 4.5 per cent to 13.5 per cent). Similarly, in the same period there has been a substantial increase in the employment of women aged 45–59. Thus the picture which emerges is one of a steady increase in the number of women in paid work, combined with an increase in responsibilities within the family itself. How women perceive this intensification in their activities has not been investigated in any detail. However, there is enough information to suggest that many women are expressing concern at the extension of their caring role into mid-life and beyond. Contrary to all expectations a crop of studies conducted in the sixties and seventies suggested that it was women rather than men who were least inclined to be retirement oriented (for Britain, see Jacobsohn, 1970; for the United States, see Streib and Schneider, 1971; Fox, 1977). Jacobsohn (1970) suggested that negative attitudes towards retirement reflected a turning away from the limited options within the home and the community. Many women saw the alternative to work as being only an extended period of care for a sick husband, with an isolated period of widowhood thereafter. Paid work, on the other hand, at least provided essential income and group support, which may be lacking within an urban community.

The problem, however, for many of these women is that the expansion in the female work force has probably ended.[7] According to Irene Bruegal (1979) many groups of women who have traditionally regarded their jobs as secure will find themselves threatened with rationalisation on a scale comparable to the wholesale elimination of jobs in traditional male strongholds. What we may see as a result of this is not only a re-emphasis on the role of women in the care of children (this, to some extent, has already happened) but also a new emphasis on the 'mothering' they can provide for elderly people. Thus Uhlenburg (1979, p. 240) has recently posed the question:

> Why should the millions of healthy and vigorous older women not be viewed as a valuable reservoir of individuals who could provide physical and mental health care and social services, and who could teach, organise recreational activities and co-ordinate activities for the elderly? With the rapid growth of the old-old, there are major opportunities for young-old women to aid in this way.

The idea that, after a lifetime of activities concerned with 'physical and mental health care and social services', women would welcome a further extension of work in this area seems questionable. What is interesting about the above argument is that it is made to appear that women are being granted a favour by being involved in social services for the very elderly. The fact that they may already be doing a vast amount of social-service work looking after a sick husband, or caring for children whilst a daughter goes out to work seems to be ignored. Clearly, what is needed is a complete break from a situation where women are given the dominant responsibility for dependents within the family and the community.

The Ageing Female

The second main issue referred to in the introduction concerns the predominantly female composition of our ageing population. This aspect is often neglected in official and academic discussions on older people. Sommers (1978, p. 124) sees this neglect as a form of de-sexualisation:

> At the chronological cut-off point of 65, a new status is acquired which falls within the purview of different laws, bureaucracies, and disciplines. These bureaucracies and disciplines tend to see their field, the elderly, as separate and distinct. They view their con-stituency as an undifferentiated category especially in regard to sex, so that the specifics are blurred. Older women tend to become invisible in statistics, theories and social programmes in the ageing field.

The consequence of this is that we know very little about the woman's experience of growing old. In particular, we have yet satisfactorily to trace sex inequalities at early phases of the life cycle into the upper stages of later life. The reason for this, however, is not only because we have an undifferentiated category of 'pensioner' or older person; there is also the point that, up until recently, growing old and retiring was largely considered a male problem. The woman's experience of ageing was seen as being marked by less dramatic changes than those facing a man upon his retirement.[8] Advocates of this view saw 'female' activities such as housework as providing a thread of continuity through the middle and upper stages of the life cycle. Women, it was argued, experienced a more gradual diminution in their responsibilities and relationships in contrast with the male, whose major social anchorage was removed with the ending of work (for a recent expression of this view, see Peter Stearns, 1977).

However, this line of argument ignores two important areas.

First the retirement of the man can bring important changes to the domestic unit. Even if only the male partner has been engaged in work outside the home, retirement will introduce many new elements into the daily life of the female partner. Whether these will generate conflict and dissension or lead to a more intimate relationship obviously depends on a number of factors, not least of which is the type of relationship enjoyed before retirement and the degree of economic security within the household. Either way, a gradual diminution in social responsibility cannot be assumed. Moreover, the event of widowhood will itself involve a degree of disorganisation at least as strong as that experienced by the male upon his retirement (Lopata, 1972).

Secondly, different assumptions about male/female roles can produce new forms of inequality at all stages of the life cycle. Thus the response that a woman makes to an event such as widowhood will depend on obvious factors such as income, health, family support, but less obviously on the type of attitudes and skills developed through the period of socialisation and education. If this process has inculcated a sense of the woman's inferiority to men, of her relative inability to handle public affairs or to administer the family budget, then it is hardly surprising that widowhood may trigger off a downward spiral of withdrawal and social isolation. In a major American study of widowhood, Helen Lopata (1979, pp. 78—9), noting that the majority of widows in her study were not involved in extensive service supports either as receivers or givers, argued that one reason

> for the lack of involvement in service supports is the traditional sex-segregated nature of everyday American life. Almost no women help anyone with care of an automobile nor do they assist on legal problems or with household repairs. These are tasks that fall into the man's domain in the usual familiar division of responsibility. If widows do perform such services, the recipients are most likely their parents or friends, people with even less experience in these areas. The widows also are not providers of transportation, since being unfamiliar with cars, they usually get rid of theirs after the death of the husband. Hence, they also do not need help in the case of a car — another consequence of a sex-segregated society.

The full impact of this segregation and conditioning may only appear in the final part of the woman's life. The likelihood of her spending a major proportion of these years living on her own is very high. On the positive side, being alone may generate a new experience of freedom. Mary Stott (1973, p. 107) has written:

> But now I am alone I am free. Sometimes I am lonely, and more painfully so when there is some small triumph or success and no one to rejoice with me, than in trouble or disappointment. But freedom has its compensations — freedom to come and go; freedom to do the things one refrained from doing before; freedom to explore new patterns of life; freedom, if one has a mind to it, to become an elderly eccentric.

But where the woman lacks economic resources (60 per cent of widows are receiving a supplementary pension) and where her confidence is low, such freedom can rarely be recognised as a positive force. In Lopata's Chicago study over half the widows claimed never to go to public places such as movie theatres or to engage in sports or play cards or other games. Four out of ten never 'entertain' or travel out of town. A study by Abrams (1980) reported that feelings of loneliness, depression and alienation were much more widespread among elderly women living alone than those who lived with others and had their ties supplemented by friendships. To understand the problems faced by such women we must consider further the main areas of social control affecting aged and widowed women.

Social Control in Old Age

To develop the arguments of preceding sections, old age can be viewed as a closing together of various patterns of control and subordination. In this process two areas seem of particular importance: the double standard of ageing; and the separation of home and work.

The Double Standard of Ageing

In a brilliant and moving essay on the position of older women, Susan Sontag (1978, p. 73) has written: 'Society is much more permissive about ageing in men, as it is more tolerant of the sexual infidelities of husbands. Men are "allowed" to age, without penalty, in several ways that women are not.' She goes on (Sontag, 1978, p. 75):

For most women, ageing means a humiliating process of gradual sexual disqualification. Since women are considered maximally eligible in early youth, after which their sexual value drops steadily, even young women feel themselves in a desperate race against the calendar.

Whilst, as Smart and Smart (1978) note, derogatory terms such as 'slut', 'scrubber', 'whore' have no male equivalent, in later life terms of abuse such as 'old bag' or 'crone' are commonly directed at women. Cultural expectations urge women to feel a lessening in their sexual desires and aspirations (even though in sexual terms women are far more stable than men, their potential being the same at 20 as at 60). The menopause itself is often thought to mean the end of sexuality and sexual pleasure. Butler and Lewis (1973, p. 89) have summarised this double standard of ageing in the following way:

> the message comes across that a woman is valuable for bearing and rearing children, and perhaps to nurse her husband in his dotage, but after that [it] is clearly useless and even burdensome to have her around. The mistreatment of old women is a national habit that has yet to be challenged even by older women themselves. They are defined as 'old' and 'women' (in the traditional sense) but rarely as viable, valuable human beings.

However, illuminating though this argument appears, it leaves unclear the source of the 'mistreatment' and double standards' experienced by older women. To understand this we have to examine the inferior position of women within the home and community, and the impact of this in later life.

Beyond Home and Work – The Female Experience

If one important argument in the critique of women's position concerns domestic enslavement, it is of some irony that women today may spend the last 20 years of their life living alone. Thus, having been brought up from childhood to regard marriage as the only acceptable state, a woman can expect to return to being single in the final phase of her life. In the absence of detailed studies (in sharp contrast to the pro-liferation of retirement studies focusing on men), we can only sketch the broad outline of the woman's experience of growing older. Three features seem of particular importance.

First, images of the 'woman's place' emphasise her position at home rather than in the world of work and production. According to Smart and Smart (1978, p. 6):

The ideology of women's place being in the home has served to perpetuate the existing sexual division of labour and to effectively limit the form of women's participation in the public domain (e.g. part-time, short-time, and temporary employment), making a withdrawal into and predominant preoccupation with, or concern for, the home and family seem natural for women.

Arguably, the constraints of this ideology appear in a more acute form in old age. A 'preoccupation with home and family' will provide limited solace for a widow whose family is geographically scattered. On the other hand, her search for alternatives will be made more difficult through the absence of support within society. The emphasis in society is to institutionalise old age on the basis of dependency (Abrams, 1978, p. 9). For women, therefore, becoming old may exacerbate conditions of powerlessness and social exclusion. Class position will be important in influencing the degree of exclusion experienced. Among some groups of older people, for example, we are already seeing important areas of innovation in the area of education (participation in study groups, self-help education classes, etc.). However, these initiatives are often by groups with a substantial background of educational involvement. The picture is less encouraging amongst those who have experienced life-long educational and social disadvantage.

Secondly, tendencies towards social exclusion may be intensified by the economic dependency of older women. Traditionally, the rights of aged women or widowed mothers have received ambiguous treatment in the area of social policy (Thane, 1978). Differences in treatment within pension schemes, the lower earnings of women and their greater life expectancy considerably reduce the income received by older women. Important areas of discrimination still remain (for example, women are prevented from receiving an age allowance until the age of 65 even though their retiring age is 60).

Women also suffer inequalities in the field of occupational pensions. In the private sector 38 per cent of employees are members – 52 per cent of men but only 17 per cent of women. In the public sector 74 per cent of employees are members – 84 per cent of men and 59 per cent of women (Reddin, 1978, p. 692). A survey by Audrey Hunt (1978) found that 51 per cent of husbands, compared with six per cent of wives, have pensions from previous employers.

The operation of the new pensions scheme and the rewards given in retirement to high earning at work create a number of problems for women. Women, unlike men, cluster in low-status, part-time employment. Although an improvement in women's earnings relative to men's may develop, even if progress is rapid (which at the present seems most unlikely) it will be at least two generations before this significantly affects retirement incomes. In the transitional period, moreover, there will be considerable inequalities based on sex and inequalities between younger and older retired women for at least four generations (Walker, 1980, p. 65).

Thirdly, women are particularly affected by the possibility of removal to some form of institution in the final years of their life. Amongst women over 85, some twelve per cent are in old people's homes, with a further six per cent confined to a hospital. It is again a source of irony that, whilst the domestic identity of women has been a pervasive theme in social policy (Wilson, 1977), this is apparently cast aside in their commital to, and treatment within, institutions. As Norman (1980) notes, the shock and grief connected with having to give up one's home and possessions is often insufficiently stressed by those concerned with the care of the elderly. Norman has documented (among other things) the failure to test the effect of providing maximum domiciliary services as an alternative to admission; inadequate consultation and care during the actual admission procedure; the authoritarian regimes within institutions; the loss of choice or control over key areas of life such as diet, times of sleeping, personal clothing, etc.

The fact that women far outnumber men in old people's homes may, to some extent, explain the low standards of care and privacy: degradation on the 'inside' reflecting external beliefs about the role of women, and the rights of elderly women in particular.

To conclude I want to consider the political aspects of ageing in relation to two areas: support by other women for older women; and joint campaigns between the young and the old.

Supporting Older Women

One of the major achievements of the women's movement in this country has been the building of a network of self-help groups covering a range of issues affecting women in the community. However, although the variety of topics covered may be impressive, the age range of the participants is still somewhat restricted. Older people themselves are minimally involved in these groups; this is hardly surprising, given the hostility which may be expressed to people in their fifties or above.[9] Yet the type of support for other women developed by feminist organisations could be crucial to the life of an individual recovering from losing a partner and experiencing, perhaps for the first time, the difficulties of living alone, of feeling useless and unwanted.

These are experiences and feelings which the women's movement has explored in depth, offering support to those attempting to live alone with a child or seeking refuge from an oppressive relationship or to those wanting an abortion. But the variety of issues needs to be expanded. *Conditions of illusion* (to use the title of a collection of papers from activists in the women's movement; Allen *et al.*, 1974) need to be challenged not only on issues concerning reproduction but also on what happens to a woman when her reproductive years are over and when her domestic role has dramatically changed. These are issues which have hardly been touched upon within the feminist movement. As a result, there is a large group of women outside it who, if not alienated by its practice, may find it difficult to relate to the kind of issues being discussed. This is undoubtedly a dangerous situation, if only because a movement unprepared for its own members to age runs the risk that historical continuity and cohesion may be lost. Moreover, challenges to the state's definition of women's rights and women's place within the community will remain limited in their scope if the exclusion of older people is maintained.

Political Work between Young and Old

Insufficient use is made of the parallel interests between groups at different stages of the life cycle. Campaigns against day-nursery closures on the one hand, and old people's homes on the other, tend to be conducted separately and by different groups, But their combined effect is the same, namely to increase the burden upon women and to perpetuate their position within the sexual division of labour. Older women caring for parents and younger women caring for children can give each other mutual support in their campaigns to maintain and expand facilities within the community. Older people can also play a role in giving examples of campaigns fought when they were mothers. As Pauline Long (1979) has argued:

Mothers of activist women in the movement today know all about activism, sexuality, abortion, unconventional relationships . . . And a lot more too. [p. 15] Sex, contraception, child care, food reform, education, the woman/man relationship, woman/woman relationship — all these things have been fought for by women of this Century. [p. 17]

Finally, older and younger women can fight together for the rights of those women who end their days in institutions of one sort or another. Though only a small minority, they may find their lives stripped of any dignity, with basic human needs and rights being ignored. The right for women to live independent lives seems important as a subject for campaign across all stages of the life cycle. An extension of the campaign to include the elderly can only consolidate the wider movement for women's liberation.

Notes

1. I haven't included in this chapter a review of social and psychological attitudes and reactions to the menopause; the work of Eileen Fairhurst, however, is making an important contribution in this area (see Fairhurst, 1979a, b).

2. Altogether, 43 per cent of women aged 65+ live alone; amongst women aged 85+, the figure is just under 50 per cent (Central Statistics Office, 1979).

3. For a statistical profile of the elderly, see Age Concern (1977).

4. In a comment on the DHSS document *A Happier Old Age*, the Equal Opportunities Commission have commented (1979, p. 7):

One of the governments stated aims is to 'keep old people active and independent in their own home, and where they have had to go into hospital, to get them back into their own home as soon as possible' . . . In practice, however, the burden of that care is often not shared by the community at all, but falls entirely on one person — usually the nearest female relative.

5. For detailed reviews of the effects of expenditure cuts, see Personal Social Services Council (1980); Association of Directors of Social Services, 1980).

6. According to Lesley Doyal (1980, p. 21), the poor

suffer and die very much more frequently from the so-called diseases of affluence — cancer and heart disease in particular. Indeed, a typical victim of heart disease is likely to be an unskilled worker with an insecure job, worried about supporting his/her family, rather than the more orthodox stereotype — the coronary-prone executive or airline pilot borne down by their awesome responsibilities.

7.   Early indications from the 1979 General Household Survey support this (see *The Economist*, 31 May 1980).
8.   For a critique of this position within gerontology, see Beeson (1975).
9.   Pauline Long (1979, p. 16) describes the following experiences:

I . . . attended a women's conference and (went) to a workshop on mother-hood. As I sat down, two younger women got up and walked to the door. Said one, 'I'm not going to stay here if a woman of *that* age is going to listen to everything I say'. At another conference I joined an 'older women's workshop. Safe here, I thought. But no. Several women in their late 30's were anxious to talk about 'what should be done with ageing parents', and found my presence and that of one or two of my contemporaries an embarrassment.

Bibliography

Abrams, M.*Beyond Three-score Years and Ten* (Age Concern Research Publication, London, 1980)

Abrams, P. (ed.) *Work, Urbanism and Inequality* (Weidenfeld and Nicholson, London, 1978)

Age Concern *Profiles of the Elderly* (Age Concern Research Publication, London, 1977), vol. 1

Allen, S. *et al*. *Conditions of Illusion* (Feminist Books, Leeds, 1974)

Arnold, J. *Sister Gin* (The Women's Press, Oakland, 1979)

Association of Directors of Social Services *Cuts in Public Expenditure* (ADSS, London, 1980)

Bart, P. 'Emotional and Social Status of the Older Woman', in P. Bart *et al*. (eds.), *No Longer Young: The Older Woman in America* (Institute of Gerontology, The University of Michigan – Wayne State University, Ann Arbor, 1975)

de Beauvoir, S. *Le Deuxieme Sexe* (2 vols., Librarie Gallimard, 1949); translated as *The Second Sex* (Penguin, Harmondsworth, 1972)

Beeson, D. 'Women in Ageing Studies', *Social Problems*, vol. 23 (1975), pp. 52–9

Bruegal, I. 'Women as a Reserve Army of Labour: A Note on Recent British Experience', *Feminist Review*, vol. 3 (1979), pp. 12–23

Butler, R. and Lewis, M. *Ageing and Mental Health* (C.V. Mosby, St Louis, 1973)

Central Statistics Office *Social Trends*, no. 9 (HMSO, London, 1979)

Doyal, L. (with Pennell, I.) *The Political Economy of Health* (Pluto, London, 1979)

Doyal, L. 'Why the Poor Suffer More', *Community Care* (13 March 1980)

Equal Opportunities Commission *EOC Response to the DHSS Discussion Document 'A Happier Old Age'* (EOC, London, 1979)

Fairhurst, E. 'A Socio-Historical Perspective on Factors Affecting the Management of the *Climacteric', Mims Magazine* (15 July 1976)

——— 'Experience of the Climacteric and the Ageing Woman', Paper presented to the joint meeting of the British Society of Gerontology and British Geriatric Society for Research in Ageing (Glasgow, 1979)

Fox, J. 'Effects of Retirement and Former Work Life on Women's Adaptation in Old Age', *Journal of Gerontology*, vol. 32, no. 2 (1977), pp. 196–202

Hessell, D.*Maggie Kuhn on Ageing* (Westminster Press, London, 1979)

Hollingshead, C. (with Katz, C. and Ingersoll, B.) *Past Sixty: The Older Woman*

202 *Women in Later Life*

in Print and Film (Institute of Gerontology, The University of Michigan — Wayne State University, Ann Arbor, 1977)

Hughes, M. *et al. Nurseries Now: A Fair Deal for Parents and Children* (Penguin, Harmondsworth, 1980)

Hunt, A. *The Elderly at Home* (HMSO, London, 1978)

Issacs, B. *et al. Survival of the Unfittest* (Routledge and Kegan Paul, London, 1977)

Jacobsohn, D. 'Attitudes towards Work and Retirement in Three Firms', (unpublished PhD thesis, London School of Economics, 1970)

Long, P. 'Speaking Out on Age', *Spare Rib*, no. 2 (May 1979), pp. 14—17

Lopata, H. 'Role Changes in Widowhood: A World Perspective', in D.O. Cowgill and L.D. Holmes (eds.), *Aging and Modernisation* (Appleton-Century-Crofts, New York, 1972)

———— *Women as Widows* (Elsevier, 1979)

Mayo, M. (ed.) *Women in the Community* (Routledge and Kegan Paul, London, 1977)

National Council for the Single Woman and Her Dependents *The Loving Trap* (NCSWD, London, 1979)

Norman, A. *Rights and Risk* (National Council for the Care of Old People, London, 1980)

Oakley, A. *The Sociology of Housework* (Martin Robertson, London, 1974a)

———— *Housewife* (Penguin, Harmondsworth, 1974b)

Phillips, A. and Rakusen, J. *Our Bodies, Ourselves* (Penguin, Harmondsworth, 1978)

Personal Social Services Council 'Local Authority Cuts in Expenditure on the Personal Social Services', PSSC Monitoring Exercise, Paper Three PSSC, 1980)

Puner, M. *To the Good Long Life* (Macmillan, London, 1978)

Pym, B. *Quartet in Autumn* (Macmillan, London, 1977)

Reddin, M. 'Who'll Pay for Pensions?', *New Society* (28 September 1978)

Smart, C. and Smart, B. (eds.) *Women, Sexuality and Social Control* (Routledge and Kegan Paul, London, 1978)

Sommers, T. 'The Compounding Impact of Age on Sex', in R. Gross *et al.* (eds.), *The New Old: Struggling for a Decent Ageing* (Anchor Books, Doubleday, New York and London, 1978)

Sontag, S. 'The Double Standard of Ageing', in V. Carver and P. Liddiard (eds.), *An Ageing Population* (Hodder and Stoughton, London, 1978)

Stearns, P. *Old Age in European Society: The Case of France* (Croom Helm, London, 1977)

Stott, M. *Forgetting's No Excuse* (Faber, London, 1973)

Streib, G.F. and Schneider, S.J. *Retirement in American Soceity :Impact and Process* (Cornell University Press, Cornell, 1971)

Thane, P. 'Women and the Poor Law in Victorian and Edwardian England', *History Workshop Journal*, no. 6 (1978)

Townsend, P. *Poverty in the United Kingdom* (Penguin, Harmondsworth, 1979)

Toynbee, P. *Guardian* (18 June 1979), p. 11

Treas, J. 'Aging and the Family', in D.S. Woodruff and J.E. Birren (eds.), *Ageing: Scientific Perspectives and Social Issue* (Van Nostrand, Wokingham, 1975)

Uhlenberg, P. 'Older Women: The Growing Challenge to Design Constructive Roles', *The Gerontologist*, vol. 19, no. 3 (1979), pp. 236—41

Walker, A. 'The Social Creation of Poverty and Dependency in Old Age', *Journal of Social Policy*, vol. 9, part 1 (1980), pp. 49—75

Walters, V. *Class Inequality and Health Care* (Croom Helm, London, 1980)

Wilson, E. *Women and the Welfare State* (Tavistock, London, 1977)

CONTRIBUTORS

Helen Evers Senior Research Fellow, Department of Sociology, University of Warwick.

Bridget Hutter DPhil Student, Nuffield College, University of Oxford.

Eileen McLeod Lecturer, Department of Applied Social Studies, University of Warwick.

Ann Oakley Wellcome Research Fellow, National Perinatal Epidemiology Unit.

Shirley Otto Co-director Detoxification Evaluation Project.

Chris Phillipson Senior Research Fellow, Adult Education Department, University of Keele.

Colin Rowett Senior Social Worker, Broadmoor Hospital.

Madeleine Simms Chairperson of the Co-ordinating Committee in Defence of the 1967 Abortion Act. Former General Secretary of the Abortion Law Reform Association.

Carol Smart SSRC Research Fellow, Centre for Criminological and Socio-Legal Research, University of Sheffield.

Phillip J. Vaughan Senior Social Worker, Heatherwood Day Centre, Formerly Senior Social Worker, Broadmoor Hospital.

Gillian Williams Probation Officer.

INDEX